Protest and Possibility
in the Writing of
Tillie Olsen

Protest and Possibility in the Writing of
Tillie Olsen

Mara Faulkner, O.S.B.

UNIVERSITY PRESS OF VIRGINIA
Charlottesville and London

THE UNIVERSITY PRESS OF VIRGINIA

Copyright © 1993 by the Rector and Visitors
of the University of Virginia

First published 1993

Library of Congress Cataloging-in-Publication Data

Faulkner, Mara.
    Protest and possibility in the writing of Tillie Olsen / Mara Faulkner.
        p.   cm.
    Includes bibliographical references and index.
    ISBN 0-8139-1417-5 (cloth)
    1. Olsen, Tillie—Criticism and interpretation.   2. Feminism and
literature—United States—History—20th century.   3. Women and
literature—United States—History—20th century.   4. Social problems
in literature.   I. Title.
PS3565.L82Z64   1993
813'.54—dc20   92-29062
                                                                                        CIP

Printed in the United States of America

Contents

Preface

BEFORE I BEGAN WRITING THIS BOOK, I believed that writing was a solitary activity. It is, in a way. But as Tillie Olsen says, all of us who write have many collaborators whose names deserve a place on the covers of our books. Among my collaborators are my parents, Hattie Miller Faulkner and Dennis Faulkner. In 1956 my mother cashed in her life insurance policy so my oldest sister could go to college, the first of our family to make that long trek away from our parents' North Dakota world. The other six of us followed—a seeming impossibility for people as poor as we were. But long before I arrived at the College of Saint Benedict in St. Joseph, Minnesota, my mother had taught me to love beauty, and my father had taught me to love stories and the music of words. My parents are not at all like the people I read about in the literature I studied in college. But thanks to Tillie Olsen, where I once saw only love and endurance, I now see courage, vision, and creativity, too.

I also want to thank a lifetime of fine English teachers whose influence is imprinted on every page of this book, and my colleagues in the English department at the College of Saint Benedict and Saint John's University for encouragement, humor, and patience. Sister Nancy Hynes, Ozzie Mayers, Florence Amamoto, Charles Thornbury, Peter Carlton, and Monza Naff deserve special thanks for reading early drafts of my manuscript, asking invaluable questions, and suggesting ways to strengthen my arguments. My sister, Judy Faulkner McGuire, the clearest thinker and writer I know, spent vacation days and long nights with me, editing every idea, every word in this manuscript for clarity and grace. I also want to thank my readers and friends at the University of Minnesota, where this book began: Toni McNaron, Elaine Tyler May, Shirley Nelson Garner, Marty Roth, and Riv-Ellen Prell. At the University Press of Virginia, I would like to thank Cathie Brettschneider and Cynthia Foote for enthusiasm, challenge, and steady encouragement. Bev Radaich has shepherded me through the thickets of computer programming, and my niece, Ellen Adelmeyer, has typed a million corrections. They kept me laughing and sane. Without all of them I would have abandoned this project long ago.

The members of my Benedictine community have influenced me in more ways than I can name. I am especially grateful to them for helping me understand what community means—an understanding that is crucial to my life, of course, but also to a careful reading of Tillie Olsen's work.

There are many others—my whole loving family and my friends who put up with several years of bad moods. And of course there is Tillie Olsen herself, who has been willing to talk with me and answer my questions, and whose wonderful writing helped create this book.

To all of you, thanks.

Acknowledgments

I GRATEFULLY ACKNOWLEDGE permission to reprint the following material:

From "The Walls Do Not Fall" by H.D. from *Trilogy.* Copyright © 1982 by the Estate of Hilda Doolittle. Reprinted by permission of New Directions Publishing Corporation.

From Poem #657. From *The Complete Poems of Emily Dickinson* edited by Thomas H. Johnson. Copyright 1929 by Martha Dickinson Bianchi; copyright © renewed 1957 by Mary L. Hampson. By permission of Little, Brown, and Company. Reprinted by permission of the publishers and Trustees of Amherst College from *The Poems of Emily Dickinson,* edited by Thomas H. Johnson, Cambridge, Mass.: The Belknap Press of Harvard University Press, copyright 1951, © 1955, 1979, 1983 by the President and Fellows of Harvard College.

From "Making Peace" by Denise Levertov from *Breathing the Water.* Copyright © 1987 by Denise Levertov. Reprinted by permission of New Directions Publishing Corporation.

From "It's the Poverty" by Cherríe Moraga from *Loving in the War Years: Lo Que Nunca Pasó por sus Labios.* Boston: South End Press, 1983. Reprinted by permission of the author.

Excerpts from "Tell Me A Riddle," "I Stand Here Ironing," "O Yes," "Hey Sailor, What Ship?" from *Tell Me a Riddle* by Tillie Olsen. Copyright © 1956, 1957, 1960, 1961 by Tillie Olsen. Excerpts from *Silences* by Tillie

PROTEST AND POSSIBILITY
IN THE WRITING OF
Tillie Olsen

Introduction

ALICE WALKER describes Tillie Olsen as "a writer of such generosity and honesty, she literally saves our lives."[1] Walker's praise is not an exaggeration. When applied to Olsen's life and work, that conventional phrase "saves our lives" takes on a half-dozen different meanings, all of them intended by Walker. Olsen's fiction—the four short stories in *Tell Me a Riddle,* her novel *Yonnondio: From the Thirties,* and the novella "Requa"— saves from forgetfulness the lives and communal histories of people still outside the visual field of most American readers, writers, and scholars.[2] Because her writing invites readers to "fill it with their own lives," as Olsen often says,[3] she also saves in memory if not in print her readers' ordinary mothers, fathers, grandparents, who are called back to life by her fictional portraits. Olsen also saves the creative lives of women and other marginal people who, through her example and her urging in *Silences,* begin to imagine themselves as writers; and she saves the characters they create. In fact, since the publication of *Silences* in 1978, *breaking silence* has become a readily understood shorthand description of the event when an individual or group tells a long-suppressed story. Finally, Olsen saves forgotten writers for new generations of readers. She has, for example, gleaned and published in *Women's Studies Newsletter* long lists of writers, almost all of them women, whom most readers had never heard of, let alone read; and at her urging the Feminist Press reprinted Rebecca Harding Davis's *Life in the Iron Mills.*[4]

I, like millions of readers, agree with Walker's estimation of

Olsen's importance and return again and again to her work for a deeper and fuller understanding of my own and my ancestors' lives. This study of Olsen's writing is then in part an expression of gratitude for lives saved, "bone by bone," as Walker says.[5] Yet there is a serene optimism, a security, in the notion of real and fictional lives rescued from oblivion that belies the anger and the sense of imminent danger I find in Olsen's writing. From the beginning of her career, Olsen has seen clearly that conservation and reclamation are hopeless, thankless tasks that have to be repeated by writers in each generation unless radical changes occur in almost every structure of contemporary society. As Annie Gottlieb says, Olsen has "taken an oath, with a character in *Yonnondio*, 'to rebel against what will not let life be.' "[6]

During a 1986 residency at the University of Minnesota, Olsen gave a lecture/reading. In the question period after the talk, a member of the audience asked her where she gets her serenity. Olsen's answer was vehement, almost angry: "I have no serenity," she said.[7] Yet, a few days earlier a newspaper interviewer had asked Olsen what she thinks of critics who characterize her works as grim and pessimistic. Her answer was again swift and vehement: "What the world has given to us doesn't have to stay as it is because we are capable and have changed it. . . . It's not unremittingly grim to know that we haven't changed enough things yet. . . . I have a lot of belief in us."[8]

These are the oppositions all of Olsen's work holds in balance: urgency and anger but never despair; hope, but never a serene or cynical acceptance of the intolerable contradictions fragmenting the lives of the people with whom she identifies—mothers, the old, working men and women, members of racial and cultural minorities, struggling artists. As I ponder her fiction and nonfiction and let myself feel the pulls of those contradictions, I, like Olsen, have no serenity. Olsen's work continues to be reprinted, widely read, anthologized, translated, and taught; and at age eighty or eighty-one, she is in demand as a speaker, teacher, and writer-in-residence.[9] Being read, of course, is the highest tribute for a writer like Olsen, who says, "There are some writers who say they don't write for an audience. Well, many of us hunger to be read, we hunger to be taught, we hunger to be known, we hunger to have our writing mean something."[10] But her work also deserves the tribute of wide and varied critical attention, an attention it is only beginning to receive. At the moment, only two book-length studies are in print—Elaine Neil Orr's *Tillie Olsen and a*

Feminist Spiritual Vision and *Tillie Olsen* by Mickey Pearlman and Abby H. P. Werlock—along with a handful of reviews, dissertations, articles, and book chapters. So another reason for this study is to help give Olsen's work the careful reading traditionally accorded writers who unsettle our comfort and trouble our sleep with their powerful challenge.

My way of approaching Olsen's work has been formed partly by my own convictions, partly by the careful work of other critics and scholars, and partly by Olsen's fiction and nonfiction, which, like all great writing, teach us how to read. My first method, which I call multiple vision, is not rightly a literary method at all but rather a way of looking at history borrowed from feminist historian Joan Kelly. The second method is what critic Marilyn Farwell calls "organic feminist criticism."

In an essay entitled "The Doubled Vision of Feminist Theory," Kelly argues that class, race, and gender modify each other in such important ways that looking at the overlap of these circumstances yields a truer picture of women's lives and the sources of oppression or liberation than does a focus on gender alone. As Kelly says, "From this perspective, our personal, social, and historical experience is seen to be shaped by *the simultaneous operation* of relations of work and sex, relations that are systematically bound to each other—and always have been so bound."[11] In Olsen's fiction and nonfiction, the intersections of gender, class, and race are evident, as are such additional circumstances as nationality, education, and age. To encompass all these broad circumstances, I change Kelly's doubled vision to multiple vision by imagining each of Olsen's characters or each of the writers she describes in *Silences* as a stack of transparent colored squares through which the sun or a brilliant light is shining. I see the squares placed at angles on top of each other. As each square is added, the color of the stack changes; at the corners, though, the color of each separate square is still visible and unchanged. Each of the transparencies represents one of the influencing circumstances in a life, particularly those that mark one as a member of a group or community and at the same time set one apart from other groups or communities.

A brief comparison of several characters from Olsen's short story "O Yes" will show what I mean. Helen is a white, middle-aged, working-class American woman, married and the mother of three daughters. Her friend Alva is also a middle-aged, working-class American woman with several children. Alva is black. If we stack up our transparencies—red for woman, white for working class—both stacks are pink. But suppose we add yellow to Alva's stack to represent her black race and blue to Helen's to represent her white race. Now, in spite of similarly colored corners, the stacks are no longer the same color—Alva's is peach and Helen's is lavender. And even this rough scheme is too simplistic to reflect the story's complexity. "O Yes" also includes as central characters two young friends, one black, one white, the daughters of Helen and Alva, whose lives are very different from their mothers' and from each others'. With the addition of a black transparency to represent the modulation of youth, their stacks turn red-orange and indigo. Olsen's multiple vision shows that, for all their commonalities, women's lives are not identical, a point that is one theme of this story, as it is of everything she has written.

In "O Yes," Olsen further refines her picture of how circumstances change lives by introducing class differences in the person of a black girl whose father is a doctor and who lives in a wealthy section of town. While she is chosen as headgirl at a prestigious white high school, the other black girls in the story face discrimination from racist teachers and classmates and are more likely to drop out of school than to be elected to office. With the addition of a brown transparency to represent the middle class, this girl's stack of transparencies is rust colored, having some shades in common with the other black characters, but with a final color different from theirs. This story, like all of Olsen's fiction, says that lumping the members of any race together is as unenlightening and demeaning as lumping women together.

Recently, Olsen seems to be disclaiming the multicolored reality created by the delineation of differences. At the annual meeting of the Modern Language Association in 1988, for example, she urged her listeners to "leap beyond race, class, and sex" in order to "recognize what is common between us."[12] Perhaps she is, understandably, appalled by the widening rifts in the United States, Africa, Eastern Europe, India, all the places around the world where differences lead not to creative coalitions against oppression but to figurative or literal wars. More likely, in her typical way of embracing contradictions, Olsen is asking her listeners to hold likenesses and differences in mind simultaneously. Her fiction and published nonfiction, at any rate, express this more complex and courageous truth. Her writing certainly does not deny the commonalities among women or among black or working people; furthermore, her multiple vision suggests that the common experiences of men and women who belong to marginal groups within

American society unite them, even as their gender divides them. But her writing also insists that ignoring or denying differences requires the suppression of some group's experiences, feelings, ideas, and history, driving them underground where they silently subvert any but the most superficial and fragile unity.

In the past, Olsen has often described her writing in terms of this multiple vision. In an interview published in 1983, she says: "As I express that which is not being said enough or said at all, that creates an additional pressure on style. To try to say that differently: when one's vision is an opposing vision to the dominant one, as it continues to be for those of us who are feminist or/and writers of color or/and write with a working class sense, whether we realize it or not, these affect how we write."[13] This vision also inevitably creates an additional pressure on critics, since most of us are trained to look at literature with single vision, or, if we are feminists, doubled vision. But as many feminist critics have discovered in the past ten years or so, the broad categories *women* and *women's literature* are both too narrow and too broad to be helpful in seeing multicolored reality. They are too narrow because they often mean *white, middle/upper class, educated, heterosexual women of the Western world*, a constricting category indeed. The experiences and responses of this small group of women are certainly not universal, but if one belongs to that group, which is the most vocal in describing itself, it is easy to think they are. The terms are also too broad, for if we make them commodious enough to envelope all women and all women's writing, they become too unfocused to be helpful—like looking for a least common denominator—and too reductive to be the source of richness that diversity can be, when freed from the tendency to rank and oppose.

The pressure on literary critics to read with multiple vision has been intensified in recent years by the brave, often angry voices of women scholars and writers who stand with at least one foot outside the white female academic mainstream. One of the most powerful of those voices is Audre Lorde's. In "The Master's Tools Will Never Dismantle the Master's House," she writes: "It is a particular academic arrogance to assume any discussion of feminist theory in this time and in this place without examining our many differences, and without a significant input from poor women, black and third-world women, and lesbians." Multiple vision shapes a literary critique that is radical in the most basic sense of the word: it lays bare in the literature it examines the many roots of oppression, which can then become the roots of pleasure and unity. Because

Tillie Olsen's writing traces so carefully both the links and the points of divergence among women but also among the other silenced people whose stories she tells, one important way of being true to her vision is to be constantly alert to both, and to the "creativity that can spark like a dialectic between polarities," to borrow Lorde's words again.[14]

As I said, the links and divisions between women and men are also crucial in Olsen's work. But the audience that literature about women has lately won is not an automatically appreciative audience for literature about poor and working-class men. As poet Robin Morgan says of her efforts to write affirmatively about men, in a "feminist ethos" that is safe for women, "celebration of a man feels crazy and you are told that it's crazy." According to Morgan, this is because the "wound" between men and women is so deep that affirmation of men seems like a betrayal of women.[15] Olsen's current feminist audience has been less than enthusiastic about "Hey Sailor, What Ship?" and "Requa," whose male protagonists Olsen presents with great sympathy. One indication of this lack of critical interest is that, unlike Olsen's stories about women and girls, these stories seldom make their way into anthologies, even anthologies of women's writing. "Requa" was first published in *Iowa Review* in 1970 and reprinted as "Requa-I" in the 1971 *Best American Short Stories;* it has been anthologized only once since then. To the best of my knowledge, "Hey Sailor, What Ship?" the second story in the collection *Tell Me a Riddle*, has been anthologized only five times.

Critical commentary on these two stories is also scanty. I have found only three extended pieces of criticism on "Requa"— Blanche Gelfant's excellent "After Long Silence: Tillie Olsen's 'Requa,'" and chapters in Orr's and Pearlman and Werlock's books. While most critics slide quickly over "Hey Sailor, What Ship?" Orr does devote part of a chapter to this story. But she offers the puzzling assessment that Whitey, the story's main character, is Olsen's least compelling protagonist, because "he does not have the resilience of spirit that arouses the reader on his behalf." Abby Werlock presents an even more puzzling reading, turning Whitey into a modernist antihero by drawing many unexamined parallels between this story and Eliot's *Waste Land* and "Love Song of J. Alfred Prufrock."[16] I will try to do these stories greater justice by looking at their male characters through the multicolored filters of gender, race, and class, rather than judging them by traditional Western standards of manhood.

My second approach, organic feminist criticism, takes into account not so much the circumstances pressing on the lives of characters as those pressing on the creative life of an author. This approach to literature is at odds with critical theories, whether modernist or postmodernist, that ignore the author or turn her or him into an abstraction. One of the motives behind the "death of the author," as it is sometimes called in contemporary critical theory, is to challenge the canon of famous male and female writers and to mute the overbearing, godlike, supposedly unique authorial voice. But in spite of these worthwhile goals, ignoring authors and their lives is pernicious for those who have had to struggle through layers of silence to find the courage to write. To deal with their work but to declare irrelevant the broad circumstances of their lives assures misunderstanding and misjudgment. It also relegates all writers to the anonymity from which women only rather recently emerged.[17]

Organic feminist criticism, as Farwell describes it, strives to put together what these critical theories take apart by exploring the fertile conjunctions between "ethics and language, text and artist, creation and relation, and ultimately art and life."[18] This approach is not, however, autobiographical in the narrow sense that it hunts for parallels between an author's life and the events in her or his stories. Organic feminist criticism searches instead for the broad historical and cultural forces that shape lives and either encourage or stifle writing. Political affiliations, marriage, even mothering, that great silencer of writers, fed Olsen's writing even as their demands all but prevented it. Far from being irrelevant to an understanding of Olsen's work, then, the circumstances of her life and even the marks of her history on her body are clues to such an understanding.

Olsen says, "It's a strange thing to suddenly recognize one is a writer . . . who can use herself or is used as a certain kind of text having to do with that which is agonizing in our lives and must be changed." She notes that her "hands were maybe two, three years of my life in water washing clothes, before the automatic washer, instead of writing on my pad."[19] The physical labor of a lifetime is, she says, "incorporated into my body," as she points to the pads on her ankles from years spent packing meat, capping mayonnaise jars, and standing at a Punch press.[20] There is neither self-pity nor self-indulgence in Olsen's recounting of those details. She does not use them to excuse her slim body of work. Yet I agree with her that if one is to understand the gaps, "the periods of stammering, of fragmented speech" of Olsen or of any writer who stands out-side the mainstream, one must also understand the tangled con-nections between that writer's personal history and her or his racial, gender, and class history.[21] In "One Out of Twelve: Writers Who Are Women in Our Century," a published version of Olsen's famous 1971 talk to the MLA Forum on Women Writers in the Twentieth Century, she writes: "The *differing past of women*—that should be part of every human consciousness, certainly every woman's consciousness (in the way that the 400 years of bondage, colonialism, the slave passage, are to black humans)" (S 26). She adds that the ratio of women writers to men who are published, anthologized, and awarded prizes can be understood "*only in the context of this punitive difference in circumstance, in history, between the sexes; this past, hidden or evident, that . . . continues so terribly, so determiningly to live on*" (S 27).

In Farwell's words, organic feminist criticism views the writer's art as "primarily communal, primarily a dialogue." In doing so, it reverses the tendency of critical theories that, when they do look for relationships between the writer and the work of art, do so only in order to "carve out a niche for the isolated and unique artist who is expressing his or her individuality, consciously or uncon-sciously."[22] Rather than "imprison[ing] her in uniqueness," to bor-row Germaine Greer's phrase,[23] I shall explore the communities that incited and shaped Olsen's writing—her "collaborators" as she calls them in *Silences*—and the readers and writers with whom she initiates a dialogue. Again, this approach seems well suited to Olsen's work. As Elaine Neil Orr says, "It is almost as if . . . [Olsen's writing] waits for an answer or echo."[24] Olsen concurs with this description, saying in an interview:

> There is something else that I learned early, and everything in my life reinforced: don't have contempt for people, don't have contempt for your readers, trust them, they are intelligent, they have lived as profoundly as you have. . . . You do not have to spell it out for them. You do not have to tell them ev-erything. You do not have to, in that particular protective way, bring them into your imagined world. They will bring to it their full beings, they'll give your writing a dimension it may not really have on the page. . . . It is you and what you bring to it . . . the common work that we do together . . . all this is part of the making of style.[25]

In uniting early and late stages of a writer's career, organic criticism also honors the slow growth of artistic talent rather than assuming that great literature springs to full-blown life from some genius's brow. The story of how *Yonnondio* came to be published is instructive in this regard. Olsen began *Yonnondio* in 1932, when she was nineteen. In 1934 the first chapter appeared in *Partisan Review*, and based on the promise they saw in it, Bennet Cerf and Donald Klapfer of Random House offered her a contract for the novel. But Olsen gave up the contract shortly after and never finished the book.[26] She thought the manuscript was lost until, some thirty-eight years later, "some of its pages were found intermixed with other old papers . . . during the process of searching for another old manuscript." Working at the MacDowall Writer's Colony, the older Tillie Olsen entered into "an arduous partnership" with that "long ago young writer," ordering the manuscript pages and choosing among the drafts (*Y* 157–58). But the vision and the words of the *Yonnondio* that was finally published in 1974 are those of her nineteen-year-old self, a self Olsen refused to touch up to make her more politically or aesthetically pleasing.

Even a sympathetic critic like Bell Chevigny says that "readers may wish the mature Olsen had not refrained, as she did, from rewriting," citing sentimentality and melodrama as the book's main flaws. In addition, the characters are inconsistent and the dialogue does not always ring true. Other critics, among them Deborah Rosenfelt, describe the difficulties Olsen faced in *Yonnondio* in combining the revolutionary polemic endorsed by the literary Left with her own chosen subject: the impact of poverty and sexism on family life and particularly on the lives of women and girls.[27] Olsen herself readily acknowledges that *Yonnondio* is unfinished and flawed. She laughs ruefully at the naïveté of the scene in which Anna Holbrook, who has suffered a miscarriage, balances a heavy laundry basket on her head in imitation of a picture she had seen in a book.[28]

But Olsen's decision not to rewrite *Yonnondio* is not a kind of downward mobility or mistrust of the wisdom and craft gained in the intervening forty years. She might agree with Adrienne Rich that revision of one's work should be more like "pruning a tree" than "retouching a photograph."[29] This fidelity to one's past work counters what Olsen calls in *Silences* "the knife of the perfectionist attitude" in art. The phrase is Louise Bogan's, and, as Olsen interprets it, it describes the intimidating attitude that leads beginning writers to devalue or destroy their work and established writers to disown their early attempts, denying their personal artistic history and, in some way, the artistic history of their race and class and gender. The way literature is usually studied does nothing to cure this blight. Olsen writes that there is "little teaching of writing as process to fortify against measuring one's earlier work against that of established writers. (No anthology of the work that admired writers were doing *their* earlier years.) Little reinforcement to the V. Woolf conception that if writing 'explains much and tells much' it is valid. Little to rouse confident sense of one's own source material—the importance of what one has to bring into literature that is not there now, and one's right to say it" (*S* 263n). Because Olsen's early work "explains much and tells much" about her growth as a writer and about the sources of her creativity, I have included *Yonnondio* and even her early poetry and journalism in this study.

Organic criticism leads me to look at Olsen's writing, reclamation and collecting, even her lists for the *Women's Studies Newsletter*, as being all of a piece, motivated by the sane generosity of spirit and the same political and ethical stance. Some critics rue the fact that Olsen spent her time putting together *Mother to Daughter, Daughter to Mother*, her 1984 "daybook and reader" that collects the writings of many women on this painful subject. And those who see *Silences* as far less valuable than her fiction say she should not have bothered with it. "Several writers could have written *Silences*," John Leonard says, "whereas only Tillie Olsen could have written her marvelous short stories."[30] But that judgment, appreciative as it sounds, takes apart what belongs together and insists upon ranking what cannot be ranked. It is as if one could say with certainty that more people will benefit more deeply from reading Eva's story in "Tell Me a Riddle" than from discovering at Olsen's generous hands the writings of Rebecca Harding Davis, Olive Schreiner, or Jean Toomer, or from hearing named in *Silences* the many economic and social circumstances that stifle artists, and in the naming being freed to create.

In practical terms, this combination of multiple vision and organic feminist criticism leads me to consider Olsen's characters, plots, and language, as well as her life as an artist, from a historical perspective rather than from the point of view of their uniqueness or universality.[31] This historical perspective has several implications. The first is that each story has whole worlds vibrating around it and within it, often worlds we do not know very well or know only from a white male viewpoint. In the eleven pages of "I Stand Here Ironing," as one critic says, "we are offered a short course in American history— . . . as it was lived in the 'personal struggles of the mother.' "[32] I have searched the texts for clues to the historical circumstances that shape the lives of Olsen's characters, and I have included some of that history in this study. This task is much easier now than it would have been ten years ago, thanks to scholars who have begun to reconstruct the history of ethnic minorities and the working class in the United States; to explore women's position in religious, social, and political movements; and to relate the fluctuations of the economy to the lives of women and children.[33]

A second implication of this multicolored historical look at Olsen's work is that it pushes readers to learn about literary contexts. If her work is to have its full power as witness to almost invisible lives, it must point us to other works that delineate those lives and to works past and present with which her stories resonate. As Catharine Stimpson writes, "Not only individual talents must be made visible, but the traditions in which they were created."[34] Specifically, it is helpful to read Olsen's stories in the imaginative tradition created by women writers of color, writers of the working class, and writers who were immigrants or children of immigrants. If we read them only within the white Western tradition, whether created by male or female writers, the danger is that we will distort them to fit that narrow mold, as if the circumstances shaping character and plot were irrelevant.

One form of distortion I have tried to avoid is pulling Olsen's work back into the very formulas from which she has struggled to free it. In *Silences,* Olsen writes that such formulas "diminish, make shallow, falsify" women's writing (253). I think they can do the same to the responses of readers and critics. Among the reductive formulas Olsen lists are some that are especially tempting, given the content of her work: "Assignment of certain characteristics, behavior, as innately female; masochism, passivity, . . . you (women) want to fail, be seduced, raped, punished. Oedipus, Electra. Mother blaming. Guilt where it is not guilt at all but the workings of an intolerable situation" (253n). As I will point out in later chapters, some critics have read her stories within these narrow and confining categories, while others have cut them to fit so-called archetypal patterns gleaned from writing by and about white middle-class women.

When Olsen does invoke stereotypes (such as the Jewish

Mother) or Judeo-Christian and classical myths (the biblical Eve, the sphinx, or Sisyphus) she does so to revise rather than reinforce them. Like the contemporary American women poets Alicia Ostriker describes in "The Thieves of Language: Women Poets and Revisionist Mythmaking," Olsen makes clear by her contexts that she is stealing the myths and stereotypes in order to argue against their traditional interpretations. Also like these poets, Olsen "simultaneously modernizes what is ancient and reduces the verbal glow that we are trained to associate with mythic material."[35] In the analysis that follows, I have traced the ways in which Olsen's stories pull myths and stereotypes out of their assumed universality into particular historical moments. Once situated in history, they reshape themselves in exciting ways to illuminate individual and communal lives.

Finally, while I believe this historical perspective is crucial to an understanding of Olsen's writings, I have read her work not as history or sociology or propaganda but as literature. Olsen has said that the women who were her companions and friends in the Communist party when she began to write did not understand her passion for the sound and shape of language. They read literature, Olsen has said, "the way women read today coming into the women's movement who don't have literary background—reading for what it says about their lives, or what it doesn't say."[36] While neither Olsen nor I scorn such reading, I am also interested in her compressed, poetic style that gives her work its revolutionary power, making it both useful and beautiful.

The criticism I have attempted in the following pages is a sometimes knotty, often tentative synthesis: with multicolored filters firmly in place I look at Olsen's works nested in each other and in her life and surrounded by ever-widening historical, social, and political contexts. I shall begin in Chapter 1 with what I consider the most important circumstances of Tillie Olsen's life and the particular stories, old and new, those circumstances have led her to tell. With that essential background in place, I shall then name the central contradictions and oppositions Olsen's work holds in balance. The remaining chapters of this study will unfold those contradictions and explore their implications for change.

Stories Old and New

T
wo excerpts from Tillie Olsen's unpublished writing show the evolution of her vision. The first is from a 1931 diary entry. In it, the young Olsen writes of the absences in her poetry: "The rich things I could have said are unsaid, what I did write anyone could have written. There is no Great God Dough, terrible and harassing, in my poems, nothing of the common hysteria of 300 girls every 4:30 in the factory, none of the bitter humiliation of scorching a tie; the fear of being late, of ironing a wrinkle in, the nightmare of the kids at home to be fed and clothed, the rebelliousness, the tiptoe expectation and searching, the bodily nausea and weariness . . . yet this was my youth."[1]

As this entry shows, Olsen was already troubled about the content of her poetry, which, according to Deborah Rosenfelt, tended to be "romantic, lyrical, full of the pain of lost or unrequited love, the anguish of loneliness, and the mysteries of nature."[2] The events of the ensuing years—political involvement, the struggle to survive the Depression, wide reading, motherhood, and work—reinforced the lessons of Olsen's girlhood, convincing her that she could and must make literature "out of the lives of despised people" (*S* 117). Later in the 1930s, she wrote in her diary of her desire "to write the history of that whole generation of exiled revolutionaries, the kurelians and croatians, the bundists and poles; and the women, the mothers of six and seven . . . the housewives whose Zetkin and Curie and Brontë hearts went into kitchens and laundries and the patching of old socks; and those who did not speak the language of their children, who had no bridge . . . to make themselves understood."[3] This steady vision has guided every phase of Olsen's writing career, leading her to work that moves powerfully against the literary and critical currents of the patriarchal mainstream, and even partially against the countercurrents created by the literary left and the feminist movement.

In this chapter, I shall discuss first the source of Olsen's vision in the shaping circumstances of her life—the sometimes fertile, sometimes barren soil out of which she grew. Her life story, and the way she tells it, are important contexts in which to read her writing. Then I shall describe in some detail the old and new stories these life circumstances have led Olsen to tell, in particular the elements in those stories that make them both "conservative" and "revolutionary," to use Bell Chevigny's terms.[4] These elements include Olsen's unusual range of characters and a triple-layered pattern that combines protest against oppression, celebration of courage and strength, and the heartening possibility of a radically transformed future world.

In a review of *Silences*, Margaret Atwood writes that the style and tone of the book are "reminiscent of a biblical messenger, sole survivor of a relentless and obliterating catastrophe, a witness: 'I only am escaped alone to tell thee.'"[5] Olsen is a survivor, but she never claims for herself special qualities that guaranteed her survival. It might enhance our opinion of her skill and pluck if she were to claim that she became a famous writer in spite of a hundred unlucky breaks. Instead, Olsen insists that circumstances, rather than lack of skill or courage, silence many potentially fine writers, silenced her for twenty years, and almost completely prevented her writing. She insists just as steadfastly that a combination of social, political, and economic circumstances, supportive communities, and "special, freaky luck" allowed her to envision herself as a writer and carved out the territory of her stories.[6]

It is important here to specify just what Olsen means by "freaky luck." It is emphatically not the self-made luck of bootstrap philosophy or self-help manuals which claim that reality is only what one makes it. Nor is it the sense of having been chosen by the gods to walk through danger unscathed. Nor is Olsen's insistence on the role luck plays in bringing talent to fruition a cynical denial of freedom and courage. It is, on the contrary, an affirmation of these qualities and a protest against the social and economic circumstances that crush them. Her insistence is also a way of bringing to consciousness the invisible, rarely credited luck of being born, let us say, white in the United States, male, in this century rather than the last, heterosexual, into a middle-class family that values education. In *Silences* Olsen suggests the kinds of luck that permit or deny "emergence into literature": "Born a generation earlier, in the circumstances for their class, and/or race, and/or sex, no Chekhov, Brontë sisters, Emily Dickinson, Thomas Hardy, Maxim Gorky, no D. H. Lawrence, Virginia Woolf, Sean O'Casey, no Franz Kafka, Albert Camus—the list comes long now: say, for a sampling, no A. E. Coppard, Charles Olson, Richard Wright, Philip Roth, Cynthia Ozick, Joyce Carol Oates, Toni Morrison, Alice Walker, etc. etc. etc. etc." (262). And we might add, no Tillie Olsen.

The first important circumstance of Olsen's life was being born in 1912 or 1913 to committed Jewish socialist parents and growing up in a socialist milieu. Her parents, Samuel and Ida Lerner, were Russian Jews who had taken part in the unsuccessful 1905 revolution. They came to America, settling eventually in Omaha. Like many revolutionary Jews of their generation, they had rejected the Jewish religion. Olsen says of her mother that she was "an incorruptible atheist."[7] But her parents had preserved what Elaine Neil Orr calls "the humanism of Yiddishkeit," and the strong sense of communal responsibility that is part of the Eastern European Jewish tradition.[8] Moreover, they had been members of the Jewish Socialist Labor Bund, a Marxist organization that encouraged members to hold on to their Jewish culture and Yiddish language, while cultivating the vision of a universal classless society.[9] Their socialist and communal sentiments were reinforced in the United States, where Olsen's father was active in the burgeoning labor movement and in the Nebraska Socialist party.

With her father secretary of the state party, the young Tillie Olsen, then Tillie Lerner, spent her childhood in a home that was a center of political activity. She remembers that she and her five brothers and sisters slept on chairs placed next to each other when guests stayed at their house. Part of her early education certainly came from the conversation and oratory of socialist leaders like Eugene V. Debs.[10] Another part came from "old revolutionary pamphlets laying around the house," as she says in a letter.[11]

Olsen began working when she was very young to help support her family, but even so she was able to stay in school through grade eleven. From the vantage point of the 1990s, the latter fact does not seem like good luck, but in the twenties, eleven years of schooling was several years more than most children of working-class parents received. Besides that, inexpensive books were avail-

able. In the 1920s, millions of Haldenman-Julius five-cent Blue
Books were published in Kansas. These books were designed and
priced to put the great literature of the world into the hands—or
pockets—of working people. (They were just the right size to fit
into a shirt pocket.)[12]

Books were "a special refuge and a special recourse" for Olsen.[13] Once, she set out to read her way through the Omaha public
library's collection of fiction, poetry, and biography. The reading
list gleaned from her journals by Deborah Rosenfelt is amazingly
broad and deep, but it shows that Olsen was especially drawn to
those writers who shared her commitment to social justice: Whitman and Ibsen, W. E. B. Du Bois and Langston Hughes, Willa
Cather and Ellen Glasgow, Upton Sinclair and John Dos Passos,
Olive Schreiner and Agnes Smedley.[14] One of her greatest pieces
of good luck was reading Rebecca Harding Davis's *Life in the Iron
Mills* "in one of three water-stained, coverless, bound volumes of
the *Atlantic Monthly,* bought for ten cents each in an Omaha junk-
shop" when she was fifteen. Although she did not discover the
author's name until many years later, this anonymously published
work said to her, "Literature can be made out of the lives of
despised people," and "you, too, must write" (S 117). In this story,
Davis's character Hugh Wolfe is one of the "despised people," a
Welsh immigrant who works in an American iron mill. He and his
fellow workers live almost like slaves with no hope for change. Yet
Hugh Wolfe has an artist's eye for beauty, and in spare moments
he carves out of korl, the waste material of the mills, the figure of a
powerful woman. In Davis, Hugh Wolfe, and the korl woman,
Olsen found a series of mirrors for her own hunger to create, a
hunger that crosses lines of class, nationality, gender, and educational level. Another ironical impetus to her writing was her discovery that the lives of the people she knew well and the language
they spoke made up an infinitesimal proportion of her reading.
What she could say had not yet been said.

The 1930s were good to writers, particularly those who were
affiliated with the political left. Elaine Hedges gives this assessment of the thirties, and though she is writing about Meridel
LeSueur, what she says fits Olsen's life as well: "In a time of
unprecedented crisis, with the American economy in collapse,
political activists could believe in radical social change as a real
possibility. Josephine Herbst . . . once described what she called
the 'beauty' of the decade as its 'communion among people, its
generosity.' This sense of communion, of being part of a collective

effort of shared revolutionary goals and expectations, both sustained and inspired LeSueur."[15] Olsen describes this decade as "a
rich, an international, period." Young activists were concerned not
only about unjust economic structures in the United States, but
also about revolutions in Russia, Africa, the Philippines, Chile,
and China, and the struggle against fascism in Europe. In her
thorough study of the socialist roots of Olsen's fiction, Deborah
Rosenfelt says that "Olsen felt herself to be part of a valid, necessary, and global movement to remake the world on a more just and
humane model."[16]

The basic literary theory of the Left was that art should express
the struggles and triumphs of the working people. Leftist literary
arbiters had narrow ideas about the form and limits of that expression, so this was a mixed blessing. Still, this theory gave Olsen and
other members of the working class the impetus they needed to
write about themselves and the work and people they knew first-
hand. In a speech delivered to the 1935 American Writers' Congress (which Olsen attended as one of a few invited women speak-
ers) Meridel LeSueur describes the coming together of language
and labor: "It is from the working class that the use and function of
native language is slowly being built. . . . This is the slow beginning of a culture, the slow and wonderful accumulation of an
experience that has hitherto been unspoken, that has been a gigantic movement of labor, the swingdown of the pick, the ax that
has hitherto made no sound but is now being heard."[17]

Even outside leftist circles, the thirties were different from the
decades before and after. Americans had become interested in the
lives of working people and even those who were out of work.
With WPA support, artists, writers, photographers, and filmmak-
ers set out to record those lives. Erika Duncan says, "Suddenly
there were photographs of people who had never been photo-
graphed before. People who had never been to the theater before
began to see plays and to create them."[18]

Since even at age eighteen Olsen was involved in the labor
movement and the Young Communist League and was at the
same time eager to write, this climate was invigorating for her. Of
course, this double dedication also created problems, because her
time, energy, and talent were divided. She worked at a wide variety of jobs, simply to stay alive (tie presser, model, housemaid, ice
cream packer, book clerk, packinghouse worker, waitress, punch-
press operator); she was a grass-roots labor organizer in a movement that demanded more than words; and she was a writer torn

between her desire to write fiction and the movement's need for someone with a perceptive eye, an understanding of history, and a powerful way with language to write pamphlets and articles.[19]

By an odd twist, these conditions came together to produce the early chapters of *Yonnondio*. Olsen was jailed in 1932 for helping organize packinghouse workers in Kansas City: "I spent some time in KC in the Argentine jail, where I developed first pleurisy, then incipient T.B. It meant I had to be taken care of, was given thinking-writing time." She recuperated in Faribault, Minnesota, where she began working on *Yonnondio*. Olsen also became pregnant and was nineteen when her first daughter was born.[20]

That same year Olsen moved to California, where she continued both her writing and her political activities. She helped organize maritime and agricultural workers and again was jailed for her activities. She wrote two accounts of the 1934 San Francisco General Strike, both of which were published—"Thousand Dollar Vagrant" in *New Republic* and "The Strike" in *Partisan Review*. *Partisan Review* also published the first chapter of *Yonnondio*, then called "The Iron Throat," and two poems. Most of this time she was holding down a job, sometimes two, and caring for her daughter.[21]

Those hard years were anything but glamorous. Olsen says of the early years of the depression: "In 1931 and '32 and '33, when a third of the nation was ill-housed, ill-clothed, ill-nourished, there were a million people riding the boxcars, most of them young, the homeless youth. . . . The family behind us cooked and killed their dog to eat. Those were the Hoover years of no welfare, no-nothingism, and denial, when there were long, long lines and apples, everything that people know about now in that shadowy mythical way."[22] Yet it is surely part of her good luck that she began to write in an atmosphere of heightened social consciousness surrounded by people who valued writing and saw it as revolutionary political work. I shall address later the problems women writers faced because of the sexist biases of the literary Left; for now, it is enough to say that Olsen found in the Left and particularly in socialist feminist writers a two-stranded tradition that did not force her to abandon her inner or outer worlds to find a suitable subject. Rosenfelt's assessment is accurate: Olsen's "profound understanding of class and sex and race as shaping influences on people's lives, owes much to that earlier tradition. Olsen's work, in fact, may be seen as part of a literary lineage so far unacknowledged by most contemporary critics: a socialist feminist literary tradition." Rosenfelt traces this lineage from Charlotte Perkins

Gilman, Vida Scudder, and Susan Glaspell, through Meridel Le-
Sueur, Tess Slesinger, Josephine Herbst, Grace Lumpkin, and
Ruth McKenney from the thirties, up to our contemporaries,
Marge Piercy, Alice Walker, and Grace Paley, to name a very few.[23]

Important as the influence of the Left was on Olsen's writing, it
would be a mistake to emphasize it to the exclusion of other
shaping circumstances, the most important being her life as wife,
mother, and worker. This combination of circumstances, while it
modified and deepened her vision, almost silenced her as a writer.
Sometime before the end of the decade, Olsen stopped writing.
She had two more daughters, married Jack Olsen in 1943, and had
a fourth daughter. During most of those years, she continued to
work at a long succession of jobs to help support her family. She
did not begin writing again until the mid fifties.[24]

Olsen's account of these years in "Silences" is not a slick ré-
sumé of obstacles overcome and awards won. It is rather the story
of her hairbreadth escape from total silencing, and mourning for
the stories in her that will never be told. When Olsen describes
herself as a writer, she says with equal conviction that she has been
extraordinarily lucky for a person from her circumstances, but also
that she has suffered irreparable harm.[25] "Silences" documents
both the luck and the harm.

First, there were the hard but hopeful nonwriting years: "In the
twenty years I bore and reared my children, usually had to work
on a paid job as well, the simplest circumstances for creation
did not exist. Nevertheless writing, the hope of it, was 'the air I
breathed, so long as I shall breathe at all.' In that hope, there was
conscious storing, snatched reading, beginnings of writing, and
always 'the secret rootlets of reconnaissance'" (S 19). Then came
the years when she lived the triple life of mother, worker, and
writer: "A full extended family life; the world of my job . . . ; and
the writing, which I was somehow able to carry around within me
through work, through home. Time on the bus, even when I had
to stand, was enough; the stolen moments at work, enough; the
deep night hours for as long as I could stay awake, after the kids
were in bed, after the household tasks were done, sometimes
during. It is no accident that the first work I considered publish-
able began: 'I stand here ironing, and what you asked me moves
tormented back and forth with the iron'" (19).

In 1954, Olsen took a creative writing class at San Francisco
State University. The story she wrote for that class, "Help Her to
Believe," earned for her a Stegner Fellowship in Creative Writing

at Stanford. In the eight months of relative freedom that followed, she finished "Help Her to Believe" (which became "I Stand Here Ironing") and began "Tell Me a Riddle." During those months, Olsen had both time and the companionship of other writers: "I was a writer. . . . I had three or four days a week—with five or six hours—that I could write. I had that extra . . . —the fact that people cared about what I'd done."[26]

The worst times of all were the in-between times, such as when her fellowship ran out just as her creative powers were at their peak and she had to return once again to full-time work:

> This was the time of festering and congestion. For a few months I was able to shield the writing with which I was so full, against the demands of jobs on which I had to be competent, through the joys and responsibilities and trials of family. For a few months. Always roused by the writing, always denied. . . .
>
> My work died. What demanded to be written, did not. It seethed, bubbled, clamored, peopled me. . . .
>
> A Ford grant in literature, awarded me on nomination by others, came almost too late. Time granted does not necessarily coincide with time that can be most fully used, as the congested time of fullness would have been. (S 20, 21)

In 1961, "Tell Me a Riddle" received the O. Henry Award as the year's best short story; in the years that have followed, Olsen's stories have been anthologized many times, and she has received numerous academic grants, literary awards, visiting professorships, and invitations to speak.

This bare-bones account of Olsen's writing career would fit the all-American, make-your-own-luck, exceptional-woman success story, except that Olsen insists on calling to our attention all those potential writers who could not afford a creative writing class, had no encouragement early or late in their lives, applied for the same scarce fellowships and literary prizes and did not get them—the women "who never come to writing at all" because they have been "diminished, excluded, foundered, silenced" (S 39). She removes herself forever from the token-woman roll by crediting the communities that surround her life in ever-widening circles, making her writing possible. Besides the support she received in the thirties, she thanks the feminist movement of the seventies for helping create an understanding and appreciative audience for her work. She also names as collaborators and nurturers all those writers who went before her, especially the little-known women writers; for, as she says, "we in art have all been contributed to, have 'collaborators,'" whether or not artists choose to acknowledge them (*S* 222).

The socialist and feminist influences of Olsen's early life, her Jewish heritage, her years as mother-worker-writer, her eclectic reading—this complex mix of silencing and enabling circumstances and lucky breaks—combined to make Olsen the survivor/witness that Margaret Atwood describes, for whom writing goes far beyond self-expression to explore societal as well as personal reasons for failure and success, suffering and joy. As I have shown, Olsen's life as a writer has been deeply fragmented, with long periods when she did not write, or at least did not publish. The past fifteen years is another of those long, silent times. Most of her writing even looks fragmented, broken, on the page. Yet both her fiction and her nonfiction express a self in conversation, supported by and responsible to many communities, some of them invisible. Her line from "Requa"—*Broken existences that yet continue*—describes her depression-era characters and their tools and tasks (65). It could also describe Olsen as a writer and the radical aesthetic that guides her work. As Catharine Stimpson writes, this aesthetic commits the artist to speak for voiceless people, "those who, though equally worthy, did not survive."[27] It asks of the writer identification rather than dissociation, rootedness rather than separation. In her analysis of Olsen's 1970 novella, "Requa," Blanche Gelfant writes that "in affirming the radical aesthetic of the thirties which identified the writer's voice with the voice of 'the people,' Olsen recovers a nearly lost legacy from the past that she values."[28] As Rosenfelt points out, this aesthetic is also traceable to feminist writers of the twenties and earlier with whom Olsen was familiar, among them Olive Schreiner and Rebecca Harding Davis, and to minority writers of every period of American history, including the present one.

This radical aesthetic has helped determine the stories Olsen would choose to tell—and not to tell. Her famous dedication to *Silences* reads: "For our silenced people, century after century their beings consumed in the hard, everyday essential work of maintaining human life. Their art, which still they made—as their other contributions—anonymous; refused respect, recognition; lost." These are the people who inhabit Olsen's stories—her displaced revolutionaries, her silent workers, her women with Zet-

kin, Brontë, and Curie hearts. Whether women, men, or children,
they are people of talent, intelligence, and social fervor in whose
lives the combined weight of patriarchy, poverty, and class and
racial prejudice prevent the full development of these qualities.
These characters and the stories Olsen tells about them appear
infrequently in Western literature.

At the center of Olsen's concern are the "common female realities," some of which she lists in *Silences:* "what goes on in jobs;
penalties for aging; the profound experience of children . . . ;
what it is to live as a single woman; having to raise children
alone; going on; causes besides the accepted psychiatric ones, of
breakdown in women" (43n). Other female realities emerge from
her fiction: growing old, social consciousness, friendships among
women and the circumstances that rupture those friendships. But
because Olsen never loses sight of the ways in which determining
circumstances both unite and divide women and men, she also
tells stories about male characters who are at the same time marginal to white patriarchal society and enmeshed in its workings.
Measured against most American definitions of success, Olsen's
male characters are failures, inhabiting a world far from that of
middle-class status and wealth. They are uneducated men and
boys, usually poor or scraping by, who look for work or do menial
and dangerous tasks that have neither glamour nor power at-
tached to them. Rather than depicting romantic forays into sex,
war, or adventure, Olsen writes about their struggles to survive in
a society that is at best indifferent to their needs, and even about
their efforts to nurture other down-on-their-luck people, including
women and children.

Olsen also includes children in all her stories. On the most
realistic level, this is because most women of her own and her
mother's generations bore and raised children. More important,
Olsen numbers children among her silenced people whose gifts
are "refused respect, recognition; lost." Although it may appear to
offer women a freer life, a fictional world in which children are
neither seen nor heard, or one in which no one has ordinary,
steady, day-to-day responsibility for them, is above all a patriarchal world.

Finally, although Olsen's stories portray individual characters
so carefully that there is no forgetting Eva or Mazie or Stevie or the
nameless mother who says, "I stand here ironing," she never
allows even the most solitary of these characters to be seen apart
from the overlapping communities and social systems in which

they live. In a 1974 talk at Emerson College in Boston, Olsen said, "What matters to me is the kind of soil out of which people have to grow, and the kind of climate around them."[29] That soil and that historical and social climate are important elements in the stories she has chosen to tell.

Olsen readily and painfully acknowledges that "experiences and comprehensions not previously admitted into literature—especially when at variance with the canon—are exceedingly hard to come to, validate, establish as legitimate material for literature—let alone, shape into art" (*S* 44n). To bring these lives and communities to art, Olsen has had to resist and counter prescriptions for fiction from various sources. Some but by no means all of these formulas are part of the Western patriarchal literary tradition; others are part of the traditions I discussed above, which were simultaneously liberating and confining for her, affirming parts of her vision and disallowing other parts.

Olsen had to reject as false, "gargoyled," or partial many of the fictional models patriarchal literature offers, which reduce women characters to the old stereotypes catalogued in *Silences:* "Earth mother, serving vessel, sex goddess, irresistible romantic heroine; victim; 'do with me as you will' stereotype" (252–53). The nasty but inevitable undersides of these stereotypes are also familiar: destructive mothers, women jealous of each other and in perpetual competition for men, whining martyrs demanding recompense from hapless children.

More difficult to resist was the silent conviction that unless women are involved in public life, there is nothing interesting to say about them, no stories to tell. This conventional point of view has been recently updated, ironically, by some feminists and is expressed by Carolyn Heilbrun in *Reinventing Womanhood:* "So far, it is men who have moved upon the earth and had adventures; it is men who have told stories . . . about women as well as about men. . . . But perhaps women have not told stories because there were no stories to tell. There was only the dailiness of life, the attention to food, clothing, shelter, the endless replication of motherhood.[30] Earlier in this book, Heilbrun briefly mentions her father's sisters, Fanny and Mollie, who at the ages of fourteen and twelve came alone to the United States from Eastern Europe, worked in sweatshops, and out of their earnings of two dollars and fifty cents a week, sent for the rest of the family, including Heilbrun's father. She says of her aunts, "I have never been able to grasp what that task required of them in the way of courage and determination." But instead of urging women writers to recover or imagine the stories of women like Fanny and Mollie, Heilbrun merely says of them that they "had been doomed," and then urges women to look to real and fictional men for models of autonomy and adventure.[31]

For if women's domestic lives are not considered good story material, the public lives of working-class women are an even less fertile source, though not necessarily for aesthetic reasons. From her earliest days as a writer, Olsen seems to have understood that keeping the stories of working women (and certainly that is most of the world's women) out of literature and particularly out of the literature that is widely read is more a question of politics than of the vitality of the material. Our society has a vested interest in not knowing. In an essay appropriately titled "The Best Kept Secret— How Working Class Women Live and What They Know," Marion Glastonbury says that one important reason why working-class women appear so rarely in mainstream literature as subjects, and almost never as authors, is that the educated public does not want to know the reality on which its comfort rests. "Muteness and invisibility," she says, "are what women are paid for." Literature demands empathy, and the reading public cannot grant that without also taking responsibility for the social conditions which keep women mute, invisible, and chronically poor. Glastonbury adds that the residue of poverty is "the dull thud of the commonplace."[32] The very words sound heavy, boring, weary—hardly promising material for fiction, whether about women or about those men whose work is repetitive, physical, dirty, and totally lacking the glitter shed by power and money.

Luckily for working men, the proletarian writing of the thirties took them and their work as its main subject; because of a pervasive sexism, however, this same writing often excluded women both as authors and as subjects. If we were to believe Mike Gold, an outspoken and influential left-wing critic from this era, the ideal proletarian writer was himself a worker "in the lumber camps, coal mines, and steel mills, harvest fields and mountain camps of America." Alice Kessler-Harris and Paul Lauter point out that even for the Left, "workplace" did not include the home, and "work" was not the endless tasks women did within the home to support their families; therefore, "only small fractions of women's lives would find their way into art."[33] The bearing and rearing of children, family life, love, and sexual politics were not considered valid subjects for literature, unless they were somehow included in the class struggle. LeSueur, Josephine Herbst, and Henry Roth all came in for negative criticism, the first two for choosing these "women's subjects" and Roth for writing the lyrical *Call it Sleep* instead of a so-called "masculine," "revolutionary" novel.[34] Proletarian literature admitted women, along with blacks and hispanics, as coworkers and corevolutionaries but not "as groups suffering their own persecution."[35]

Moreover, leftist theory often viewed children alternately as traps pulling committed intellectual radicals back into the bourgeoisie and as tools in the service of the revolution. Tess Slesinger satirizes the first attitude in her 1934 novel, *The Unpossessed*. In the last chapter Maggie Flinders reflects with bitter sarcasm on her husband's reasons for urging her to have an abortion: a baby, Miles says, "means the end of independent thought and the turning of everything into a scheme for making money."[36] On the other hand, in the same year the editors of *Partisan Review* introduced Tillie Lerner's "Iron Throat" with the approving comment that the author had taken time out from writing and political work "to produce a future citizen of Soviet America."[37] But for Olsen, children are not tools of any ideology, and she accords her young characters personhood by making their inner and outer worlds as weighty as those of her adult characters.

Olsen's determination to write about communal roots and social circumstances ran with the grain of leftist thought but decidedly against the grain of the individualistic, conformist fifties when she was writing the four stories contained in *Tell Me a Riddle*. Given their affiliations with the American Communist party and the labor movement, it is not surprising that both Olsen and her husband Jack were hunted down by the House Committee on Un-American Activities during the McCarthy years. In 1953 Jack was subpoenaed to testify before HUAC and later blacklisted, which meant that he could no longer work on the ships in the San Francisco docks. Though Olsen was not called before the committee, she has said in a recent interview that she was fired from several jobs when FBI agents arrived at her workplace to reveal her affiliations.[38]

In *Homeward Bound: American Families in the Cold War Era*, historian Elaine Tyler May describes the fifties as the decade of "containment," during which everything from the McCarthy probes and bomb shelters to nuclear families in their newly bought suburban ranch houses enforced conformity of thought and action. Although there were exceptions, as there are in every era, women and men were safely ensconced in gender roles that were much more rigid than they had been in the two previous decades. Rather than working to change society, people were urged to adapt to it, even to undergo therapy if necessary in order to "feel better about their place in the world." As Tyler May says, "Domestic containment and its therapeutic corollary undermined the potential for political activism and reinforced the chilling effects of anticommunism and the cold war consensus."[39]

McCarthy was disciplined by the Senate in 1955, but the fact that the days of purges and loyalty oaths were over did not make the second half of the decade a hospitable time for writers like Olsen who were in the socialist feminist tradition. Kessler-Harris and Lauter state that "within a few years, the entire world of left-wing culture was ploughed under by the attacks of McCarthyism." Books by such writers as Agnes Smedley, Josephine Herbst, and Tess Slesinger were removed from libraries in the United States and overseas and disappeared from used book stores, not to reappear until the 1970s and 1980s. The whole climate was one in which voices of protest and radical social analysis simply could not be heard. "As the cultural soil dried up," say Kessler-Harris and Lauter, writers who had been nurtured by the ideals of the thirties "lost their audience."[40] While many writers of this era portray rebellious individuals asserting themselves against the System, very few suggest, much less insist on, communal solutions as Olsen does in each of her stories from the fifties. It seems just a little short of miraculous that during those repressive years she was able to write "I Stand Here Ironing," "Hey Sailor, What Ship?" "O Yes," and "Tell Me a Riddle." As I will show in later chapters, in each of these stories Olsen challenges the domestic, social, and political ideologies of the fifties. It also seems obvious that the silences pervading the lives of the characters in those four stories are symbolic of the silencing in the United States of the radical voice of protest.

Olsen's conviction about the importance of untold stories and forgotten people has led her to resist these formidable literary and social currents. Her resistance becomes art, as she puts all her craft as a writer at the service of the people she honors. As Stimpson writes, Olsen "signifies her respect for [the dignity of her characters] . . . in the exactitude and scrupulous effort of her work."[41] In Glastonbury's "dull thud of the commonplace," we hear the thump of the iron on the ironing board, the "clawing dinning jutting gnashing noises" of the meatpacking plant, the clatter of a mother's sewing machine. Suddenly, lives too dull and people too undifferentiated for fiction become unforgettable, touched by the alchemy of her writing.

But Olsen frankly admits that she wants not only to reveal and conserve lives rarely seen in print but also to "write what will help change that which is harmful for human beings in our time."[42] Does Olsen's fiction perform that revolutionary task, or has she, in Audre Lorde's words, settled for "a shift of characters in the same weary drama" of sadness and defeat?[43] While this question is not limited to feminist criticism, feminists have been asking it with special insistence. It is not rhetorical or academic. Writers struggle with it, as do women searching in literature for models, and parents trying to decide what books to give their daughters to read. The critics ask in various ways whether the stories about women told by women are liberating or just so many more overheated rooms that shut out the sky and help keep women readers from imagining and living different lives.[44]

For a writer like Olsen who is committed to showing the circumstances that thwart human development, the problem is especially thorny. Yet I find Olsen's fiction, as well as *Silences* and *Mother to Daughter, Daughter to Mother*, hopeful, liberating, and challenging. For no matter what story of loss, fragmentation, or destruction she tells, she also delineates the strength and courage that explain "the mystery of survival in a wasteland," to borrow Blanche Gelfant's fine description of "Requa."[45] But because survival is not enough for Olsen, her stories go even further. In every story, stylistic patterns running sometimes with, sometimes against the plot sturdily challenge long-accepted patterns of passivity and defeat, and assert alternatives.

I can best explain Olsen's balancing of these apparently contradictory perceptions in terms of two of her favorite quotations, the first from Blake, the second from Dickinson. Together they give clues to the structure of her work and its unsettling power. Blake's words are quoted twice in *Silences:* "Blight never does good to a tree. And if the blight kill not the tree but it still bear fruit, let none say that the fruit was in consequence of the blight" (38, 117). But Olsen always adds her amazed qualifier, "And yet the tree did— does—bear fruit" (*S* 177, 258). The Dickinson quotation, which Olsen cites often in talks and interviews as a way of explaining her vision, is "I dwell in Possibility—/a fairer House than Prose—"[46]

I confess I cannot find a literary term that adequately describes these three conflicting yet intertwined perceptions. What comes closest is Olsen's description of a black choir singing a gospel hymn in which "many rhythms rock apart and yet are one . . . rhythm" ("O Yes," 50). The shorthand phrase I have settled upon to describe these intricate verbal rhythms is *blight-fruit-possibility paradigm*. I do not mean to suggest by that phrase that Olsen's stories have the slickness of fictionalized theory or the serenity of archetype. This paradigm is a pattern that emerges from Olsen's life and the lives of the despised people about whom she writes. "I would never be so presumptuous," Olsen recently said, "to think I was writing for all women. . . . I write out of my time, out of myself, out of what I and others are experiencing."[47] Nor does this phrase suggest the paradoxical reconciliation of opposites; rather, it describes just the reverse: a precarious balancing of contradictions in which blighting circumstances always threaten to obliterate the memory of past achievements and destroy future possibility.

As I have said, Olsen pictures in all their harsh contours the lives of silenced people who cannot speak for themselves. She also defends them from labels like "loser," "passive victim," or "evil mother" by naming the causes outside of them that trap and maim and by rejecting mainstream definitions of lives untouched by mainstream privilege. She always asks what she calls "the writer's question": "is this true? is this all? if indeed gargoyled, then what misshapen?" (*S* 250). She does this sometimes by showing in meticulous detail the constricting circumstances of their lives and sometimes by painting with broad strokes the oppressive economic and social systems that surround them. This is the blight.

Gelfant writes that for Olsen "history is a dump-heap strewn with broken promises and wrecked hopes, among which lie examples of human achievement. Someone must sort through the junk. . . . This is the task of reclamation Olsen has assumed as a writer and assigns to her characters."[48] The human achievements Olsen salvages are the fruit borne not because of but despite oppression. Although only "Requa" is actually set during the thirties, in every story a character, an image, a place evoke the Great Depression experience of scavenging for the necessities of life. In "Tell Me a Riddle," Eva, the aging grandmother, sorts through boxes of old clothes, looking "with a life-practiced eye" for "what is still wearable within the worn" (77). In "Requa," Wes and his nephew Stevie dig through mounds of machinery, tools, and old cars—the discards of migrant families—sorting the "discarded, the broken, the torn from the whole: weathereaten weatherbeaten: mouldering, or waiting for use-need. *Broken existences that yet continue*" (65). More important, in both "Requa" and *Yonnondio*, where children search the town dump for treasures, the characters themselves are junk, a wasteful society's throwaways whom Olsen salvages for her readers.

For Olsen this salvaging of gifts from the past is an act of respect and love; it is also an act of self-preservation. For the failure to remember with unsentimental love dooms us to a futile search for meaning and direction begun anew in every generation. Olsen's way of remembering and rendering her memories is something like that of Maya Angelou, who says black Americans can choose to scorn their ancestors as "shuffling and smiling" Uncle Toms and Aunt Jemimas; or they can remember that Uncle Toms shuffled and smiled to feed and protect their families, and Aunt Jemimas tended white children so their own could go to school.[49]

In the same vein, Olsen says emphatically that she did not intend her characters to be victims and does not want her readers to see them as such. In 1982, drama students at Southwest Missouri State University staged *Yonnondio*. Olsen attended the premiere and afterward commented on how deeply moved she had been by this tribute to her work: "What went so deep was that I felt, on that stage or behind that stage making it happen, were the grandchildren of Anna and Jim. . . . They were proof that these are not just victims, lower-class . . . 'losers,' 'basically not very smart or why would they be where they were,' . . . 'people without will,' all of the canards."[50] She would say that anyone who refuses to lie down and die, anyone who resists destructive conditions with courage, humor, and resourcefulness is not a victim. Even mobility, that destroyer of memory, continuity, and community, is evidence of such courage: "That's part of what being human is: you push yourself up and move . . . to try to make life better."[51]

Adrienne Rich's distinction between feminist history and women's history is pertinent to Olsen's search for the fruit of previous generations: "As feminists, we need to be looking above all for the greatness and sanity of ordinary women, and how these women have collectively waged resistance. In searching that territory we find something better than individual heroines: the astonishing continuity of women's imagination of survival, persisting through the great and little deaths of daily life."[52] While women's history concentrates on the lives of exceptional women who were active in some public sphere, feminist history brings to light the often invisible communities that made those noteworthy accomplishments possible. Feminist history also tells the story of the nameless women who, even in patriarchal societies, used power and brought about change.[53]

Olsen's writing is alive with the conviction that creativity, strength, and adaptability are far more common in women than most people think, though one's vision has to shift to see the unconventional, sometimes desperate, manifestations of these qualities. Mothers in *Yonnondio*, "Tell Me a Riddle," and "I Stand Here Ironing" hold their families together. These are not the literary mothers Heilbrun describes in *Reinventing Womanhood*, who use their motherhood "as an excuse not to succeed outside a domestic role, not to try, or, trying, not to persevere through the necessary pain."[54] They are "essential angels," in Olsen's terminology, who "must assume the physical responsibility for daily living, for the maintenance of life." Although these women are *"so lowly as to be invisible, . . . without [them] no art, or any human endeavor, could be carried on for even one day"* (S. 34). But Olsen goes beyond feminist history in claiming creativity and endurance for working men, the very young, and the old. The children in *Yonnondio*, for example, create elaborate structures and dramas on the city dump. The men in "Requa" make a family for each other and an orphan boy. Olsen would agree with Rich that remembering such creativity and persistance is "nutriment" and that "seeds stored for centuries can still germinate" in the pages of fiction, bearing fruit for present and future generations.[55]

Valuable as these memories are, however, Olsen's writing insists that courage in the face of destructive conditions is not the best human life has to offer. In the terms of the paradigm I am tracing, she insists on possible alternatives to oppression. Again, the literary Left of the thirties provides clues to the earliest roots of this conviction. According to such leftist theorists as Mike Gold and Edward Seaver, writers were to urge workers on "through the maze of history toward Socialism and the classless society."[56] They were to show both suffering and triumph over suffering as a result of the revolution.[57] Olsen's earliest poem, "I Want You Women Up North to Know," satisfies to some degree the leftist demand for revolutionary optimism. She describes the terrible working conditions and wages of Chicana seamstresses in a Texas sweatshop, and while the poem does not end triumphantly, it includes the following stanza, which offers the 1917 Bolshevik revolution as a model of salvation for American workers:

Her brother lies on an iron cot, all day and watches,
on a mattress of rags he lies.
For twenty-five years he worked for the railroad then they laid
     him off.
     (racked days, searching for work; rebuffs; suspicious eyes of
        policemen.)
     goodbye ambrosa, mebbe in dallas I find work; desperate
        swing for a freight,
     surprised hands, clutching air, and the wheel goes over a
     leg,
     the railroad cuts it off, as it cut off twenty-five years of his
        life.)
She says that he prays and dreams of another world, as he lies
     there, a
     heaven (which he does not know was brought to earth in
        1917 in Russia,
     by workers like him).[58]

While Olsen soon moved beyond such explicit propaganda, I see
this poem as a step in her struggle to bring together protest and
dream.[59] Like other writers of the thirties, Olsen faced the challenge described by Kessler-Harris and Lauter: "How can a writer
bring alive the vision of a triumphant socialist future, which no
one has seen or fully imagined, with anything like the power to
evoke the struggles and devastation of capitalism in decline?"[60]
And because Olsen's vision has always encompassed more than
socialism, she faces the additional tasks of imagining a nonpatriar-
chal and nonracist future.

The chapters that follow will explore Olsen's images of possibility, sometimes misshapen as if battered by history, sometimes
lightly sketched as if alternatives do not yet exist, even in imagination. While her possibilities are rooted in historical gifts we have
not known how to perceive or receive, she never takes refuge in
nostalgia. Nor is Olsen utopian. She shows what might be, what
must be in this world, in our time. In fact, the most subversive
function of her work is the assertion that human life can be more
than and other than it is. Her hopeful promise of full creative life
aims to make people forever dissatisfied with the numbness of
physical, emotional, and intellectual starvation.

In the next four chapters I will discuss four themes in the light
of this paradigm. I express them as potentially fruitful tensions
which, because of blighting circumstances, become instead con-

tradictions that fragment and destroy. The first theme is that motherhood, potentially a source of creativity and social change, is
often the most formidable silencer in women's lives. When circumstances force women to choose between mothering and other
creative work, children are not miracles but enemies destroying
their mothers' lives. The second theme is that although working
women and men could be allies and supporters, identifying with
each other's needs and aspirations, patriarchy and poverty turn
men into enemies of women and children, and the patriarchal
family into an isolated, dangerous unit that cannot shelter its
members. The third theme is that familiar American tension between community and solitude, between being for oneself and
being responsible for others. This tension becomes a forced choice
between cynical individualism and isolation on the one hand and
absorption in protective but dehumanizing communities on the
other. The communities are either so embroiled in power structures that they demand betrayal from their members, or so ghet-
toized that they lock in ripples of violence and turn responsibility
into powerless guilt. The fourth theme is the necessary rhythm of
silence and language. This natural rhythm also becomes a terrible
contradiction, especially for women, but also for black people,
workers, and children, all of whom are caught between silence
and a language that erases or distorts their experiences and even
the fact of their existence.

I have chosen to follow this paradigm through Olsen's work for
reasons I have already mentioned. It challenges readings that
declare Olsen's writing either grim or serene. It is neither. Rather,
Olsen has been able to do in her fiction and nonfiction what most
writers accomplish only in poetry or fantasy: portray simultaneously oppression, strength, and the possibility of intense, liberating joy. This combination makes Olsen's writing both "conservative" and "revolutionary," asking of us as readers "tireless
research and the skill of adjusting our vision so that we can understand and value, *see* what has been neglected before," as Chevigny
writes.[61] It also asks us to imagine and value what does not yet
exist.

But crucial questions about the paradigm itself immediately
arise: Is this pattern truly empowering? For whom? Is it mislead-
ing, elitist? Has it been empowering for Olsen, whose most recent
period of silence disappoints and troubles her readers? I will offer
here only the beginning of an answer to these questions.

One of the truisms about art, writing included, is that great art grows out of great suffering. One can easily line up examples of writers whose genius seems to be directly proportioned to the oppressions they labored under. Tillie Olsen could be one of those examples. It is tempting to say that grueling days spent in the heat of Omaha packinghouses helped produce *Yonnondio;* that out of her struggle to balance necessary work, mothering, and writing came "I Stand Here Ironing" and "Tell Me a Riddle"; that Olsen's most recent silence as a writer (she has published very little since *Silences* in 1978) suggests that blight does produce fruit, and that when circumstances are favorable, the tree healthy, the climate mild, both the necessary resistance and the material disappear. But that truism, whether applied to art or to the rest of life, is both simplistic and cruel; for its logical conclusion is to leave suffering intact and to do nothing to ease hungers or oppressions, all in the interest of human achievement. That attitude is commoner than one might expect, though it is usually phrased more subtly. Critic Sally Cunneen, for example, said of Olsen, "Luckily, Tillie Olsen was never rescued" by education and cut off from her working-class roots.[62] Cunneen is a great admirer, but I do not believe she would want such dubious luck for herself. One of the values of Olsen's paradigm is that it powerfully challenges the exaltation of suffering and deprivation. I think Olsen is right in asserting over and over that the blights of racism, sexism, and class prejudice produce nothing but death. Though they sometimes produce the material of art, they cannot grant the environment that brings it to fruition. I will return to these questions in my conclusion after I have shown how the paradigm works itself out in the four themes I have chosen.

If in the chapters that follow I seem to move back and forth between blight, fruit, and possibility, that is because they are woven together in Olsen's prose, where words, images, and rhythms are so rich that they suggest all three and ask the reader to keep all three in mind. I have also followed Olsen's lead by reading her works in dialogue with each other rather than as isolated entities. Anyone who has been to a Tillie Olsen reading knows how she weaves her writing together. She might interrupt her reading of "I Stand Here Ironing" to interject the triumphant description from *Yonnondio* of Baby Bess discovering her power to act; or she might juxtapose a description of silenced writers and a description of Eva, her silenced revolutionary from "Tell Me a Riddle." Read together, Olsen's stories and essays are like the call and response of black preaching or impassioned political oratory. Perhaps one story asks a question while another provides the answer. Or one story might sketch the bit of history essential to understanding a character in a different story. Phrases, images, and myths travel by metaphorical leaps from one work to another, gathering meanings as they go and suggesting startling links that tie story to story.

Finally, although an examination of language might logically come first in a study like this one, I have chosen to discuss it last because I do not want an early focus on Olsen's admirable style or her pondering on language to divert attention from mothers, children, working men, or communities. Mothering, labor, and efforts of people to join together are not only or even primarily metaphors for writing. While thwarted artists haunt her pages, she never lets us forget the life circumstances that hinder their efforts; and while both *Silences* and her fiction are certainly about making creativity possible for writers and other artists, they are also about making mothering, fathering, and community possible.

Motherhood as Source and Silencer of Creativity

F|ROM ONE of her earliest pieces of writing—"I Want You Women Up North to Know" (1934)—to one of her most recent—*Mother to Daughter, Daughter to Mother* (1984)— Tillie Olsen has been passionately interested in mothers as writers and as subjects of literature. Motherhood as both source and silencer of creativity is one of Olsen's main themes, and she has spent her life rescuing mothers from silence, inarticulate awe, distortion, and sentimentality.

In her afterword to *Mother to Daughter, Daughter to Mother*, Olsen says that even in this book about mothers, "least present is work written by mothers themselves. . . . Whatever the differences now (including literacy, small families), for too many of the old, old reasons, few mothers while in the everyday welter of motherhood life, or after, are writing it. That everyday welter, the sense of its troublous context, the voice of the mother herself, are the largest absences in this book. And elsewhere" (275–76).

It does not take much imagination to discover what the "old, old reasons" are. One reason mothers have not written their stories is that women have been told, blatantly or subtly, that they must choose between motherhood and other creative work, including writing. (Olsen lists in *Silences* the many women writers who were childless, some by choice, many because they were convinced they had no choice.) Another old reason is the myth that motherhood is ineffable, that it is an experience so immured in nature that no one can find the words to write about it. According to this myth, mothering is something mothers intuitively know how to do but cannot explain to anyone else. This notion sets them apart from everyone—their childless sisters, the fathers of their children, and a sterile society. The underside of the myth of ineffability says that even should a woman have the confidence and time to write about motherhood, that experience is too ordinary, narrow, and dull to interest anyone except, perhaps, mothers themselves. A third reason why mothers have not told their stories is "the patriarchal injunction" Olsen describes in *Silences*, which tells women writers to avoid subjects belonging to the "woman's sphere," not because they are ineffable but simply because they are female. This injunction says to women, "If you are going to practice literature—a man's domain, profession—divest yourself of what might identify you as a woman" (250). Since mothering is an undeniably gendered mark of identification, women writers who want to succeed should avoid this subject at all costs.

Mothers have not fared much better as subjects. Their sons and daughters have often settled for grim or glowing stereotypes, and those stereotypes have passed for truth. As Adrienne Rich writes in *Of Woman Born*, it is "easier by far" for daughters to "hate and reject a mother outright than to see beyond her to the forces acting upon her."[1] Of course, some few writers in every generation have challenged the stereotypes. Daughters of immigrant mothers and daughters growing up in poverty have created portraits of mothers that are both loving and unstintingly honest, and are filled with grief, anger, and, sometimes, admiration. Edith Sumner Kelly's *Weeds* comes to mind, as do Agnes Smedley's *Daughter of Earth* and the novels of Anzia Yezierska. This is the tradition in which Olsen wrote her stories about mothers and mothering. But because most of these works went out of print soon after their publication and have only recently been reprinted, the tradition has been invisible to most readers.[2]

A more contemporary reason for the silence by and about mothers is that feminist writers and critics disagree about the value of this subject. While many contemporary feminists share Olsen's interest, there is by no means a consensus. In a review of May Sarton's 1985 novel, *The Magnificent Spinster*, Valerie Miner reveals this uneasy split: "For anyone dismayed by the current feminist infatuation for motherhood, it is refreshing to read a novel in which the women do stand on their own."[3] Olsen's interest in mothering can hardly be termed infatuation—it is neither fleeting nor romantic—yet she is determined to bring to light not only the oppression mothers have suffered but also "the yields possible in circumstanced motherhood," as she says in *Silences*. She is well aware that loving and admiring depictions of motherhood might be read as reproaches by women who have chosen to remain childless. Several years after her famous 1971 talk at the Modern Language Association Forum on Women Writers in the Twentieth Century, Olsen reflected that she barely touched the subject of the gifts mothers give, fearing that the many childless professional women in the audience would hear her remarks as one more version of the "traditional (mis)use" of the joys of motherhood "to rebuke and belittle the hard-won achievement of their lives; more of the societal coercion to conform; family as the only suitable way of life for a female" (*S* 202).

A stanza from "Cellar Door," a recent poem by Sue Standing which Olsen includes in *Mother to Daughter, Daughter to Mother*, expresses another familiar dilemma Olsen shares with other women writing about their mothers:

> Her hands stained and nicked
> from all the peeling, cutting, blanching—
> beautiful how she touched things,
> how quickly she could thread a needle.
> I'm not supposed to love her for this—
> smoothing our hair, sewing our clothes,
> or on her knees waxing the floor.[4]

Showing mothers' domestic work as beautiful and admirable might seem to women readers like reinforcements of limiting roles or as calls to duplicate the patterns of their mothers' lives.

Olsen's life and the content of her work stand in direct opposition to these reasons, old and new, that have made motherhood "the least understood, the most tormentingly complex experience to wrest to truth" (*S* 254). Her life as writer and working mother of four daughters contradicts the idea that mothering and writing are by their very nature mutually exclusive activities. Although she writes eloquently in *Silences* of the domestic and economic structures that limited her writing and almost prevented it altogether, she writes just as eloquently of the ways in which her life as mother gave her the substance of her work.

In almost everything she has written, Olsen delineates the distorted shape motherhood has taken in patriarchal society and critiques the cluster of beliefs about it that have been passed on as truth from generation to generation. It is part of her revolutionary work of helping to change "what will not let life be" for women. But Olsen's repudiation of patriarchal motherhood, that "last refuge of sexism," as she calls it,[5] is not in any sense a rejection of mothers or mothering. On the contrary, Olsen considers mothering one of the great untold stories of women's lives and one of the great unmined sources of literary marvels. (Unlike Rich, who uses the word *mothering* to mean the experience and *motherhood* to denote the institution, Olsen uses these words interchangeably. Only the context makes her meaning clear. I will follow Rich's usage throughout this chapter, however.) Olsen insists in *Silences* that the losses to literature and to many other fields of knowledge and endeavor have been incalculable "because comprehensions possible out of motherhood *(including,* among so much invaluable else, *the very nature, needs, illimitable potentiality of the human being— and the everyday means by which these are distorted, discouraged, limited, extinguished)* . . . have had . . . to remain inchoate, fragmentary, unformulated (and alas, unvalidated)" (202). The task she has set for herself is to bring those comprehensions to "powerful, undeniable, useful expression" (*S* 202).

In the mid thirties, when Olsen began writing about mothers and their lives, the American Communist party had already entered the phase Paula Rabinowitz calls the Popular Front era. As a way of distancing itself from Stalinist repression in the U.S.S.R., the party turned toward mainstream American values and "adopted images of wholesome family life that conformed to stereotypes of Mom and apple pie." In literature by both men and women, this Popular Front ideology "produced a sentimental portrait of motherhood as a natural well for political consciousness."[6] Olsen, along with other Socialist women writers, resisted this sentimental ideology, asserting through her characters that the constrained and limited lives of mothers in patriarchal society was a dry well indeed, from which women could draw neither political consciousness nor the energy for political action.

On the other hand, she writes in *Silences* that "conscience and world sensibility are as natural to women as to men; men have been freer to develop and exercise them, that is all" (42). This conviction seems to have come to her not by way of party ideology but from her own life experiences and from knowing committed socialist women like her mother and the Bundists Seevya and Genya Gorelick, the three women to whom she dedicates "Tell Me a Riddle." This is the story in which a mother's "world sensibility" is most evident, and it seems to be more than coincidence that Olsen began writing it in 1955–56, the year in which all three women died.[7] Olsen found in them and in her own life the combination of experiences that do lead mothers to political consciousness and a commitment to change that reaches far beyond their own families. That combination includes early political involvement, wide reading, and a knowledge of history. In several of her characters, most notably Eva in "Tell Me a Riddle," Olsen brings to "useful expression" a mother's world consciousness.

Finally, Olsen understands well the chasms that exist between mothers and their daughters, and between women who are mothers and those who are not. Yet her work reveals her belief that only full and honest remembering, neither distorted by bitterness nor softened by nostalgia, can bridge those chasms. One of the ways in which Olsen accomplishes this many-faceted task is by embodying in three complex sets of images the blight-fruit-possibility paradigm I described in the previous chapter as the fluid structuring principle of her work. Specifically, she uses three constellations of images, centering on hunger, stone, and flood, to describe the blighted circumstances of mothers' lives, to express wonder at the fruit of endurance and beauty their lives have borne, and to sketch the joyful possibilities that mothering could hold for women and for the world. But Olsen transforms these three sets of images into one another with the logic of poetry or dream, setting up echoes and oppositions both within and between works. In the discussion that follows, I will try to show what these image patterns mean and, at the same time, follow their intertwined, shifting course through Olsen's work.

The first of these image patterns revolves around hunger and food. In everything Olsen has written—her poetry, fiction, essays—she uses the language of eating, of feast and famine, of nurturing and starvation, of fat bellies and skeleton children to show a blighted world. In several works—most notably *Yonnondio*—hunger is a literal fact of life, the obvious result of chronic, institutionalized poverty; but in every work, spiritual, emotional, and intellectual hungers gnaw even at those characters who are well fed.

The images of food and eating also suggest that life is meant to be a banquet in a plentiful, generous world. In a world of possibility, feeding is an expression of gracious and generous nurturance in an interlocking human and natural ecology; and hungers for food, justice, knowledge, and beauty are all part of the healthy reaching out to life. Even the dead become nourishment for the living. But, at least on the surface, that is not the world of Olsen's stories. She shows us instead a world where to survive one must take food from others. Hunger, of necessity, becomes savagery; food snatched from others and hastily devoured is tasteless; and nourishment given binds people to each other through unending need.

Although Olsen is concerned with all hungry people, the hungers of mothers and children preoccupy her most. Even one of her earliest poems, "I Want You Women Up North to Know," is filled with the familiar images of starving mothers and their children. There is Catalina Rodriguez, age twenty-four, her "body shrivelled to a child's at twelve, / and her cough, gay, quick, staccato, / like a skeleton's bones clattering"; and Catalina Torres, who "to keep the starved body starving, embroiders from dawn to / night," spurred on by "the pinched faces of four huddled / children / the naked bodies of four bony children, / the chant of their chorale of hunger."[8]

Yonnondio picks up these images of physical deprivation, showing impoverished mothers and their families living in a world that feeds on them instead of providing nourishment. Through Olsen's multiple vision we see both men and women caught in poverty; this same vision, however, shows us the further devastation suffered by poor women, as the additional overlay of sexism leads husbands to feed off their wives and forces mothers and children to devour each other's substance.

While Jim and Anna share the want their poverty imposes, Anna carries the additional burden of Jim's assumed ownership of her body. Because he sees her and her "damn brats" both as his possessions and as dead weight, he demands from her all the sustenance an unjust and uncaring society refuses to give him. One night at supper, not seeing how sick Anna is, Jim pushes aside his plate saying, "Anytime I want sewage to eat I can get it on the job" (89). But he is hungry, so he shoves down the tasteless food. That night he comes home drunk and rapes Anna. Before this meal, Jim says to Mazie, "Git in there and help your ma git dinner on the table. You might tell her Bess aint the only one in the house that wants to eat" (87). This seemingly harmless statement ominously foreshadows Anna's rape and miscarriage. Anna becomes the victim of Jim's ravenous hunger and the two actions part of the same meal. As Olsen's context makes clear, Jim hungers not for food or sex, but for his manhood; or, more accurately, he hungers for the human dignity that is being taken from him.

Anna's repeated pregnancies are the inevitable result of Jim's attitude toward her. Olsen describes these pregnancies, too, in terms of hunger, but this time it is Anna and her children who feed on each other. When Anna becomes pregnant for the fifth time in seven years, she sinks into a stupor, neglecting her family and her house. She is "caught in the drowse" of her pregnancy, trapped in "a dream paralysis." "Drugged by the warmth," she sits by the stove for hours at a time, "her hands over her belly, a half smile of wisdom on her mouth." Anna grows "monstrous fat" with this new child while her other children go hungry, "thinning . . . as if she was feeding on them" (52).

But Anna's monstrous size is deceptive, just as the protruding stomachs of starving babies are deceptive. After this fifth child is born, the image of Anna feeding off her children is reversed, and she grows gaunt and sick, with Baby Bess perpetually tugging at her breast. Olsen wants us to hear the unconscious irony in Jim's statement, "Jesus Christ, woman . . . where does the money go to? God knows we're eatin worse'n animals, and Bess eatin off you don't cost more" (71). Firmly entrenched in the sexist attitude that women are good for nothing but sex and childbearing, Jim refuses to see that each succeeding pregnancy devours more of Anna's health and energy—more of herself.

Olsen shows that mothers living in poverty are doubly starved, bearing their children's deprivations as well as their own. Though Anna's sensitivity makes her attentive to each child's needs and gifts, the knowledge that she cannot meet the needs or cultivate the gifts drains her energy as surely as repeated pregnancies. One of the tragedies of this story is that even though Anna holds herself to the task of making a better life for her children, she is unable to give them even physical necessities, much less a taste for beauty or the education she believes means freedom for them.

In Olsen's view, one reason mothers are devoured in patriarchal culture is that the family, and more often than not the mother, is solely responsible for the children's well-being. During the "dream paralysis" of her pregnancy on the South Dakota farm, Anna is rooted as one is in a nightmare, unable to wrench herself free from the mesh of social expectations that holds her fast. During the ice-locked winter on the prairie, the solitude and the cramped house drive Jim almost to distraction. He escapes to do chores and disappears in the afternoons to talk and drink with the neighbors. But what Jim cannot endure, Anna must, spending her pregnancy shut up in a room with four small, sniffling children and no adults to talk to. The harshness of Anna's lonely struggle to nurture her children comes through clearly in the scene in *Yonnondio* when, after a physical and emotional breakdown, Anna drags herself out of bed to plant a garden. Jim finds her there, but when he tries to get her to go back to bed, she says fiercely:

> "Who's to do it if I'm not up? Answer. *Who?* Who's to . . .
> look out for . . ." Gasping hoarsely. "Who's to care for 'em if
> we dont? Who? . . .
>   "*Who?* Answer me . . . Oh Jim," giving in, collapsing into
> his reaching embrace, "the children." Over and over, broken:
> "the children. What's going to happen with them? How are
> we going to look out for them? O Jim, the children. Seems like
> we cant do nothing for them in this damn world." (106–7)

All of Anna's children suffer as their physical and spiritual hungers grow and Anna becomes less able to meet their needs. But her repeated pregnancies have the most disastrous effect on Mazie. They deprive her of the beauty and tenderness she needs, force terrifying responsibilities on her, and make her see the cycle of her mother's life in some confused way as the pattern of her own.

The chapter describing Anna's fifth pregnancy graphically shows this harmful progression. Early in the chapter, Olsen shows that both nature and words help Mazie resist attacks on her self-confidence and keep her faith in the goodness of her family. They feed her hunger for beauty and for creative control of her world. Sometimes Mazie stands near the road and watches buggies roll by: "When there are gay little girls sitting high and proud in the buggies, ribbons in their hair blowing a long streamer in the wind, shame and envy shudder over her, and she draws herself together to make herself nothing, to lose herself in the faded gray dress on her body. Then the sun and wind rippling over her skin, and the gold corn moving against the sky lull her into beauty again with the slenderest arms of rhythm" (41). Another passage shows that words, too, afford Mazie a refuge from poverty. After she and Will start school, she sees clearly her own "rag-bag clothes"; and when the sadness for herself and her family is more than she can bear, she gathers her little brothers together and recites a nonsense rhyme that their neighbor, Mr. Caldwell, taught her:

Oh Were I a Lum Ti Tum Tum
In the land of the alivoo fig
I'd play on the strum ti tum tum
To the tune of the thinguma jig.

It does not matter to Mazie that the words do not make sense; that is their charm. Their playful mystery lifts her out of poverty: "Reciting it, the sadness would ebb; the autumn would become blue and gold again" (47).

But during the long winter, Mazie feels herself being pulled into the "dream paralysis" of patriarchal motherhood; and soon even nature and language—as necessary to her as food—are turned into grotesque reflections of pregnancy and birth. One early spring day near the end of Anna's pregnancy, Mazie and her brother Will escape to a daisy-sprinkled hillside. Mazie shuts her eyes and presses her fingers over the lids so that she will see butterflies, "their wings all colored," rather than the burgeoning shapes around her that remind her of her pregnant mother:

> Trees fat with oily buds, and the swollen breasts of prairie.
> Ugly. She turned her eyes to the sky for oblivion, but it was
> bellies, swollen bellies, black and corpse gray, puffing out bag-
> gier and baggier, cloud belly on cloud belly till at the zenith
> they push vast and swollen. Her mother. Night, sweating
> bodies. The blood and pain of birth. . . . She could feel words
> swollen big within her, words coming out with pain, bloody,
> all clothed in red. She began to hit Will, hard, ferocious. . . .
> "Oh Will, Oh were I a Lum Ti Tum Tum." Ugly. Swollen like
> bellies. (55–56)

In this brilliantly written passage, the images and realities of pregnancy, starvation, and bloated death are superimposed on each other. Words and nature are pulled into Mazie's nightmare and turned into caricatures of themselves. The magic drains out of Mr. Caldwell's rhymes, as they too become "ugly. Fat bellies."

Immediately after the scene on the daisy-covered hillside comes the birth of Anna's fifth child. Olsen begins her description with these terse lines: "[Mazie] wakened that night to a nightmare of Jim's savage hand on her shoulder. 'Wake up now. Your mother's goin to have a baby, and you've got to help her'" (56). Jim goes to get the neighbor women, leaving a terrified eight-year-old to help her mother prepare to give birth. When they return, Mazie runs out to the barn, away from the pain on her mother's face and the half-understood words of the adults. "Then, strangely, hunger came. Trickles of it in her mouth, battling under the nausea. Food—the smell of it yearned in her nostrils. She found an egg, warm. It slipped down her throat, then it was washed up again, spurting over the ground. Yes Momma. I'm sick, Momma. Butterflies lives behind your eyes. Perhaps there were stars above, known stars" (57). The story's imagery underlines the irony of this description: it is predictable rather than strange that the events of her mother's life stir in Mazie a persistent hunger food cannot satisfy. Significantly, this scene, like Anna's hungry pregnancy, is set on the South Dakota farm where for once food is plentiful and good. But because Anna and Mazie are hungry for more than food, easing physical poverty cannot ease other kinds of starvation nor preserve Mazie's hopes for a different future for herself.

It is not farfetched to say that Mazie realizes in some intuitive way that she has escaped her mother's fate only because of her age, and that only temporarily. Here and throughout *Yonnondio* she runs away as often and as long as she can from the seemingly irrevocable facts of her mother's life—childbirth and miscarriage, rape, endless work, and bondage—escaping into the barn, the street, the dump, or her fantasy world. But her defiant flight is always temporary, and the bonds that tie her to her family always bring her back. When Mazie looks at her gaunt or pregnant mother "with pain and fear and pity in her eyes," those feelings are certainly as much for herself as they are for Anna.

In "Tell Me a Riddle," Olsen shows even more clearly than in *Yonnondio* the grotesque shape of motherhood in the patriarchy and the immense cost of the institution to mother and children. Again, she totals up the cost by filling this story with the language of starvation, feeding, and eating. Eva, the central character, is a grandmother, with her years of pregnancy and child rearing far behind her. Yet in describing her, Olsen uses images that suggest both pregnancy and starvation. Eva is a little gnome, "all bones and swollen belly," with clawlike hands and a "yellow skull face"—the portrait of starvation that stares at us daily from posters and television screens. Those closest to her see her as something edible. David, her husband, and Nancy, her daughter-in-law, try to persuade her to move from her familiar home to the Haven, a "cooperative for the aged" run by David's lodge. When she refuses, they leave her to "stew a while," as Nancy puts it. But perhaps more important, the language of food both expresses and shapes Eva's perception of herself and of the people and events surrounding her. When David complains to the children about her harsh tongue, she thinks, "(Vinegar he poured on me all his life; I am well marinated; how can I be honey now?)" Her quarrel with David over selling the house becomes a "bellyful of bitterness," her sickness she feels as a "ravening inside," and her children are "morsels" with "lovely mouths" that "devour."

Linda Yoder describes well one purpose of this "overwhelming concentration of [food] imagery." It underlines, she says, Eva's overidentification with her role as mother "against which Eva will wisely, though painfully, struggle."[9] In other words, Eva's life has been so completely absorbed by nurturing others that these activities have taken over her ways of thinking and feeling and even her language. To borrow Olsen's imagery, they have eaten her up.

It was a brilliant stroke on Olsen's part to make Eva a grandmother living in the relatively affluent fifties rather than in the hungry twenties of *Yonnondio*. For Eva, the tasks of mothering that used up Anna's life are only memories, or have dwindled into unimportance. Instead of skimpy meals stretched to feed nine, now "a herring out of a jar is enough." While David worries about money, Eva shrugs, "In America, who starves?" The ironic answer to this question is that mothers starve even in America and even long after they have stopped being responsible for their children and no longer have to contend with physical hunger.

Against her family's urging, Eva refuses to nurture her grandchildren in the traditional mothers'/grandmothers' ways—holding, comforting, feeding—because she knows she dare not let herself be drawn again into the "long drunkenness" of needing and being needed, of devouring and being devoured by trusting children. Yet it is significant that she never abandons the language of food and hunger, and at the end of her life talks deliriously about "bread, day-old" and "one pound soup meat." Furthermore, Olsen's omniscient narrator continues to use this language to describe Eva, suggesting that motherhood as defined and structured in patriarchal society starves mothers by absorbing them body and spirit. Eva is hungry for all the nourishment that her life has refused her or that she has resolutely given away to be true to herself and her beliefs. As later chapters will show, she is hungry for both solitude and community, silence and language. (Eva even *tastes* and *chews* words and ideas.) Unaware that he is accurately describing her spirit as well as her body, David reminds Eva that she is "all bones and a swollen belly." All David sees are the symptoms of her illness; but here, as in *Yonnondio,* Olsen wants her readers to see mocking visual echoes of starvation and pregnancy which, mirroring each other and her illness, together form the shape of Eva's life.

In her fine essay "The Hungry Jewish Mother," Erika Duncan sets "Tell Me a Riddle" in the context of Jewish-American literature by women. In this literature, writes Duncan, "mothers are the 'bread givers' who try to make feeding into a replenishing, ecstatic act. But the mothers are themselves starved in every way, sucked dry and withered from being asked almost from birth to give a nurturance they never receive. They are starved not only for the actual food they are forced to turn over to others, but for the stuff of self and soul, for love and song."[10] That is the blighted life mothers lead in patriarchal society. As Olsen would say, that is the life of most women, past and present, as they carry the full weight of gender, class, and sometimes racial bias. We also see clearly the ways in which the mothers' hungers are visited upon their children, especially their daughters, who, like Anna's Mazie and Eva's Clara and Hannah, are reduced to "hands to help."

But to stop with grief and anger is to stop far short of Olsen's destination. The second element of her structuring paradigm, the fruit borne by the blighted tree, is nowhere more evident than in her portraits of mothers. For Olsen's fictional mothers possess intelligence, courage, and a gritty determination to survive, no matter how insurmountable the obstacles they face. What is more, in every story, mothers reach beyond survival to make their children's lives richer and wider than theirs have been. Sometimes they succeed; more often they fail. But even in failure, Olsen says, the most nourishing bread they give future generations is the coarse grain of their courageous effort. An important part of the task Olsen has set for herself is to acknowledge this nurturance. She does so by setting remembered moments of beauty and exaltation in mothers' lives in their context of pain and struggle.

This combination of beauty and struggle is evident in a remarkable passage from *Yonnondio,* in which the rhythms of Olsen's prose transform work that might be seen only as absolute drudgery into grace. It is no accident, of course, that the work Olsen describes is that of preserving food. The scene occurs on an unbearably hot day in a long line of such days, and Anna is in her kitchen canning fruit, making jelly, and tending her children all at the same time. Here is a portion of that scene. Read aloud, its rhythms work their way into the body:

In the humid kitchen, Anna works on alone. . . . The last batch of jelly is on the stove. Between stirring and skimming, and changing the wet packs on Ben, Anna peels and cuts the canning peaches—two more lugs to go. If only all will sleep awhile. She begins to sing softly—*I saw a ship a-sailing, a-sailing on the sea*—it clears her head. The drone of fruit flies and Ben's rusty breathing are very loud in the unmoving, heavy air. Bess begins to fuss again. *There, there, Bessie, there, there,* stopping to sponge down the oozing sores on the tiny body. *There.* Skim, stir; sprinkle Bess; pit, peel and cut; sponge; skim, stir. Any second the jelly will be right and must not wait. Shall she wake up Jimmie and ask him to blow a feather to keep Bess quiet? No, he'll wake cranky, he's just a baby hisself, let him sleep. Skim, stir; sprinkle; change the wet packs on Ben; pit, peel and cut; sponge. This time it does not soothe—Bess stiffens her body, flails her fists, begins to scream in misery, just as the jelly begins to boil. There is nothing for it but to take Bess up, jounce her on a hip (*there, there*) and with her free hand frantically skim and ladle. *There, there.* The batch is poured and capped and sealed, all one-handed, jiggling-hipped. There, there, it is done. (148–49)

In a recent talk, Olsen said that only when she read this scene aloud to an audience did she realize that Anna's movements had the economy and disciplined grace of dance. "We gladly applaud for dancers on the stage," she said, "but do not recognize the similar grace and miracle of synchronization" of a mother, her baby on one hip, canning and tending her other children. Olsen added that she likes to imagine Anna's granddaughters as dancers, whose freer lives Anna had made possible with her hard work and loving determination.[11]

There is danger in this kind of writing. Turning relentless work into a dance could lead to the kind of sentimentality that perpetuates the work by casting the softening glow of nostalgia over it and that encourages daughters to repeat the surface patterns of their mothers' lives. That Olsen is alert to this danger is clear from the scenes following this domestic dance, in which the same event is seen as a mother's daily deadly toil; her skilled and useful labor to feed her family; and a moment of beauty that is as necessary and nourishing as canned peaches and amber jelly.

The multiple tasks push Anna to trembling, and her tenderness with the children is mixed "with a compulsion of exhaustion to have done, to put Bess outside in the yard where she can scream and scream outside of hearing and Anna can be free to splash herself with running water, forget the canning and the kids and sink into a chair, lay her forehead on the table and do nothing" (149–50). But Anna does not stop; she keeps working through the afternoon, surrounded by her heat-sickened children. Late in the day, as Anna still works, the sun—shining through a prism salvaged from the dump—sheds rainbows on the room. Mazie watches as the rainbow falls on Anna: "Not knowing an every-hued radiance floats on her hair, her mother stands at the sink; her knife seems flying. Fruit flies rise and settle and rise." Mazie, with her quick appreciation for beauty of any kind, says lovingly, "Momma" (152).

Light and shadow chase each other across these few pages, as Olsen's style turns drudgery into dance and back into drudgery, and then, for a fleeting moment casts "the stammering light" of beauty and promise over the whole scene. The cycles of poverty and sexism that rule *Yonnondio* will end this moment and perhaps steal it from Mazie's memory. (In "Tell Me a Riddle," Eva's delirious, deathbed singing reminds her oldest daughter, Clara, of a sound she has not heard or remembered since childhood. Clara cries in silent anguish, "*Where did we lose each other, first mother, singing mother?*" [116].) Even knowing well that moments like this one are often lost to daughters, Olsen has chosen to preserve it as precious and nourishing without in any way exalting the toil or urging future generations of daughters to repeat it.

To return to Duncan's phrase, Olsen's fictional mothers are "bread givers" dedicated to feeding their children's bodies, minds, and hearts. But Olsen shows another, equally important yield of "circumstanced motherhood." Because the experience of mothering, coupled with the other crucial experiences I described earlier, gives them what Olsen calls "a profound feeling about the preciousness of life on earth,"[12] the other fruit their lives sometimes bear is an awareness of justice and injustice that reaches beyond the walls of home and family. Olsen dramatizes this sense of justice most powerfully in Eva, who like the Seevya and Genya of Olsen's dedication, had been a revolutionary during her girlhood in Russia, has memorized her few books, and knows both past history and the United States of the 1950s. To understand what Olsen is saying about Eva's wide-ranging consciousness we need to return to the image of bread, this time superimposed on the recurring image of stone.

Bread and stone run parallel to each other through most of "Tell Me a Riddle." In the scene just before Eva's death, they leave their parallel tracks, meet, and undergo that transmutation of shape and meaning that Olsen uses so powerfully. In Eva's last delirious words, these two images reveal that her embattled love for her family and her desire to create a more just world for everyone are somehow the same passion, felt with the same intensity and fed by the same springs. David keeps watch by her deathbed and listens as she repeats bits from her memorized books, the facts of destruction in human history, snatches of songs, and speeches from their revolutionary past. They are litanies of courage, hope, and terror for the human race:

> Slaveships   deathtrains   clubs   eeenough
> The bell   summon what enables
> 78,000 in one minute (whisper of a scream) 78,000 human
> beings   we'll destroy ourselves?

and:

> Lift high banner of reason (tatter of an orator's voice) jus-
> tice   freedom   light
> Humankind   life worthy   capacities
> Seeks (blur of shudder) belong   human being   (118, 119)

As David listens, it seems to him that Eva is "maliciously . . . playing back only what said nothing of him, of the children, of their intimate life together." He says to her, knowing she cannot hear him, "A lifetime you tended and loved, and now not a word of us, for us." Finally Eva's words work their way into his consciousness, and he too remembers the idealism of their youth, the ways he has conspired with society to betray those ideals, "and the monstrous shapes of what had actually happened in the century." To ease himself, he thinks of their grandchildren, "whose childhoods were childish, who had never hungered, who lived unravaged by disease in warm houses of many rooms, had all the school for which they cared, could walk on any street, stood a head taller than their grandparents, towered above—beautiful skins, straight backs, clear straightforward eyes. . . . And was this not the dream then, come true in ways undreamed?" (121).

The answer to David's question is *yes*, but only if one is thinking in individualistic terms. For Eva, *family* and *children* have meanings that extend far beyond tight biological definitions. Thoughts of the well-being of her own family have never allowed Eva to escape into complacency, and now, having fallen under her spell, David cannot escape either. He answers his own question "as if in her harsh voice":

> *And are there no other children in the world?* . . .
> *And the flame of freedom, the light of knowledge?*
> *And the drop, to spill no drop of blood?* (121)

Eva's sense of responsibility for all the children of the world also deepens her sense of helplessness and grief. One of her hungers is surely the hunger and thirst for justice, and her starving body, that "swollen thinness," imitates as if by sympathetic magic the bodies of children not so well-fed as her own. Now, under Eva's influence, David begins to feel her lifelong starvation. He piles a tray with food, eats it, but "still was there thirst or hunger ravening in him."

As David realizes how much of his own idealism has been lost, he is filled with wonder that Eva has not lost or betrayed her dreams. But when David asks her to affirm their wide-ranging vision, Eva answers with memories of their private life together, and bitter memories at that:

> *Still she believed?* "Eva!" he whispered. "Still you believed? You lived by it? These Things Shall Be?"
>
> "One pound soup meat," she answered distinctly, "one soup bone."
>
> "My ears heard you. Ellen Mays was witness: 'Humankind . . . one has to believe.'" Imploringly: "Eva!"
>
> "Bread, day-old." She was mumbling. "Please, in a wooden box . . . for kindling. The thread, hah, the thread breaks. Cheap thread"—and a gurgling, enormously loud, began in her throat.
>
> "I ask for stone; she gives me bread—day-old." He pulled his hand away, shouted: "Who wanted questions? Everything you have to wake?" . . .
>
> Words jumbled, cleared. In a voice of crowded terror:
>
> "Paul, Sammy, don't fight.
>
> "Hannah, have I ten hands?
>
> "How can I give it, Clara, how can I give it if I don't have?"
>
> "You lie," he said sturdily, "there was joy too."
>
> Bitterly: "Ah how cheap you speak of us at the last." (123)

This short scene is, among other things, a small masterpiece of ironic humor; even this close to death, David and Eva talk in parallel monologues, their memories as unsynchronized as their lives in America have been.

What interests me most, though, is David's remark, "I ask for stone; she gives me bread—day-old." This is a witty reversal of the New Testament passage in which Jesus describes the mercy of God with this homely comparison: "Is there a man among you who would hand his son a stone when he asked for bread?" (Matt. 7:9).[13] The reversals move in every direction. David asks not God or his father for sustenance, but rather his dying wife. He also reverses the usual connotations of bread and stone. The nourishment David asks for to feed his ravenous hunger is the stone of unshakeable faith in life rather than bread, which at best is perishable; day-old, it is a mark of poverty and defeat. Of course, David attributes Eva's refusal to give him the nourishment he needs to her contrariness. The fact is that she is not answering his questions at all, but following the associative drift of her own memories. What Olsen gives us is a picture of Eva's thoughts and a hint of her influence, finally, on David. Although Eva can articulate the link only in fragments, in her mind, the personal and the political are knitted together. In the early part of this scene, Eva will not let David rejoice in his own family's health and lose sight of the world's hungry children; here she will not let him take refuge in dreams of political change that do not encompass the often dreary realities of family life, where mothers must struggle alone to make ends meet.

That familiar split between the personal and political has no place in Olsen's writing. As Catharine Stimpson writes: "Given her sense of American politics, Olsen cannot show the achievement of the good dream, only its transformation into terror or its dissolution. When the dream is dissipated, as it is for the American-born children of Russian revolutionaries in 'Tell Me a Riddle,' its political contents, its sense of 'the flame of freedom, the light of knowledge,' are lost. Only its personal contents are gratified. Without the political, the personal is merely materialistic."[14] I would add, however, that in Olsen's feminist vision, the reverse is also true: in patriarchal America, without the personal, and especially without a consideration of the lives of women and children, the political is empty theory, espousing equality on street corners or in labor halls while ignoring the deep ills of family life.

Just as the personal and the political, reality and idealism are fused in this scene, so are the images of bread and stone. If we read the rest of the story with this fusion in mind, earlier references to stone take on unexpected meanings. Two such references give insights into the marvels Eva's life can yield to the alert reader and the ways in which her life breaks out of the isolation of motherhood.

Early in the story, as part of his campaign to get Eva to move to the Haven, David shouts at her, "You sit, you sit—there too you could sit like a stone" (78). Critic Mary DeShazer says that this description, along with David's epithet, Mrs. Word Miser, turns Eva into a "silent, Sphinx-like hoarder of words" who, in struggling with the Sphinx's question, "What is Man?" finds both the question and the answer inadequate to human experience, and more specifically, to women's experience. As DeShazer writes, "Man has been too long the seeker of and answer to the riddle . . . ; woman too must identify the quest. Traditionally woman has been unable to riddle, for she has lacked the power to name her own experience."[15] While David glibly matches his grandchildren riddle for riddle, the silent, searching Eva says she knows no riddles. It would be more accurate to say that she knows no answers to the riddles that torment her and certainly none that she could tell a child.

While this image of Eva as Sphinx is provocative, I think Olsen expects or, more realistically, hopes that her readers will also see in this woman sitting "like a stone" Rebecca Harding Davis's korl woman from *Life in the Iron Mills,* the book Olsen rescued from oblivion. The korl woman is rock hard, "crouching on the ground, her arms flung out in some wild gesture of warning." She is hungry, her maker Hugh Wolfe says, not for meat but for "summat to make her live." Far from being inscrutable like the Sphinx, she has a "wild, eager face like that of a starving wolf's." She is the product not of an ancient civilization, but of American industrial society, carved from the waste material from the iron mill. Her maker is an illiterate miller who, with no hope of ever becoming anything better, is cursed or blessed with an artist's eye and hands and heart. The korl woman's form is "muscular, grown coarse with labor"; one of the visitors to the mill, looking at the "bony wrist" and "the strained sinews of the instep," describes her as a "working woman,—the very type of her class." The visitors see in her gesturing arms both "the peculiar action of a man dying of thirst" and "the mad, half-despairing gesture of drowning." Finally, the sympathetic narrator of the story, who keeps the carving after Hugh Wolfe's suicide, says that the korl woman has "a wan, woeful face, through which the spirit of the dead korl-cutter looks out, with its thwarted life, its mighty hunger, its unfinished work. Its pale, vague lips seem to tremble with a terrible question. 'Is this the End?' they say,—'nothing beyond?—no more?'"[16]

These are Eva's questions. She asks them not only about her own life and the life of her son, Davy, who was killed in World War II, but also about all those lives wasted by war and by many kinds of starvation. In her delirium, she says: "Tell Sammy's boy, he who flies, tell him to go to Stuttgart and see where Davy has no grave. And what? . . . And what? where millions have no graves—save air" (113–14). Her most tormenting questions are "when will it end?" and "Man . . . we'll destroy ourselves?" (108).

Whether as Sphinx or korl woman or both, after a lifetime of being bread, Eva has conspired with the circumstances of her life to change herself into stone. This becomes clear if we look at another important passage, shortly after she has refused to hold her newest grandson. She spends the afternoons shut in the closet in her daughter's home, trying to protect herself from her family and their needs. As her mind travels impressionistically from subject to subject, she repeats to herself her grandson Richard's lesson on rocks: "Of stones . . . there are three kinds: earth's fire jetting; rock of layered centuries; crucibled new out of old (igneous, sedimentary, metamorphic). But there was that other—frozen to black glass, never to transform or hold the fossil memory . . . (let not my seed fall on stone). . . . (stone will perish, but the word remain). And you, David, who with a stone slew, screaming: Lord, take my heart of stone and give me flesh" (99). Shortly before this, Richard had given her two specimens to start her own rock collection, the first a trilobite fossil, the second a piece of obsidian, shiny and impervious as glass. It is as if Eva is pondering which kind she is, seeing the risks of being stone rather than bread. In her pondering, the meanings of stone shift, reach back into myth and history, and take on a dizzying ambiguity. Eva wants to become, and somehow leave for the world, something that will last, outliving her body and keeping her beliefs alive, green and burning in its heart. She knows that bread spoils or is devoured, leaving children always hungry for more. She wants instead to be the kind of rock that is shaped by history or the kind that holds "the fossil memory," to be cherished by a future generation of children collecting the wisdom of the past.

The line, "And you, David, who with a stone slew, screaming:

Lord, take my heart of stone and give me flesh," is puzzling at
first. David is of course the biblical David who killed Goliath with a
stone from his slingshot, but from there on, the scriptural refer-
ence will lead us astray if we follow it too closely. (The David story
is from the first Book of Samuel [17:36–58], while the second half of
the quotation comes from the Book of Ezekiel where it is reported
as the word of God spoken to the people of Israel through the
prophet [36:26–27].) By this time Olsen has made it clear that Eva
is not an observant Jew, having rejected her religion as a young
girl. What she knows of Scripture is probably meant to be a mix-
ture of early memories and gleanings that are simply a part of
Judaeo-Christian culture. Olsen frequently shifts the meanings of
biblical passages, sometimes slightly, sometimes radically, often
with ironical results. Here David is not the heroic savior of his
people but a slayer in a world where death breeds death. He might
represent David her husband, whose imperviousness to her needs
has been in some way deadly to both of them; he might be her son
Davy, who killed and was killed in World War II; he might be her
gentle friend Lisa, who killed an informer with her teeth; he might
be humankind, all of us implicated in death even as we pray for
the ability to love. David might be Eva herself, hardening her
heart, and in so doing betraying herself and others. For Eva faces
the danger that she will simply be "frozen to black glass," closed to
love or pity, a stone on which no seed can grow. (In another
kaleidoscopic shifting of images, seed comes to mean life itself, the
grain made into bread, children, and the word.) Eva continues her
pondering, "(stone will perish, but the word remain.)" She is no
doubt thinking of her beloved authors and orators and, with despair, of all her own unspoken words, which, if she could only say
them, would outlive her.

    In creating a character like Eva, a woman and a mother who has
somehow kept all these supposed opposites alive within her, Olsen shows that even in the patriarchy mothering bears fruit. In the
scene from the end of the story that I described earlier, day-old
bread and inedible stone are transformed into a feast, as Eva and
her granddaughter Jeannie teach each other the intricate relationships between life and death and together teach David. Jeannie
gives Eva the easeful knowledge that at last someone has heard
and understood the lessons her life taught her.

    I have said that in describing Eva's swollen body, Olsen super-
imposes the images of fatal illness, starvation, and pregnancy in
order to show the terrible cost exacted by poverty and patriarchal

motherhood. For Olsen, even this nightmare image suggests possibilities that for me were completely unexpected. In this scene David finally comes to understand the breadth and fidelity of Eva's life. For the first time in years, perhaps for the first time in their marriage, he sees her in her full humanity, "dear, personal, fleshed," and instead of coining one more ironic epithet, he calls her by name. He sees Jeannie's sketch of himself and Eva, their hands clasped, "feeding each other"; obeying the images, he lies down, "holding the sketch (as if it could shield against the monstrous shapes of loss, of betrayal, of death) and with his free hand [takes] hers back into his" (124). In this scene, David and Eva feed each others' starvation (the "ravening" each feels) and in some way give birth to each other, their hands umbilical cords, and Jeannie the midwife. The tragedy here is that it is her life as mother, as bread and bread giver, that made Eva's perceptions possible and at the same time commanded her silence. For Eva the birth and the saving nourishment come too late. But Olsen gives the wisdom of Eva's life to her readers through the words of this story, this imperishable stone.

Although Olsen is convinced that even "circumstanced motherhood" is the source of marvels in life and in literature, her writing always urges her readers to look beyond the circumstances, beyond marvels that can be enjoyed by future generations but never by mothers themselves and rarely by their own children. Her radical subtext—the possibility beneath her prose—insists that mothering in its literal meaning and in all the extended meanings she gives it in her fiction and nonfiction is meant to be tender, ecstatic, explosively creative, and revolutionary, not in some yet-to-be-created utopia, but in this world. This may seem at first like a rash misreading, since Olsen continues to argue as she has throughout her writing career that the circumstances in which mothers and children live make full human development impossible. Almost fifteen years ago, she wrote in *Silences:*

> Except for a privileged few who escape, who benefit from its effects, it remains a maiming sex-class-race world for ourselves, for those we love. The changes that will enable us to live together without harm . . . are as yet only in the making (and we are not only beings seeking to change; changing; we are also that which our past has made us). In such circumstances, taking for one's best achievement means almost inevitably at the cost of others' needs.

> (And where there are children. . . . And where there are
> children. . . .) (258)

One might expect her view to have changed to match the changes
that have occurred in women's lives in the intervening years.
But while Olsen acknowledges gratefully that at least in some
places technology and the women's movement have combined to
broaden mothers' horizons and lessen the drudgery of their lives,
she insists rightly that mothers still bear "the major responsibility
for the maintenance of life, for seeing the food gets there, the
clothing, the shelter, the order, the cleanliness, the *quality* of life,
the binding up of wounds, the attention to what is happening,
roof after roof." She also asserts that societal structures in the
United States still make it impossible for mothers to raise their
children except "at the cost of [their] . . . best, other work."[17]
Finally, she continues to point out to anyone who will listen that
for many mothers, in the United States and throughout the world,
even the meager gains of the past few decades are out of reach.

On the other hand, since the beginning of Olsen's writing
career, she has implied that things do not need to be the way they
are for mothers. *Silences,* for example, is filled with statements like
these: "No one's development would any longer be at the cost of
another" (222n); the silencing of mother-writers is "(unnecessarily
happening, for it need not, must not continue to be)" (39); and of
the mother-artist Käthe Kollwitz, she marvels at what might be
"if—needed time *and* strength were available simultaneously with
'the blessing,' the 'living as a human being must live' . . . (as, with
changes, now could be)" (212). "Could be," "not yet," "so far"—
these persistently hopeful phrases, scattered like seed in *Silences*
and in her talks and interviews, are the explicit counterparts of the
hopeful subtext of her fiction.

I do not believe that Olsen's sketching of the creative possibilities of mothering falls into the "current infatuation with motherhood" Valerie Miner deplores. In her fiction, Olsen never suggests
that mothering should take the place that romantic love, or more
recently, sexual experience, has held in literature as the one and
only route to maturity and selfhood available to women. On the
contrary, in suggesting the possible, Olsen deflates many over-
blown features of the motherhood mystique. That deflation is an
important strategy in making the possible real. Once again, the
imagery of hunger, eating, and feeding shows us how she accomplishes this multilayered task.

In Olsen's fiction, the language of hunger almost always holds two elements of her basic paradigm folded within one image: starvation, greed, and something close to cannibalism on the one hand, and a passionate give-and-take that replenishes body and spirit on the other. This imagery suggests that when hunger of any kind is not distorted by inequality and injustice, it is healthy, generous, curious, and eager for connections. It leads to equality rather than domination. Even on the most literal level, hunger expresses a desire to stay alive; and giving food both sustains life and expresses a faith that life is worth sustaining. On the figurative level, her imagery acknowledges that, consciously or unconsciously, each generation feeds on the wisdom and work of ancestors and contemporaries as well as on the promise of children. In the face of no matter what betrayal or hypocrisy, meals in Olsen's work are communal, the flat-out denial of individualism.

A few examples will serve to show that, for Olsen, being healthily hungry is almost synonymous with being healthily human, not just for mothers and children but for everyone. In a fine passage from *Silences*, she quotes Whitman's belief that "American bards . . . shall be Kosmos, without monopoly or secrecy, glad to pass anything to anyone—hungry for equals by night and by day." Olsen adds her impassioned interpretation of what this hunger for equality means:

> O yes.
> The truth under the spume and corrosion. Literature is a
> place for generosity and affection and hunger for equals—not
> a prizefight ring. We are increased, confirmed in our medium,
> roused to do our best, by every good writer, every fine
> achievement. Would we want one good writer or fine book
> less? . . .
> Hungry for equals. The sustenance some writers are to
> each other personally, besides the help of doing their best
> work.
> Hungry for equals. The spirit of those writers who have
> worked longer years, solved more, are more established;
> reaching out to the newer, the ones who must carry on the
> loved medium. (174)

Given favorable conditions, creation and relation feed each other. Again from *Silences*, "So long they fed each other—my life, the writing—; —the writing or hope of it, my life" (20). Even the conscious and subconscious levels of the human person feed each other: "Subterranean forces can make you wait, but they are very finicky about the kind of waiting it has to be. Before they will feed the creator back, they must be fed, passionately fed, what needs to be worked on" (S 13). In Olsen's fiction, everything is meant to be tasted and chewed. David urges Eva to taste the beauty of the California seacoast, and in "Hey Sailor, What Ship?" Lennie and Whitey share the pleasure of "chewing over . . . the happenings of the time or the queerness of people" (R 46). For Olsen, literal and figurative images of hunger express the healthy, essential needs of every part of the human psyche and of the human community, becoming a wedding of body and spirit and a powerful force drawing people out of isolation toward each other.

The logic of Olsen's imagistic connections between hunger and mothering raises a further question: What would mothering look like if it were not maimed by the "sex-class-race world" in which it now exists? I believe Olsen's answer is exactly the same as the answer to the same question about hunger: mothering could be, *can* be healthy, generous, curious, eager for connections, even rapturous. Olsen's language again suggests possibilities of both starvation and plenty. Eva calls her children *morsels*. Suggesting something small, fragile, and tasty, this word holds both potential menace and tenderness. David says to Eva, "You are the one who always used to say: better mankind born without mouths and stomachs than always to worry for money to buy, to shop, to fix, to cook, to wash, to clean." Eva's answer—"How cleverly you hid that you heard. I said it then because eighteen hours a day I ran. And you never scraped a carrot or knew a dish towel sops"— reveals that she was not renouncing hungry people or the task of feeding them but rather the unspoken rules of the patriarchal family (R 74).

David calls Eva "a woman of honey," meaning, of course, the opposite; Eva concurs with his opinion of her, thinking during an argument, "(Vinegar he poured on me all his life; I am well marinated; how can I be honey now?)" (80, 84). This exchange would seem to reinforce the image of Eva as food, and bitter food at that, but Olsen gives neither David nor Eva the last word. As she often does, here she uses David's ironical epithet to tell some deeper truth about Eva. In an oblique way, Meridel LeSueur's autobiographical essay, "Annunciation," helps me understand what Olsen might mean. In this essay, LeSueur explains why she wants to write down her feelings about her first pregnancy. This urge, she says, "is something perhaps like a farmer who hears the swarming of a host of bees and goes out to catch them so that he will have honey. If he does not go out right away, they will go, and he will hear the buzzing growing more distant in the afternoon."[18] Though Eva is certainly not honey-sweet, I do not think it distorts Olsen's meaning to say that she wants to capture the wisdom of Eva's life before it grows distant in the afternoon, and that she wants her readers to taste that wisdom and find it nourishing and even delicious.

Another important passage linking mothering and hunger goes even further in suggesting possible yields. It is the famous one in which Eva tries to explain to herself why she cannot hold her grandson: "Immediacy to embrace, and the breath of *that* past: warm flesh like this that had claims and nuzzled away all else and with lovely mouths devoured; hot-living like an animal—intensely and now; the turning maze; the long drunkenness; the drowning into needing and being needed" (93). Eva uses similar words to describe her daughter Vivi, caught in "the maze of the long, the lovely drunkenness" of mothering (96). With some justification, critics have described this passage on mother love as "violent" and the language that of addiction or even cannibalism.[19] I propose a parallel—or perhaps subterranean—interpretation, suggested by words like *intensely, maze, lovely drunkenness,* and *drowning,* all of which say that mothering can be an ecstatic experience having much in common with intense creative and communal activity. Olsen creates here something far more interesting than a new version of the cliché that turns mothering into a metaphor for the creative process. Instead, she suggests that mothering is one of many analogous human experiences that involve one wholly, dissolving tight boundaries and sweeping one into "the seas of humankind." Because of their power, such experiences are both dangerous challenges and exhilarating adventures; they threaten annihilation and at the same time promise fullness of life.

The images Olsen uses for all these experiences—the flood, the high tide, the powerful underground river—seem to have come to her early from the 1934 San Francisco longshoremen's strike. At any rate, they appear for the first time in "The Strike," her account of that event. The longshoremen are a river "streaming ceaselessly up and down, a river that sometimes raged into a flood, surging over the wavering shoreline of police, battering into the piers and sucking under the scabs in its angry tides. HELL CAN'T STOP US. . . . That was the meaning of the seamen and the oilers and the wipers and the mastermates and the pilots and the scalers torrenting into the river, widening into the sea."[20] Flood images almost disappear in the landlocked heat of *Yonnondio;* we hear them only briefly in Anna's songs—"Oh Shenandoah I love your daughter / I'll bring her safe through stormy water," and "I saw a ship a sailing / And on that ship was me." They reappear more than twenty years later in the stories collected in *Tell Me a Riddle* and later still in *Silences.* I suspect that the expanded meaning of this imagery in later works reflects what twenty years as mother and writer taught Olsen about the hidden emotional similarities among seemingly disparate experiences. Several passages that use flood images to characterize such experiences will show what those lessons were.

In "O Yes," innumerable images of drowning and baptism mingle with each other to describe Carol's experience of being drawn into black religious experience and into caring for lives other than her own. The church choir sings:

> *Wade,*
> *Sea of trouble all mingled with fire*
> *Come on my brethren it's time to go higher*
> *Wade wade (R 57)*

Carol tries to separate herself from the explosive pain and joy of the black congregation by focusing on "a little Jesus walk[ing] on wondrously blue waters to where bearded disciples spread nets out of a fishing boat." But the voices sweep over her "in great humming waves" and she feels herself drowning into "the deep cool green": "And now the rhinestones in Parry's hair glitter wicked; the white hands of the ushers, fanning, foam in the air; the blue-painted waters of Jordan swell and thunder; Christ spirals on his cross in the window—and she is drowned under the sluice of the slow singing and the sway" (57–58).

A passage from "Tell Me a Riddle" picks up similar images of flood and drowning to describe Eva's experience of mothering: "It was not that she had not loved her babies, her children. The love—the passion of tending—had risen with the need like a torrent; and like a torrent drowned and immolated all else" (92). Olsen then describes Eva's early revolutionary spirit and the new tasks she believes old age holds for her; the flood imagery declares the commonalities between these three phases of Eva's life: "On that torrent she had borne [her children] on their own lives, and the riverbed was desert long years now. Not there would she dwell, a memoried wraith. Surely that was not all, surely there was more. Still the springs, the springs were in her seeking. Somewhere an older power that beat for life. Somewhere coherence, transport, meaning" (92–93).

Finally, Olsen echoes both "O Yes" and "Tell Me a Riddle" when she describes in *Silences* the experience of writing and how it feels when writing has to be deferred. For her and for the writers she quotes (James, Woolf, Gide, Kafka), writing is *"rapture; the saving comfort; the joyous energies, pride, love, audacity, reverence wrestling with the angel, Art—"* (173). She describes the many times in her life when she had to "leave work at the flood to return to the Time-Master, to business-ese and legalese" (21).

In using this flood imagery to forge links between mothering and other absorbing, creative work, Olsen obviously is not repeating the "moldy theory" that all women must be biological mothers in order to claim their womanhood (*S* 16); nor does she mean that mothering can or should absorb a woman's whole life. Finally, she is not bitterly or ironically setting mothering alongside political action, religious experience, or writing only to reveal by contrast its dull passivity. On the contrary, her imagery suggests that, far from being dull and repetitive, mothering could and should be high adventure, calling forth compassion, courage, and wonder. It could and should be like art, Olsen says in *Silences*, in "the toil and patience," but also in the "calling upon total capacities; the reliving and new using of the past; the comprehensions; the fascination, absorption, intensity" (18). In addition, viewing mothering as art and as a source of art can help dismantle the walls between women who are mothers and women engaged in other creative work and, at the same time, help bring together the often fragmented selves within individual women.

By demonstrating that her life as mother was one of the main sources of her writing, and in taking the further step of making mothers' lives the center of much of her fiction, Olsen counters one of the old notions about mothers I described at the beginning of this chapter. This notion claims that mothering is an experience so immured in nature there are no words to express it. Olsen's imagery tells a homelier truth: that mothering is neither more nor less expressible, neither more nor less sunk in silence than any other experience that involves one's whole being. Just as it is difficult but possible to write about making love, creating a poem, teaching well, marching on a picket line, or nursing a dying grand-mother, it is difficult but possible to write about mothering.

Annie Gottlieb's 1976 book review entitled "Feminists Look at Motherhood" helps me to understand the weight of Olsen's influ-ence in bringing mothering out of the hazy, romantic half-light that has obscured it for so long. Gottlieb writes about an honest and joyous dialogue between her, a writer with no children, and her youngest sister, who had just given birth to her first child. It is a dialogue, says Gottlieb, that would have been impossible only a few years earlier:

> The birth of my sister's baby would have divided us irrevoca-bly from each other—and from ourselves. She would have passed, for me, into a closed, dim world, inarticulate, seduc-tive and threatening, made up of equal parts of archetypal power and TV-commercial insipidity. And for her, it would have been hopelessly beyond the reach of words she could not begin to formulate and would in any case not have dared to utter, because they would have violated all the accepted canons of motherhood.
>
> She might have feared my educated contempt, for mother-hood, while cloyingly idealized, was in no way honored as ei-ther a source or an accomplishment of human intelligence.[21]

Gottlieb attributes the newfound possibility of communication between herself and her sister to the women whose books about motherhood she is reviewing (Alta, Jane Lazarre, and Adrienne Rich). Their work was made possible, she says, by the Women's Movement, "which in turn has drawn inspiration from the work of a few pioneers—foremost among them Tillie Olsen." For Gottlieb, Olsen "*feels* like the first, both to extend 'universal' human experi-ence to females and to dignify uniquely female experience as a source of human knowledge."[22] Although Olsen would hasten to name many predecessors to whom she herself is indebted, I agree with Gottlieb that Olsen is certainly the first whose works have been widely read, studied, and discussed.

In the fifteen years since Gottlieb wrote that tribute, dozens of books about mothers, mothering, and motherhood have ap-peared, and it is true that what Valerie Miner terms "this current infatuation with motherhood" might be traced to Olsen. But Olsen never sets mothers against women like May Sarton's magnificent spinster who "stand on their own." In fact, she does the opposite. As Gottlieb says, Olsen's writing has directly and indirectly helped to create connections "between body and mind, between female experience and the realm of thought, between a woman who at this moment is predominantly a mother and one who at this moment is a writer."[23] While Olsen continues to show clearly the differences among women, including those between women who are mothers and those who are not, she steadfastly affirms that those differences are not inherently divisive, ought not to be used as weapons of reproach or sources of guilt, and do not lend themselves to ranking except when one is obeying the dictates of patriarchal thought.

Gottlieb writes that "between the 'experience' of motherhood and the patriarchal 'institution,' a system of man-made myths and 'false-namings' exists that twists the experience itself into something far more anguished and confining than it would naturally be. What it could be under vastly different circumstances we cannot fully know."[24] Olsen's stories express more powerfully than those of any other writer I know the needless anguish and confinement, asking that her readers, sons and daughters all, "enter the pain" of their mothers' lives.[25] But Olsen never gives up on the possibility that pregnancy, birth, and the essential arts of mothering could be one way for a woman to give birth to herself; they could be replenishing acts for mothers, their children, and a hungry society. In the imagery of Olsen's fiction, they could be hearty bread, stone that preserves the valuable lessons of the past, and a flood filled with life.

CHAPTER

3

The Gnarled Roots of
the Patriarchy

O LSEN ADDRESSES directly in *Silences* and implicitly in her
fiction the difficulties women of every class and race en-
counter in dealing with, living with, and writing about
men, whether they are husbands, lovers, fathers, grandfathers,
sons, or friends. At the end of *Silences* she expresses the familiar
anguish many women writers have articulated in the past two
decades:

> The oppression of women is like no other form of oppres-
> sion (class, color—though these have parallels). It is an op-
> pression entangled through with human love, human need,
> genuine (core) human satisfactions, identifications, fulfill-
> ments. . . .
> What compounds the personal agony for us, is that portion
> of the harm which comes to us from the beings we are close
> to, who are close to us. Their daily part in the balks, lessen-
> ings, denials. Which we must daily encounter.
> And counter? (258)

In writing about men and about women and men together,
Olsen has set herself the difficult task of distinguishing the "chains
from the bonds, the harms from the value, the truth from the lies"
(*S* 258). To this end, she has chosen not to present men as faceless
stereotypes nor to create a world where women's only support
comes from other women. Her women and men do not inhabit

mutually exclusive worlds in which men are responsible for all the wrongs done and women are hapless, helpless victims.

Every story includes male characters who are to some degree sympathetic; and in Olsen's two least-read stories, "Requa" and "Hey Sailor, What Ship?" the protagonists are men, the orphan boy Stevie and his uncle Wes in the former and an alcoholic sailor named Whitey in the latter. Olsen presents these characters with affection, admiration, and respect: they have lives of their own, and their feelings, thoughts, and memories are central to the stories.

Olsen's multiple vision adds another layer of complexity to the task of writing about men, for the modulations of class, race, and nationality create many breaches in the boundary between the sexes. Catharine Stimpson says that a feminist writer might use working-class male characters "to make palpable a theory, like that of John Stuart Mill, of a cross-class male drive towards rule; of a cross-class male fear, at once brutal and skittish, of sexual equality." She adds that Olsen's faith in the goodness of her working-class characters makes such a theory untenable for her.[1] I would say rather that while Olsen certainly is a feminist, her early immersion in socialist theory and practice as well as her experience as a coworker, daughter, and wife of working men radically changed her feminist vision. Olsen recognizes that men who do not belong to the white mainstream are victimized in obvious and subtle ways, sometimes in the same ways as women, often differently.

Olsen is not alone in seeing and naming the ambiguous relationships between women and men who stand outside mainstream culture. In fact, this is one of the main themes running through the works of contemporary minority women writers. One powerful description of this painful linkage is poet Andrea Canaan's from her essay "Brownness": "It is hardest to see my enemy as brown men yet in order to see myself clearly I must face the closest threat to my survival for it is he who most rapes me, batters me, devalues my strength, will not allow my weakness. He is closest to me for he is my father, my brother, my son, my man, my lover. I love him, I glory in his maleness and agonize in his degradation. I must refuse to allow him to oppress me while I must be concerned for his survival."[2] For Olsen as for Canaan, women and men are both enemies and allies. In Olsen's simple phrase, men and women "share want" (R 10), standing together against poverty, racism, and class prejudice.

Olsen never denies that women living in poverty or under

racial discrimination are doubly or triply victimized. Nor does she deny the terrible ruptures between women and men or men's often total lack of understanding of their wives or daughters. But she does imply that men's abusive actions toward women must be seen in their historical context, neither as unique instances of cruelty nor as universal aspects of behavior, always and everywhere the same and attributable to so-called masculine nature or even to the configuration maleness has taken on in our society. For Olsen, this domination is attributable rather to a whole assortment of historical factors that modify what on the surface might look like the same old stories of possessiveness, ignorance, and cruelty.

It is almost impossible to write about Olsen's view of men without also discussing her view of the family, for she sees clearly that it is within the patriarchal family that women's and men's lives converge and diverge with the greatest pain and bitterness. As critic and historian Deborah Rosenfelt writes, for Olsen the family is "at once a source of strength and love, and a battleground between women and men in a system exploiting both."[3] In other words, Olsen portrays the family as one of the institutions that blights the lives of men as well as women and almost guarantees that men will pass oppression on to their wives and children, perpetuating in their homes the very structures and values they struggle against outside. At the same time, Olsen says, in an uncaring society, "the family must often try to be the center for love and health the outside world is not" (S 18).

Olsen's paradigm of blight, fruit, and possibility again provides a helpful way of looking at the family and at the lives of men and boys who, for reasons of class or race, stand outside the mainstream. She shows the harm done to working men by an economic system that thrives on exploitation, harm which men often carry home like bitter pay, converting economic exploitation into domestic abuse. But with her intense desire to salvage human dignity and concern from wasted lives and relationships, Olsen also shows the heroic perseverance of her working men, bound like their wives to making a better life for children and to creating a more just society. She shows rare moments of beauty and tenderness in their lives, suggesting still uncreated possibilities. For just as she claims intelligence, world consciousness, and the desire and ability to create as women's birthright, so she claims for men gentleness, intuition, and the desire and ability to nurture. Finally, she reconceives the family as the place where this more humane balance could be achieved.

The blighted condition of men's lives is most evident in Olsen's descriptions of the conditions under which so many of them are forced to work. Their jobs in mines, sewers, packinghouses, and junkyards require skill, agility, and strength. But these jobs do not repay the workers with self-respect, choice, or a chance for advancement. At their worst, they do not even repay them with a living wage.

This blight infects the lives of poor boys while they are still children. In *Yonnondio*, Olsen's narrator describes the "man's burden" thirteen-year-old Andy Kvaternick must carry as he goes down into the mines for the first time:

> And no more can you stand erect. You lose that heritage of
> man, too. You are brought now to fit earth's intestines, stoop
> like a hunchback underneath, crawl like a child, do your
> man's work lying on your side, stretched and tense as a
> corpse. The rats shall be your birds, and the rocks plopping in
> the water your music. And death shall be your wife, who
> woos you in the brief moments when coal leaps from a burst-
> ing side, when a cross-piece falls and barely misses your head,
> when you barely catch the ladder to bring you up out of the
> hole you are dynamiting. (13–14)

The men's release from danger, disease, and crushing toil is alcohol. At the end of this first day of work, the other men call Andy to complete his initiation into manhood: "'Andy,' they are calling you, in their lusty voices, your fellow workers—it is an old story to them now. 'Have one on us.' The stuff burns down your throat, the thoughts lie shipwrecked and very still far underneath the black sea of your mind; you are gay and brave, knowing that you can never breathe the dust out. You have taken your man's burden, and you have the miner's only friend the earth gives, strong drink, Andy Kvaternick" (14–15).

Wives and mothers watch helplessly as men's bodies and spirits are eroded. In a 1937 journalistic essay called "Women Know a Lot of Things," Meridel LeSueur writes that women know how the economy is doing without reading about it in the newspaper, because they read it on the bodies of their husbands. By reading this "Braille" of "hunger and want and terror," a woman can know with helpless compassion that her husband is "like a fine uncared-for precision machine, worn down in his prime, or eaten by acids in Textile, or turned to stone by Silicosis."[4] Olsen lets us read this language of bodies in *Yonnondio*, showing us men's feet swollen from working far underground, standing in water inside and outside their boots. We see Jim at the end of a day in the packing-house, asleep, but his hands still twitching as if he cannot stop them from working. Yet no matter how hard Jim and others like him work and how much they endure, an exploitative economic system guarantees that they will not be able to provide for their families.

In showing us the ways in which her male characters are worn down by intolerable working conditions, Olsen does not mean to say that they suffer more than the women. She shows rather that men, women, and children are all reduced by class, race, and gender to whatever economic or social function the society needs to perpetuate itself. In such adverse circumstances, an oldest daughter is a pair of hands to help with childcare or housework; a worker in a packing plant becomes a machine or the meat she or he is processing; a working man is a pair of twitching hands, and a woman "a maternal breast or belly" (to borrow critic Judith Kegan Gardiner's description of Eva.)[5] All of these reductions erode human dignity; all of them are linked to each other and help perpetuate each other; and, under Olsen's careful touch, all of them offer men and women the chance to identify with each others' sufferings.

Olsen's male characters, like her women, desperately want a supportive, nonexploitative community. Every story holds examples of this desire. In "Hey Sailor," Whitey mourns "the death of the brotherhood": "*Once, once an injury to one is an injury to all. Once, once they had to live for each other. And whoever came off the ship fat shared, because that was the only way of survival for all of them, the easy sharing, the knowing that when you needed, waiting for a trip card to come up, you'd be staked*" (R 45). In "Tell Me a Riddle," David wants to go to the Haven, partly to put an end to money worries and partly to make life easier for himself; a more important reason is that there "it matters what one is, not what one can afford" (75). But for these working men, as for women living in a man's world, advancement is possible only if they give up solidarity with their peers. For example, in *Yonnondio*, Jim says that the only way a fellow worker can become a straw boss is to drive the men unmercifully and to agree with his supervisor that they are lazy (133). In "Hey Sailor, What Ship?" Whitey talks about "Kissass Karnes," who had "nimbly, limberly clambered up" the ranks by separating himself from the brotherhood of seamen (44, 45).

Both men and women are misshapen by roles and by the press

of circumstance on their lives, and then blamed for the unattractive result. Eva is bitter, a compulsive worker, silent. David is whoever others want him to be; in Eva's words, he is "clown, grimacer, floormat, yesman, entertainer, whatever they want of you" (*R* 75). Finally, though *Silences* deals in greatest detail with the many stifling layers women have to fight their way through to write, Olsen is also attentive to all marginal people, whether women or men, whose class, color, or nationality raises barriers between their aspirations and the world of literature. She writes that "for any male not born into a class that breeds . . . confidence," it is very difficult to achieve "the measureless store of belief in oneself to be able to come to, cleave to, find the form of one's own life comprehensions" (*S* 256). Though some critics have taken Olsen to task for using so many male voices in *Silences*,[6] that varied chorus clearly shows the oppressions shared by men and women.

This sympathetic portrayal of shared oppression has not led Olsen to romanticize her male characters or excuse their violent treatment of women. On the contrary, she assigns responsibility and explores the causes of domination and violence. In her dissertation, "Patterns of Survival: Four American Women Writers and the Proletarian Novel," Joan Wood Samuelson writes that in Olsen's fiction, the "proletarian man does not abuse his wife simply because his poverty frustrates him, but also because he views his wife as his inferior, his property, subject to his whims and punishments."[7] This abuse takes several forms. Some of Olsen's male characters desert their families, claiming for themselves a desperate freedom their wives do not have. Early in "I Stand Here Ironing," the mother reflects on the beginning of her daughter's life when she herself was nineteen and struggling to support them. Emily's father had walked out on them, saying in his good-bye note that he "could no longer endure . . . sharing want" with them (*R* 10). In that phrase, understated but edged in bitterness, the lives of mothers and fathers living in poverty simultaneously converge and diverge. They do share want; but mothers are "at once stranded and rooted at home with the children" (in Stimpson's phrase), and if they flee at all, they flee like Anna Holbrook "into illness and depression."[8] Fathers, on the other hand, often walk out, sometimes permanently. The threat of desertion carves itself into the women's dreams. In *Yonnondio,* Jim Holbrook leaves his family only temporarily, but in Anna's dreams he is always "fleeing, shrinking to a tiny dot on the lurid sky" (68). Most of the fathers in Olsen's stories stay with their families, held by love and duty. But they shore up their threatened manhood by imposing on their families the patriarchal structures they despise on the job. Born into these structures and enslaved by them, they also help keep them firmly in place. Although they hold themselves heroically to the task of supporting their families and often try to give them the protection of loving arms, they also ensure, ironically, that their protection will be useless.

Men's unthinking oppression of their wives and daughters is epitomized in the devastating scene from *Yonnondio* in which eight-year-old Mazie hears her drunk father rape her mother. That she can only imagine what is happening makes the experience even more terrible for her. Mazie is forced to witness an act of male violence she cannot prevent, change, or forget. She hears her father come home singing. She knows he is drunk, and there is no use telling him that Anna, sick from nursing one baby and pregnant with another, had fainted earlier in the evening. Then:

> What was happening? It seemed the darkness bristled with blood, with horror. The shaking of the bed as if someone were sobbing in it, the wind burrowing through the leaves filling the night with a shaken sound. And the words, the words leaping.
>   "Dont, Jim, dont. It hurts too much. No, Jim, no."
>   "Cant screw my own wife. Expect me to go to a whore? Hold still." (91)

Mazie finds her mother on the kitchen floor. Unable to awaken her drunk father, she is forced to watch Anna miscarry. Mazie runs out of the house, but she cannot run away from the horror or block it out of her mind. Olsen conveys Mazie's fear and confusion in impressionistic flashes:

> Running, so much ugliness, the coarse hair, the night bristling, the blood and the drunken breath and the blob of spit, something soft, mushy, pressed against her face, never the farm, dont cry, even baby's cryin get away from me ya damn girl, the faint gray vapor of river, run, run, but it scares you so, the shadows the lamp throws in the wind.
>   The cold, the world was so cold. (94)

Although Jim would not deliberately harm Mazie, his mindless violence against Anna robs Mazie of her childhood, turning her life into a waking nightmare in which it is "useless to resist, to cry out, because it is a voiceless dream to be endured" (89).

Olsen does nothing to soften the brutality of Anna's rape and its effects on Mazie or to excuse Jim, yet she takes pains to show us that in other areas of his life he, too, is caught between responsibility and helplessness. After Anna's miscarriage the doctor comes to look after her and Baby Bess and leaves directions with Jim for their care. Jim goes out to look for Mazie, and as he carries her home, he says to her, "Momma's sick, awful sick, Bigeyes. Awfully sick, and the doctor says she needs everything she cant get . . . everything she needs but not how to get it." And about the baby, "And Bess' pretty sick, me not noticing, blind as a bat. And medicine, he says. Everything, but not how to get it." The narrator's voice breaks in to describe Jim's despairing love as a "cry from a million swollen throats" (95). These are the million fathers like Jim whose sense of responsibility drags them to grueling and demeaning jobs every day and makes them repeat old vows to do better, "vows that life will never let [them] keep" (107).

Olsen shows men stripped of their self-respect by the same societal standards that urge them to prove their manhood through competitiveness, brute force, and sexual domination. She weaves this grim pattern into her description of events leading to Jim's rape of Anna. At the end of a long day's work in the sewer, the contractor waddles up to Jim and his workmates, spits tobacco juice "square into Jim's empty boot," and says to them, "so ten foot is all you women made today, huh? What I want to know is what the hell you do when you're on the job, suck titty?" The men must swallow his insults or quit, an option only unmarried men can consider. During a night of drinking, Jim turns that tormenting thought around and around: "Alright for Tracy to talk, he doesn't have a wife and brats. But no man has any business having 'em that wants to stay a man. Having to take all that goddamn crap" (75). That night he rapes Anna. Because he cannot turn on his boss, forced sex becomes Jim's way of proving his manhood to himself.

The terrible irony is that Jim's brutal attitude and actions both reflect and reinforce those of a society where every woman—whether wife, prostitute, or little girl—is fair sexual game. He offers Mazie the protection of his arms—"Kiss Poppa and we'll go home and I'll make a farm and warm you, a nice fire, and you can fall asleep on daddy's lap" (95); but whether Jim knows it or not, Olsen shows her readers that in such a society a father's arms are no protection at all. Early in the story, Mazie narrowly escapes being thrown down a mine shaft by Sheen McEvoy, whose face and mind were destroyed by a gas explosion in the mine. He thinks that if he sacrifices a child, the mine will not claim the lives of any more men. In Mazie's mind sexuality is always connected with that experience, Sheen's breath smelling of liquor, his face "a red mass of jelly" pressed against her, kissing her (20–21). It is one of the images Mazie tries to banish from her mind, along with the sights and sounds of her mother's rape. Jim was not able to protect her from McEvoy, and the logic of the world he was born into and helps keep intact says he will not be able to protect her from other men, including himself, who are bent upon reclaiming their manhood.

A striking similarity between *Yonnondio* and "Tell Me a Riddle" bears out Samuelson's statement that in Olsen's fiction patriarchal attitudes and not just poverty lead proletarian men to dominate their wives. In the thirty or so years that intervene between the events of *Yonnondio* and those of "Tell Me a Riddle," the economic status of many working men has changed greatly. Several decades of union activity and an improved economy obviously have yielded good enough wages so that David can own a home and retire with a pension and the promised security and pleasures of the union Haven. With the frustrations of extreme poverty gone, we might expect David to treat his wife differently than Jim treats Anna. Of course, in many ways he does, in part because Olsen draws him more skillfully and subtly than she does Jim. David does not beat or rape Eva, but he still manipulates her to fulfill his needs, still tries to make her into the person he wants her to be, and most important, is still blind to the fact that Eva *is* a person to be known and respected. Olsen seems to be showing us through David that healing "the hidden injuries of class" does not inevitably heal the injuries of gender. Her socialism does not delude her into believing that once economic inequalities are righted, social equality for women and men will follow, or that committed socialist men, of whom David is a fictional example, will necessarily renounce or even be aware of the immeasurable harm their patriarchal attitudes inflict on wives and daughters.

While Olsen documents that harm in meticulous detail, she does not make Jim, David, or her other focal male characters into easy targets for her readers' wrath. In spite of the many blighting circumstances of their lives and in spite of the ways in which they spread that blight to their families, these characters are capable of great endurance and, surprisingly, a rough nurturance of women and children. In the words of Olsen's paradigm, these lives, though blighted, still bear fruit. Olsen breaks open the meaning of mothering and lifts the burden from the shoulders of biological mothers by presenting a circle of other nurturers who perform one or another of the tasks usually delegated to mothers. In Olsen's stories, men stand side by side with women in that sheltering circle.

For some of them, the care is sporadic, called forth only by the extremities of birth, sickness, and death. This is true of Jim and David, who are so firmly entrenched in patriarchal roles that in ordinary day-to-day life they rarely lift a finger to help their wives with the children and the house. Eva rages at David that through the raising of seven children he "never scraped a carrot or knew a dish towel sops" (R 74). Once when Jim offers to help Anna, she blazes at him, "If you cant see what needs doin, just dont trouble to ask, you hear, just dont trouble to ask. . . . Why dont you go set like you always do; done. . . . 'Cept that one wintertime on the farm I was carryin Bess. And that didn't last long" (Y 108–9). Olsen shows us Jim drawn into a nurturing role as he tries to mend the hurt caused by his brutal misuse of his wife. As Anna lies bleeding from her miscarriage, Jim carries her to bed and "with tremor hands he kneads the flesh above her womb till the blood stops pouring, and stillness comes" (92). He goes out to find and comfort Mazie, and while Anna is sick he feeds the baby and tends the children. David, too, takes on this role as Eva is dying. He tends her gently "with his knotty fingers as Jeannie had taught," and the story's final, powerful image shows David and Eva with their hands clasped as though they were feeding each other.

But these moments of nurturing by Jim and David are responses to crises. Olsen leaves unanswered the question of whether in calmer, more ordinary times these husbands and fathers would return to their old habitual blindness. By contrast, in "Hey Sailor, What Ship?" and "Requa," stories in which the main characters are unmarried, childless men, Olsen blurs patriarchal notions of gender differences and all but obliterates gender roles. Through these shifts, she also reveals the deforming and transforming power of the family.

In "Hey Sailor," Whitey is the longtime friend of Helen and Lennie and their three daughters, Jeannie, Carol, and Allie (the same family Olsen writes about in "O Yes" and "Tell Me a Riddle"). Whitey is a sailor and a union man, who for complex reasons has become an alcoholic, "a Howard Street wino," as Jeannie calls him. His life has degenerated into a hopeless pattern: jobs on board ship fewer and farther between, and during the time on shore "gin mills and . . . cathouses," "sidewalk beds and doorway shelters, . . . flophouses and jails" and sometimes the hospital for his drink-induced sickness (R 25). More and more rarely he comes to visit Helen and Lennie in San Francisco. This is the story of one such visit. It could be an altogether different story. Whitey has led an adventuresome life. We learn from Jeannie that he saved Lennie's life in a 1934 strike. To all appearances, he is a rough-talking, hard-drinking man's man who lives in an all-male world at sea and visits prostitutes at every port. When he comes to see Lennie and Helen and their daughters, he sails gallantly into their lives, bringing with him heroic speeches, bragging sea stories, and funny songs, and lavishing money and presents on them. He is a fighter, as his broken nose and battered face show, and he stands up for his shipmates. For the whole family Whitey is a link to adventure.

Yet, in Olsen's story, none of his bravado is important, or, more accurately, it is important for what it hides. When Jeannie objects to Whitey's drunken profanity, Helen says, "Jeannie, I care you should understand." What Helen wants her teenage daughter to see is that Whitey's bravado, rough talk, and expensive gifts mask tenderness and a longing to be part of a family. Olsen encourages this understanding in her readers by according Whitey the same generosity and respect she grants her women characters. She tells most of the story from his point of view, letting us know his feelings, memories, and tortured thoughts.

In contrast to most of Olsen's other male characters, Whitey's alertness to Helen and her needs is remarkable. Even half-drunk or wholly hung over, he recognizes the little signs of hard times— a single row of cans in the cupboard, tired lines in Helen's face, the working mother's house never quite clean or neat. He knows how to respond to what he sees, offering *the ear to hear, the hand that understands how much a scrubbed floor, or a washed dish, or a child taken care of for a while, can mean*" (46). Whitey's fading dream of what he wants to do for this family is thoroughly domestic: to arrive when they are all gone and have them come home to a house really cleaned and dinner on the stove. In this house, it does not occur to Whitey that this "woman's work" is beneath him, or even that it is woman's work.

In a heartbreaking scene, Olsen also shows Whitey's love for children, using another of her startling reversals to portray the same reality from opposite sides. In "Tell Me a Riddle," Eva must resist the feel of a child and her response to it—"the love—the passion of tending" that rises up to drown her life. In "Hey Sailor," when six-year-old Allie curls up in Whitey's lap and falls asleep, Olsen's description of his feelings is very close to her description of Eva's, with one important difference: "It is destroying, dissolving him utterly, this helpless warmth against him, this feel of a child—lost country to him and unattainable" (20). That last phrase holds a world of pain. The mothering that uses up Eva's life is unavailable to Whitey, but the feeling (falsely called maternal instinct) is the same for both of them.

The great irony is that the structure of home and family that shuts women like Eva in often also shuts men out, especially men like Whitey, who have no assigned role within the domestic patriarchal family. When he is with Lennie's and Helen's family, he bounces the little girls on his knee and says the old rhyme:

> *What is life*
> *Without a wife* (bounce)
> *And a home* (bounce bounce)
> *Without a baby?* (37)

Whitey has neither wife nor baby and knows he never will. But this story is no triumphant assertion of male freedom from bonds or bondage. In Whitey, Olsen reverses the familiar literary pattern of men running off to the sea or some other handy wilderness to escape marriage and family life and the threat to manhood that domesticity represents. Whitey's only escape is alcohol, and he is escaping not from domesticity but from loneliness and his *"curious inability"* as a young man to engage in casual, purchased sex. It is not clear whether Whitey is gay or simply unable to fit the patterns of male behavior his adventuresome life demands; all we hear in this regard is the *"torn-out-of-him-confession"* to Helen and Lennie: *"—don't you see, I can't go near a whore unless I'm lit?"* (46). The closest Whitey comes to marriage is in his memory of four-year-old Jeannie announcing that she is his wife: "(He had told the story so often, as often as anyone would listen, whenever he felt good, and always as he told it, the same shy happiness would wing through him, how when she was four, she had crawled into bed beside him one morning, announcing triumphantly to her mother: I'm married to Whitey now, I don't have to sleep by myself any more)" (39).

Whitey loses even this remembered union when Jeannie rejects the old story as an embarrassing link to this "Howard Street wino." The story's closing paragraph shows him cut adrift and lost: "He passes no one in the streets. They are inside, each in his slab of house, watching the flickering light of television. The sullen fog is on his face, but by the time he has walked to the third hill, it has lifted so he can see the city below him, wave after wave, and there at the crest, the tiny house he has left, its eyes unshaded. After a while they blur with the myriad others that stare at him so blindly" (47). When Whitey leaves this family behind, it is not because he wants to save himself from tendrils that clutch and bind but because he sees himself as an outsider who is beyond salvation. He goes back to his flophouse room where he and another wino can drink without facing the sorrow in his friends' eyes, drowning among other things his love for children and his sensitivity to women's feelings. Through Whitey, Olsen asserts that love and sensitivity are little understood qualities that are common to men as well as to women but too rarely acknowledged in life and in literature.

"Requa," Olsen's little-known 1970 novella, presents the most complete and affirmative portrait of a male character. In this deceptively simple story, Wes sticks with his recently orphaned nephew Stevie through the long haul, giving him a rough, unsentimental companionship that looks at first glance like the opposite of mother love.

The year is 1932. Wes brings Stevie from San Francisco to a boarding house in Requa, a forest-encircled town on the Klamath River near the California-Oregon border. West works at a combination gas station–dump–trading post, sorting and repairing the junk that migrant families barter for a few gallons of gas. Stevie's father was killed in the war before Stevie was born. The only legacy the father leaves to his son is a medal pinned to the yellow envelope announcing his death. Stevie's mother raised him by herself, and after her death, Stevie is alone except for Wes, his mother's brother, whom he hardly knows.

This is not a promising combination. There is nothing childishly attractive about Stevie. He is a pale, skinny fourteen-year-old, always "snuffling scratching swallowing." Devastated by his mother's death, he seems to be *"gone," "not all there,"* a "dummy," and a "loony." He is used to city streets and entertainments and finds no comfort in hunting or fishing or in the towering natural beauty around Requa. To endure his pain over his mother's death, he lives deep inside himself and is oblivious to pleading or commands. Wes, caught in the barrenness of his own life, tries nevertheless to make good on his promise to take care of Stevie. His resolve, the familiar resolve of Olsen's mothers and fathers, is that Stevie will have a better life than he and his sister had: "I'll tell you this, though, he's not goin through what me and Sis did: kicked round one place after another, not havin nobody. Nobody" (56).

In spite of harsh words and a beating when Stevie refuses to go to school, Wes holds to his promise, taking him to the junkyard so he can pass on to Stevie his skill with tools. As Stevie comes to know Wes, he sees his uncle as "capable, fumbling; exasperated, patient; demanding, easy; uncomprehending, quick; harsh, gentle: *concerned* with him. *The recognizable human bond*" (65). Wes discovers the depth of patience in himself as he performs the menial tasks of child rearing, and, in spite of his own need for love, he offers love to this "ghostboy." A gentle hand on the shoulder, rough apologies, a backhand compliment, spoken and tacit understanding of Stevie's loss, are the *"habitable known, stealthily, secretly, reclaiming"* (65).

That Whitey and Wes give their love from outside the structure of the patriarchal family seems to say that such homely, steady tenderness is unlikely within that rigid framework. Olsen shows at every turn that the framework damages men, women, and children; yet she stops far short of an outright condemnation of the family. In her essay "Tillie Olsen: Witness as Servant," Catharine Stimpson offers a helpful description of Olsen's attitude: "Olsen's attraction to the home—no matter how sorrowfully or frequently or regretfully she qualifies it—helps to distinguish her ardent feminism from that which would abolish the family, be it nuclear or extended, altogether. Since the domestic sphere has such promise, its difficulties must be attributed to other institutions. The organism of domesticity must be remedially diseased, not intrinsically destructive."[9] I would modify Stimpson's assessment by saying that Olsen's ardent feminism, shaped by her equally ardent class and race consciousness, leads her to blame the family's blighted condition both on its patriarchal structure and on a hostile outside society. And in spite of its diseased condition, in Olsen's stories, the family shelters lives and assures that broken existences will continue.

A powerful scene from *Yonnondio* uses the image of a gnarled tree to show the Holbrook family's heroic, doomed efforts to create a better life for themselves. On the morning the Holbrooks are to leave the South Dakota farm and head for the meatpacking town, Jim and Anna stand together in the early morning:

> Two figures moving with pain in the dawn darkness, in the vapor mist. Two voices lashed by a dry and savage wind, bringing strangely the scent of lilac.
> "Almost time now, Anna. We'd better go. . . ."
> "Right away now, Jim. . . . Jim, what's the matter, life never lets anything be? . . . Just a year ago . . . I tried for us to have a good life. You tried too, Jim. . . ."
> Two figures blur into one, gnarled and lonely. Very low he says: "You're shivering. Cold?"
> "Awful cold. Let's go. Now."
> "But you cant take it lying down—like a dog. You just cant, Anna." (58–59)

In this passage two separate figures blur and two separate voices become interchangeable, with Anna echoing Jim's "Right away now" and "Let's go. Now." Either of them could offer Jim's despairing effort to bolster their courage or Anna's insistence that they both had tried. We see Anna and Jim as if through tears; and although their lives are twisted together by love, effort, and failure, nothing can alleviate their loneliness in a harsh, unhospitable world. But that very loneliness convinces them that they provide their children's only hope, and so they set out again.

Given the harm the family inflicts on its members, one might expect Olsen's gnarled tree to be barren or to produce nothing but bitter fruit. But that is not the case. Olsen's stories reflect a more ambivalent view of the family as a flawed institution that nevertheless has kept generations of people alive in spite of the indifference and outright hostility of the surrounding society. Even the apparent rootlessness that plagues the Holbrooks is deceptive, for each migration attests to Jim and Anna's deeply rooted commitment to each other within their embattled family. Beyond the struggle for survival, Olsen's fictional families pass on essential lessons about responsibility, understanding, and the usefulness of work. They also strive to "transmit a moral sense to their children," as Stimpson says, teaching them an ideology that "may be at odds with and better than the dominant society."[10]

But in Olsen's revisionary storytelling, the very word *family* often means something other than the nuclear family, that tight, explosive modern entity whose very name ticks like a bomb. Olsen stretches the skin of that word to accommodate all sorts of odd and wonderful shapes: a mother and child alone ("Requa" and "I Stand Here Ironing"); a mother, several children, nieces and nephews, and a church community ("O Yes"); parents, children, and a beat-up sailor ("Hey Sailor"); a boy, his uncle, and a chance assortment of faces around a boardinghouse table—male, female, black, Chinese, white—all of whom help in "reclaiming" the lost boy ("Requa"). In all of these families, the meanings of mothering and fathering blur, shift, and become one meaning. Mothers earn or help earn a livelihood while fathers, uncles, and male friends do the work of "the essential angel" that even the most modern technology cannot dispense with. They soothe and hold; they wipe noses, clean up vomit, and empty bedpans; they help create the *"recognizable human bond,"* the *"habitable known,"* weaving trustworthy domestic rituals of word, story, song, and gesture. Within these oddly shaped families, children are miracles to the people who form each protective circle. They are loved, and the love shelters them or, as with Stevie, calls them back from a numbed depression.

Yet Olsen makes it clear that each of these families is too fragile to ensure "survival in a wasteland" (to borrow Blanche Gelfant's phrase).[11] At the end of "O Yes," Helen tries to comfort her daughter, searching for words to explain the grief Carol is feeling, settling for silence, and finally "sheltering her daughter close, mourning the illusion of the embrace" (71). That last phrase could mean several things, among them that a mother cannot tell her daughter at thirteen the things she needs to know to survive betrayals. Olsen's use of the same image in other contexts, however, suggests a more frightening meaning. In "Hey Sailor," Whitey strokes Allie's hair *"as if* the strokes would solidify, dense into a protection" (*R* 30, my italics); in *Yonnondio* Jim holds Mazie and strokes Anna's hair, "silently making old vows . . . that life will never let him keep" (107). Taken together, these "illusions of the embrace" imply dangers from within and without the family. Within the patriarchal family, the greatest danger comes from gender relationships. But in a family of whatever shape, size, or configuration, sheltering arms cannot protect a child in a world that is not safe for children. Even in "Requa," the most hopeful of Olsen's stories, there are disquieting hints of outside forces threatening the small group of people Stevie has come to see as family. The shifting assortment of faces around the table and snatches of overheard conversation suggest joblessness, poverty, and forced moves:

> Highpockets is gone. When had he gone, and why? The
> blurredness will not lift. A new man, thready, pale, sits in his
> place and has his room.
>
> The talk eddys around him: aint going to be no season, not
> in Alaska Vancouver or Pedro . . . like crabs feedin on a dead
> man, like a lot of gulls waitin for scraps . . . the Cascades the
> Olympics the Blues . . . nickel snatchin bastards (71)

In a world like ours, Olsen suggests, even the wisest care provides
shelter that is temporary or illusory. To release the creative possibilities of family love, the surrounding world must change.

Olsen creates tough family bonds from gnarled roots and
clasped hands—bonds she will not split by separating out men
and boys. In so doing, she asks of her readers a complex response
for which even a sympathetic feminist audience might be un-
prepared. It seems to me no accident that "Requa" and "Hey
Sailor, What Ship?" are the least read and critiqued of Olsen's
works. For in writing sympathetically of Wes and Whitey, of Jim
Holbrook and David, Olsen gives up the apparent safety and
defiant joy of women's separatism, risking that her affirmation of
men might be read as a betrayal of women. But just as her stories
ask us not to despise our mothers and grandmothers as passive,
hostile, and weak, they ask us to look behind the gargoyled faces
of fathers, grandfathers, and friends for the life circumstances that
shaped and misshaped them. They ask us to respond not with
hatred but with the painful, fruitful tension of anger and love.

Community as Necessity and Danger for the Self

I N A 1974 TALK, Olsen said, "My vision is very different from that of most writers. . . . I don't think in terms of quests for identity to explain human motivation and behavior. I feel that in a world where class, race, and sex are so determining, that that has little reality."[1] As I understand this statement, Olsen does not mean that she is unconcerned with the full flourishing of individual lives. In fact, she expresses in every story, every essay or interview unshakeable faith in human possibility and steadfast anger at whatever keeps people young or old from "flowering, experimenting, trying, learning . . . in a world whose season was, as still it is, a time of winter."[2]

The important difference between Olsen and many of her contemporaries lies rather in her conception of how the self flowers. In Olsen's work, selfhood is never for the self alone, but always for the self and the community. Without community, each person is caught up in competition, hermetically sealed away from compassion, and denied the full range of human feeling and activity. In Olsen's vision, as long as self-fulfillment is defined in individualistic terms, the winter continues, with only a fortunate few escaping to more gentle climates. Although many of her characters (especially but not exclusively the women) are sensitive and original people whose visions challenge mainstream culture, they are not romantic rebels standing alone against the sky. They are instead bound to communities and in fact often grow out of the fertile soil of a community that is somehow invisible because we have been trained not to see it or even to suspect its existence.

A rich definition emerges from Olsen's fiction: a community is any group that is not simply an aggregate of individuals but rather people who are bound together for support and protection or to achieve a common cause, and who feel themselves mutually responsible. First, there are the unchosen and sometimes unacknowledged communities into which one is born—gender, class, and ethnic group. Then there are visible and to some extent chosen communities, such as religions, labor unions, political organizations, and friendships. Olsen's fiction also hints at the invisible communities I mentioned—people joined across time and space by virtue of shared joy or suffering, ideals or beliefs, or people from past generations who are sources of inspiration and courage in the present. Finally, there is the human community, though I hesitate to use a phrase that has come to suggest a bland, homogenized mass, unmarked by all the other communities to which its members belong. For Olsen, on the contrary, the human community is infinitely varied, and the differences among its members are at least as important as the likenesses. I have chosen not to include the family in this gallery of communities, partly because it is infected in unique ways by patriarchal attitudes, as I tried to show in the previous chapter. Another reason for excluding it here is that the family, like the isolated, individualistic self, often stands in opposition to larger communities and is itself lonely and vulnerable.

Olsen's efforts to make all these communities visible link her to socialist, socialist feminist, and Jewish writers; but the modifications created by her multiple vision link her even more closely to women writers of color, and especially to black writers. In *The Third Woman: Minority Women Writers of the United States*, Dexter Fisher writes that Toni Morrison, Audre Lorde, Ann Petry, and other black women writers give the community "back to itself by elevating the commonplace to the artistic." The careful depiction of community also "implicitly connects . . . the individual to her history."[3] Olsen's fiction accomplishes these same tasks.

In her essay "The Master's Tools Will Never Dismantle the Master's House," Audre Lorde writes: "Without community, there is no liberation, only the most vulnerable and temporary armistice between an individual and her oppression."[4] Olsen's fiction dramatizes that assertion. But there is no sentimentality in her portrayal of the bonds linking the person to the community; even my general description above suggests that these sometimes overlapping, sometimes exclusive communities are often at odds with one another. For example, the community that supports one as a worker might oppress one as a woman, and a supportive community of women might be racist or class-bound. The blights of class, race, and gender reach into communities of all kinds, but especially into those of marginal people, often turning the communities into ghettos whose most honest and sensitive members must escape in order to preserve their integrity and their bonds with people outside the walls. Olsen shows clearly the costs of this escape as well as the costs of remaining within limiting and divisive communities with their prejudices and alignment with power. On the other hand, blighted though they are, the embattled communities in Olsen's fiction provide essential protection for their members and often confer the sturdy selfhood that comes from loving support and from the call to be responsible for lives other than one's own. Like the family, communities exhibit both inertia in the face of insufferable social conditions and the strength to change those conditions; they call their members to betrayal—and to integrity and hope.

In the imagery of the paradigm I see running through Olsen's fiction, the blighted, many-branched tree of community did—and does—bear fruit. But survival within a ghetto is no ideal, and being forced to choose between the self and the community is neither natural nor inevitable. Olsen's vision of possibility is like Eva's in "Tell Me a Riddle": "To smash all ghettos that divide us— not to go back, not to go back—this to teach" (R 90). With imagery, revised mythology, and the interplay of shifting points of view, Olsen presents the radical possibility of communities that both honor differences and reach through them toward identification; that lift guilt from innocent shoulders by asserting communal responsibility; and that free the individual from the tight prison of self-absorption, making possible the full development of a generous creativity.

I shall begin this perusal of blighted community by examining a fairly common critical reading of the character of Eva in "Tell Me a Riddle," for she is the character most likely to be wrenched out of her social context and set on a forced march toward self-fulfillment, defined in individualistic terms. This critical reading pulls the story and its elements out of their historical context and into reductive interpretive formulas. In so doing, it reinforces an individualism that contradicts the communal, historical vision central to the story. In general terms, this interpretation says that Eva's great failure is the failure to achieve selfhood. In this failure she is Everywoman; Eve; the universal, literally selfless first mother who must be punished for her failure. This reading is seductive even to critics who are otherwise sensitive to Olsen's circumstanced characters and stories.

In "De-Riddling Tillie Olsen's Writing," Selma Burkom and Margaret Williams write that Eva "has lived in the isolated world of the home, is not socially adept, and does not wish now to become so. Bitter over her antisocial, unself-fulfilled life, it is symbolically appropriate that she be riddled with cancer."[5] Susan Corey Everson expresses a similar view in her dissertation, "Bodyself: Women's Bodily Experience in Recent Feminist Theology and Women's Literature":

> [Eva as] Eve, the biblical mother of all, has been reduced to an unattractive martyr role, unable to become herself.
> Eva's fascination with the Book of Martyrs throughout her life is a fitting symbol for the way in which she has interpreted her role. . . . Her sin is the common sin of women[,] . . . the sin of failure to become a self and failure to take responsibility for her life.[6]

Translating Eva into Eve or Everywoman is a common reaction, and whether she is seen lovingly as the first mother or critically as the evil first woman, the interpretation holds obvious dangers. Judith Kegan Gardiner says that by the end of the story, "Eva is no longer the evil first woman, not the female body or the busy and worn hands to which her roles under patriarchy have assigned her; she is the agent of a revolutionary and transcendent ideal that can be passed from woman to woman, of a commitment to fully human values." She adds, however, that "Olsen must murder Eva's 'poor body' . . . as scapegoat for all the evils of female roles."[7]

I see two problems with the verdict that Eva is being punished for her failure to become a self. First, for Olsen the failure of women to become as fully themselves as they might is rarely "sin" or irresponsibility; it is rather the sad result of pressing life circumstances or, as she puts it, "the workings of an intolerable situation" that pits women's needs against the real, felt needs of others (S 253). Second, although Eva's family does not acknowledge it, she *is* a person to the extent that the circumstances of her life permit. She has lived forty-seven years within the confines of a family that cannot "endure her separateness," as Jacqueline Mintz writes.[8] They blame her for becoming to some degree the person they demanded she be. Denied a wider scope for her energy, she is a compulsive cleaner of her own house and those of her daughters-in-law; denied companionship all her life, she has become a solitary; denied words, she has become stubbornly silent. Yet Eva maintains an ironic distance from the roles that appear to have absorbed her life, never succumbing to them but rather seeing them for what they are: a diminution and distortion of her strength and intelligence. I do not want to minimize the arduous struggle required to preserve the self within the role, yet I am amazed at the weightiness of Eva's person, and at how well she knows her own mind, feelings, and desires, in spite of her family's best efforts to force upon her what they need or what they think she ought to need. Mary DeShazer points out that the first italicized sentence in the story—*"Never again to be forced to move to the rhythms of others"*—expresses Eva's unspoken determination to follow her own bent rather than the whims and desires of her family. As DeShazer notes, "Olsen is underscoring the fact that it is Eva's *inner* life which is real, vital, rhythmic."[9] As Eva nears death, even David is amazed that she has kept her early beliefs alive, defending them against the "monstrous shapes" of loss, betrayal, and death. He says in wonder, "Eva! . . . still you believed? You lived by it? These Things Shall Be?" (123).

Gardiner says that Eva is no longer the evil first woman at the end of the story. In a sense the reverse is true: this nameless woman becomes Eva only at the end of the story. For the first fifty pages of this fifty-three-page novella, Eva does not have a name. To the children she is *Ma* or *Granny* or half of an indivisible unit referred to as *they*. DeShazer says that "to David, Eva is 'she,' the other." When he addresses her it is with a string of epithets, preceded, of course, by *Mrs.* The pronoun *you* "becomes a verbal weapon hurled back and forth between them during arguments: '*You* are the one who always used to say . . . '; '*You* scratched in your dirt with the chickens and thought Olshana was the world'." (DeShazer's italics).[10] Eva finally receives her name when she is close to death, as Jeannie's, David's, and the reader's knowledge of her individuality deepens. David calls her by name at the moment when he sees her as a person with a history, a person whose inner life is more spacious and complex than her roles and his ironic interpretation of her behavior. In her delirium, Eva has been traveling back through her life; in this beautiful scene, David travels with her:

> She sang clearly, beautifully, a school song the children taught
> her when they were little; begged:
>   "Not look   my hair   where they cut. . . ."
>   (The crown of braids shorn.) And instantly he left the mute
> old woman poring over the Book of the Martyrs; went past the
> mother treading at the sewing machine, singing with the chil-
> dren; past the girl in her wrinkled prison dress, hiding her
> hair with scarred hands, lifting to him her awkward, shamed,
> imploring eyes of love; and took her in his arms, dear, per-
> sonal, fleshed, in all the heavy passion he had loved to rouse
> from her.
>   "Eva!" (123–24)

Seeing Eva as Everywoman denies this history and erases crucial differences among women, which Olsen takes pains to delineate even within the small space of this story.

Moreover, by story's end the martyr stereotype is in shreds and so is any concept of Eva either as an ideal mother or as an evil mother guilty of some cosmic failure. Besides being a mother, she is also a thinker, a dreamer, a lover, a revolutionary set down in a particular time and place and shaped by a particular set of communal experiences. It is true that Eva spends much of her energy closing herself into a smaller and smaller space where the demands of her family and the polite chatter of acquaintances can no longer reach her. But as Olsen portrays her, she is not a rugged individualist leaving all human community behind in a final, desperate climb to self-fulfillment. She is, on the contrary, a woman shaped by early community experiences but forced into isolation by the blighting circumstances of her life.

The central conflict of this story arises from the different ways in which David and Eva have experienced solitude and community during their marriage. David wants to sell their house and move to the Haven; Eva refuses to leave her home and the "reconciled solitude" she has finally found. For David the Haven is aptly named. There he will not have to struggle with wheezing vacuum cleaners and scarce money; he will be "*care*free" in a community of his friends "where success was not measured by accumulation, and there was use for the vitality still in him" (73).

But the sociable, voluble life promised by David's Haven comes too late for Eva, who can no longer live "between people," as she puts it. Her daughter Vivi protests, "you lived all your life *for* people." Vivi does not understand the distinction, but Eva does. "Not with," she answers (85). For Eva's experience of solitude has been like her experience of silence. Just as there is a necessary, fertilizing silence, there is also a necessary solitude that lets the mind and imagination range by closing out for a time the bewildering press of everyday life. Everyone from hermits in their cells to children sheltered in caves made of blankets and chairs knows the need for this replenishing solitude.

But there is another kind of solitude that is sheer loneliness, the kind Eva suggests when she insists that she has lived her life between people but not with them. The details of Eva's isolated life as a wife and mother of many young children emerge in her quarrels with David. When he promises her a reading circle at the Haven, Eva answers bitterly, "Now, when it pleases you, you find a reading circle for me. And forty years ago when the children were morsels and there was a Circle, did you stay home with them once so I could go? Even once? You trained me well. I do not need others to enjoy" (75). While David has many friends, Eva has only the memory of Lisa, the young Russian rebel who taught her to read. In Los Angeles, where David takes Eva after he discovers she is dying, a woman runs up to them in the street, crying, "'dear friends, old friends.' A friend of *hers*, not his: Mrs. Mays who had lived next door to them in Denver when the children were small" (105). That little stressed word *hers* shows how rare women's friendship was for Eva, but not, as David says, because she is "Mrs. Live Alone and Like it," or because she considers herself "better than everyone else." For Eva, as for many women of the twenties, thirties, and forties, frequent moves and a husband who obviously believes a woman's place is at home prevented friendship until she no longer had the talent or the taste for it—until she needed other things. Even David must admit that "she had not always been isolated, had not always wanted to be alone. . . . But . . . he could reconstruct, image, nothing of what had been before, or when, or how, it had changed" (119).

All her married life Eva has been denied the first, reflective kind of solitude and had the second, isolating kind forced upon her, until in her old age she has made her peace:

> *Being able at last to live within, and not move to the rhythms of oth-*
> *ers,* as life had forced her to: denying; removing; isolating; tak-

ing the children one by one; then deafening, half-blinding—
and at last, presenting her solitude.
And in it she had won to a reconciled peace. (77)

In this reconciled peace, her home, "now stilled of clamor," "no longer an enemy, for it stayed clean," has become a sanctuary, a shell, a second protective skin. Her home is the Haven that a busy "cooperative for the aged" could never be for her. It is a spacious yet sheltering place where every cranny fits her and where her mind and spirit can range free and at the same time be protected from the endless interruptions and invasions that characterized the rest of her life. The familiar walls offer both protection and vulnerability.

Eva's desire for solitude sets up a regular chorus of literary echoes, especially in the writings of women. Writers as diverse as Virginia Woolf, Anzia Yezierska, Mary Wilkins Freeman, and Elizabeth Stern, to name a few, ask in essay, fiction, and autobiography for rooms of their own with doors to shut. Other echoes carry the voices of American women poets, like Emily Dickinson, who chose to live within the shell of her Amherst home in order to protect "That polar privacy / A soul admitted to itself—."[11] Another voice is that of H. D., who writes in "The Walls Do Not Fall":

> I sense my own limit,
> my shell-jaws snap shut
>
> at invasion of the limitless,
> ocean weight . . .
>
> so that, living within,
> you beget, self-out-of-self,
>
> selfless,
> that pearl-of-great-price.[12]

Marianne Moore and Elinor Wylie also play with images of shells, skins, and rooms to describe the friendly shelter their creativity needs.[13]

Eva's solitude sets up more discordant echoes as well: Sylvia Plath's Esther, suffocating under her bell jar; Charlotte Perkins Gilman's nameless woman, driven mad by her yellow-wallpapered prison; Emily Dickinson again, who records in many poems the hunger and chill she suffers in her polar privacy. (Significantly, in a section of *Silences* titled "Restriction, Deprivation, Exclusion," Olsen includes opening lines from many poems in which Dickinson expresses her desolation [244–46].) In Olsen's own work, Anna Holbrook from *Yonnondio* tells her son wistfully of far-off lands where boys get to go but not girls. As a sorry substitute, Anna moves her washtubs and the baby's basket outside and works in her garden instead of cleaning her house: "She would have liked to range the stove alongside too, even cook over an open fire. Inside suffocating her . . . [and] a need was in her to be out under a boundless sky in unconfined air, not between walls, under the roof of a house" (113, 109–10).

Eva's solitude, like Dickinson's, exacts a price. Listen again to those repeated phrases, *reconciled peace* and *reconciled solitude.* Eva treasures her solitude, but she has had to reconcile herself to the "Restriction, Deprivation, Exclusion" that made it possible. Even though partially chosen, there is infinite loss in a solitude that must be complete in order to exist at all. Though Eva says she will at last move to no one's rhythms but her own, she has no chance for the natural rhythms of solitude and companionship, because the voices of her family pour through the smallest chink, drawing her again into the press and bustle of their lives. What is more, a life lived only within a house, voyages of discovery launched only within a mind, communal bonds that exist only in memory and imagination, are a kind of death for a woman who, as a girl, was part of a revolutionary movement that aimed to change the world.

Annette Bennington McElhiney writes, "In contrast to her life as a submissive housewife and mother in America, in Russia Eva was already a rebel at age sixteen."[14] The story offers fragmentary allusions to Eva's early political activity. From David's comments and Eva's memories we learn that she had been an orator in the failed 1905 revolution during which her "girl's voice of eloquence" had spoken "their holiest dreams" (90, 119). She had spent a year in solitary confinement in a Siberian prison, "where only her eyes could travel and no voice spoke" (92). These clues tell us that Eva had probably been a member of the Bund, or General Jewish Workers' Union. This is the "older power" that has never died in her and that still pushes toward expression and action. To understand what this membership means in Eva's life, it is helpful to turn to histories of the Bund that have recently become available in English. It is especially important to understand what the place of women was in this revolutionary organization. Two good sources of information are Henry J. Tobias's *Jewish Bund in Russia: From Its*

Origins to 1905, and *The Jewish Woman in America* by Charlotte Baum, Paula Hyman, and Sonya Michel.[15]

By the early twentieth century the Bund had thousands of members who were committed to overthrowing the czarist empire and making Russia a socialist society. Many women from the proletariat and the upper middle class joined, even though to do so meant a break with family and with a thirty-five-hundred-year-old Jewish religious tradition. Tobias writes, "Arguments, if not beatings, were sure to follow, once . . . [a woman's] affiliation was discovered. The gradual move toward the emancipation of women shook the very foundation of social life."[16] Women labor activists were certainly motivated by their concern for the Jewish community and for all workers, but according to Baum, Hyman, and Michel, women had another important motive for joining this community. With its opposition to patriarchal religion and its promise of political equality, the Bund opened to women a "society in which they could be fully enfranchised."[17]

For women and men alike, belonging to the Bund usually meant imprisonment and early death. A woman Bundist who was still alive in 1975 recalled, "Thirty years is a lifetime for a revolutionary. None of us expected to live longer than that." In fact, women demanded equal treatment from the government, even when that meant equal risk of death. At her trial, Bundist Anna Heller Rosenthal said: "I speak in the name of all the women. The women fighters want no favors from the Czarist powers. There was no division . . . between men and women. We were treated equally. Together with men we stood up in a just struggle and we feel that for the realization of the ideals toward which we strive, a human life is not too dear a price to pay. We take upon ourselves complete moral responsibility for all that has happened." An account of the death of one woman Bundist testifies to the strength this community gave its members. Pati Srednitsky Kremer was one of the founders of the Bund and a lifelong member. In 1943, when Kremer was seventy-three, the Nazis rounded up the Jews from her hometown of Vilna and took them out to execute them. A woman who somehow escaped the executions told about Kremer's courage and remembered her words to the women Bundists gathered around her: "We will join hands and together sing the Bundist hymn, 'The Oath'; . . . then death won't be so terrible."[18]

Eva remembers her early membership in the Bund as something that gave her life meaning, not only when she was a girl in Russia, speaking boldly and risking imprisonment and death, but throughout her life. But the very qualities that made Eva a revolutionary—her outspoken eloquence, independent thought, and active membership in a political community—made her singularly unfit for the familiar American mold of passive wife and mother whose world is her home. If she left behind in Russia the ignorance of *shtetl* life and the danger of the Bund, she had also lost the camaraderie of that life and, more important, the sustaining political community that would permit her to translate conviction into action.

While labor union activities in America gave David a brotherhood, they did not give Eva a sisterhood. Newly written or reprinted histories of women's place in the American labor movement reveal that "no strike was ever won without the women," as labor organizer Mother Jones says.[19] Fascinating accounts of the 1937 Flint, Michigan, Women's Emergency Brigade and the 1934 Minneapolis Teamsters Strike, and Olsen's own account of the 1934 General Strike in San Francisco show women marching on picket lines, facing police guns, dogs, and tear gas, tending wounds, and helping prevent violence.[20] But the labor movement was deeply sexist both in its leadership and in rank and file male members; and after the strikes were over, women were expected to go tamely back to their isolated lives. Genora Johnson, one of the members of the Flint Emergency Brigade, said, "The brigade disbanded with the victory. . . . The husbands began saying, 'Well, you women did a wonderful job, but now your duty is back there getting those kids in school, getting the wash done, and regular meals again.' "[21] There is no indication in "Tell Me a Riddle" that even the activity of a women's auxiliary was available to Eva. Her only memory of "that winter of the strike" is the one called up by her daughter Vivi, of Eva taking the children to the railway station to keep warm because they had no coal to heat their house. But for Eva, rather than an experience of solidarity, that was one more instance of isolation: she and her small children, alone, huddled in a public depot.

I have said that people of integrity often feel compelled to withdraw from communities when they can no longer tolerate the community's narrowness of vision. Eva's rejection of the community provided by the Jewish religion is such a choice, based on her conception of Judaism as a patriarchal religion that tolerates injustice. As a Bundist, she would probably have rejected her religion as a young woman; her words within the story show that she never returned to it. When Eva is in the hospital, she frightens away the visiting rabbi and demands that the hospital change their description of her from Jewish to "Race, human; Religion, none." Eva's daughter Hannah asks her one Friday evening to light the Sabbath candles. Her reaction to Hannah's and David's explanations for the request is angry and uncompromising. Hannah wants to pass on the Jewish religious heritage to her boys, David says. But for Eva that heritage is superstition: "From our ancestors, savages, afraid of the dark, of themselves: mumbo words and magic lights to scare away ghosts." When David argues that the lighting of the candles has always meant peace in the house, Eva blazes at him:

> Swindler! does she look back on the dark centuries? Candles bought instead of bread and stuck into a potato for a candlestick? Religion that stifled and said: in Paradise, woman, you will be the footstool of your husband, and in life—poor chosen Jew—ground under, despised, trembling in cellars. And cremated. And cremated. . . .
>
> Heritage. How we have come from our savage past, how no longer to be savages—this to teach. To look back and learn what humanizes—this to teach. To smash all ghettos that divide us—not to go back, not to go back—this to teach.
> Learned books in the house, will humankind live or die, and she gives to her boys—superstition. (90)

Given Eva's background, it is easy to take these passionate statements at face value and see Eva as someone who rejects both her nationality and her religion without a moment of regret.

But in spite of all evidence to the contrary, I see Eva's necessary rejection of Jewish religious community and ritual as one of the most painful strippings of her life because it means the loss of communal links in the present as well as invisible links with past generations. My understanding of just what this loss might mean comes from Barbara Myerhoff's *Number Our Days*, an anthropological study of Jews living in a California retirement center; from Elaine Neil Orr's careful tracing of what she calls a "feminist spiritual vision" through all of Olsen's writing; and from reading "Tell Me a Riddle" alongside "O Yes" as question and response.

Myerhoff describes Jewish ritual among the women of the Aliyah Center as actions that bond them not just with each other but also and perhaps more importantly with their mothers and grandmothers. Basha (the name Meyerhoff gives one of the women) eats her meals alone, easing her loneliness by reenacting rituals her mother taught her when she was a girl. Her supper is soup made of free chicken feet, the fare of the poor and the old; but she sets the bowl of soup on a clean linen handkerchief, a practice her mother taught her, and she always prays before she eats, another lesson from her mother. Basha says, "Whenever I sit down, I eat with God, my mother, and all the Jews who are doing these things even if I can't see them." As Myerhoff remarks, because of Judaism's "particular richness" in ceremony and symbol, "Center people were able to elevate mundane affairs, bringing to each moment a heightened consciousness that rendered suffering and scarcity explicable, and because explicable, bearable."[22]

On the last Friday night before Basha leaves the Center to move to a nursing home, she is asked to bless the Sabbath candles. Even though the blessing is a weekly event and Basha had not expected to be moved by it, she weeps as she blesses the candles and says the blessing prayer. Myerhoff describes the blessing as "a powerful and complex event in Basha's life, in which she experienced a unification with her mother, and with herself as a child. Such rare moments of personal integration may happen when early memories stored in the body are triggered by the enactment of ancient long-known ethnic ritual gestures." Basha's own explanation is simple and moving: "When I was a little girl, I would stand this way, beside my mother when she would light the candles for Shabbat. We were alone in the house, everything warm and clean and quiet with all the good smells of the cooking food coming in around us. . . . My braids very tight, to last through Shabbes, made with my best ribbons. Whatever we had, we wore our best. To this day, when the heat of the candles is on my face, I circle the flames and cover my eyes, and then I feel again my mother's hands on my smooth cheeks."[23]

Myerhoff identifies another important quality of rituals that helps explain their power. They are, she says, "capable of making improbable, impossible claims. Because they are dramatic in form, rituals persuade us by our own senses . . . lulling our critical faculties. We perform in rituals, and doing becomes believing."[24] Myerhoff illustrates this power in her description of a Center Sabbath service held in a lounge transformed for the evening into a *shul*, or synagogue. Because many of the men were Orthodox, they would not pray with women present. So the women stood outside, where Jewish women have stood for centuries. Myerhoff watches them, the men inside, praying with intense devotion, the women outside, leaning against the walls and mouthing the men's chanted words. From her conversations, Myerhoff knows that many of the women have since childhood felt angry and humiliated at their exclusion from the most sacred rites of their religion, and she feels "sad and resentful" for them and for herself.[25]

Myerhoff then sees Sylvia, a woman who in daily life moves in and out of lucidity. On this Sabbath evening Sylvia has combed her hair and covered her head with a bit of toilet paper. She prays the long-remembered prayers, and for this moment she is not only sane but feels joyfully connected to God, the past, and the present. Myerhoff comments, "Truly she had come forth from the ruins and put on glorious garments." Myerhoff's reflection on this segregated Sabbath service is enlightening. She had been to many Jewish religious rituals, she says, in which the women were "fully included as participants in the ceremonies, sitting in dignity and comfort with the men," and had found them empty of religious meaning. "But I would return to the Ocean Beach Kosher Guest Home on Friday afternoons as often as I could," she writes, "even though as a woman I would have to stand outside. I had never been to so religious a service nor had I ever beheld an object so sacred as the covering on Sylvia's head."[26] Myerhoff's experience dramatizes her description of ritual's power to lull the critical faculties of the participants and lure them into accepting contradictions that they would never accept in the absence of ritual.

But in Eva, Olsen has created a woman whose critical sense is rarely lulled; and while Eva is not by any means coldly rational, it is impossible to imagine her finding solace in a ritual that excludes her from participation because she is a woman. For the Jewish Sabbath ritual, like the rituals of other patriarchal religions, sanctifies and strengthens this injustice, which remains unjust no matter how lovely the glow from the candles or how beautiful the chant.

Through Eva, Olsen is asking a further question: what happens to people's lives when they lose or discard communal religious rituals and have no others to put in their place? Eva feels compelled to reject a blighted religion that to her means sexist oppression, betrayal, and money spent on candles when children are hungry. But as Olsen has said, the Eva's of the world are deeply religious, in their "reverence for life, a sense that there was something far greater than their individual lives, . . . the need for ritual, for observance, for helping each other."[27] As Eva knows, a life that gives potatoes and lights no candles is mean and threadbare. One day when Eva is close to death, her granddaughter Jeannie brings her a cookie cut and decorated to resemble a little girl. It is, Jeannie explains, the *Pan del Muerto*, the Bread of the Dead, made by a grieving mother to commemorate the death of her child. Eva instantly grasps the paradox this bread ritualizes—that the dead feed the living—and she appreciates its importance to the mother. She has Jeannie set it on her dresser where she can see it; it is, she says, "something of my own around me" (110). But Eva's own Jewish bread-baking rituals are gone, those precious, silent links to her mother and grandmothers and to her daughters; there is nothing in her life to take their place, except this bread come to her by chance from another culture and another religious tradition. Along with religious ritual, Eva has lost the gifts ritual gives: ecstasy, history, the fragile balancing of paradoxes, and perhaps most important, the loving support of a community.

To understand fully the depths of this loss, it is helpful to read "Tell Me a Riddle" alongside "O Yes." When Carol goes to her friend Parry's christening in a black Baptist church, she sees for the first time people experiencing the ecstasy, the complete letting go, that some religions not only permit but encourage. Carol hears women scream and faint and sees them carried out of church by calm, white-gloved ushers who have "the look of grave and loving support on their faces." Her mother's friend, Alva Phillips, tries to explain what is happening:

> "Maybe somebody's had a hard week, Carol, and they locked up with it. Maybe a lot of hard weeks bearing down." . . .
> "And they're home, Carol, church is home. Maybe the only place they can feel how they feel and maybe let it come out. So they can go on. And it's all right." . . .
> "Get Happy, we call it, and most it's a good feeling, Carol. When you got all that locked up inside you." (*R* 61)

But in spite of Alva's explanation, the experience is traumatic for Carol, and doubly so because it comes at the same time as her realization that she has turned away from Parry to be accepted by her white friends. She weeps, "Mother, I want to forget about it all, and not care. . . . Oh why is it like it is and why do I have to care?" (71).

Carol's mother has no words of comfort, for she too is filled with unexpressed pain and has no loving community where she can let it out. The last lines of the story refer, of course, to Carol's mother, but they could just as well describe Eva: "While in her, her own need leapt and plunged for the place of strength that was not—where one could scream or sorrow while all knew and accepted, and gloved and loving hands waited to support and understand" (71). Rejecting organized religion and its rituals does not take away the need for community support and understanding, and these Eva's reconciled solitude cannot give her.

Olsen says that "we have to find our way to what religion offers without the unhappy associations it had in the past and still has in the present when it was and is so misused to keep oppressive power."[28] In her reader *Mother to Daughter, Daughter to Mother*, Olsen has included "Dream-Vision," her retelling of a dream her mother had shortly before she died. It describes the kind of ritual in which Eva would gladly have participated. I include a long section of it here because many Olsen readers may not have seen it:

> It seemed to her that there was a knocking at her door. Even as she rose to open it, she guessed who would be there, for she heard the neighing of camels. (I did not say to her: "Ma, camels don't neigh.") Against the frosty lights of a far city she had never seen, "a city holy to three faiths," she said, the three wise men stood: magnificent in jewelled robes of crimson, of gold, of royal blue.
>
> "Have you lost your way?" she asked, "Else, why do you come to me? I am not religious, I am not a believer."
>
> "To talk with *you*, we came," the wise man whose skin was black and robe crimson, assured her, "to talk of whys, of wisdom."
>
> "Come in then, come in and be warm—and welcome. I have starved for such talk."
>
> *But as they began to talk, she saw that they were not men, but women:*
>
> *That they were not dressed in jewelled robes, but in the coarse everyday shifts and shawls of the old country women of her childhood, their feet wrapped round and round with rags for lack of boots; snow now sifting into the room;*
>
> *That their speech was not highflown, but homilies; their bodies not lordly in bearing, magnificent, but stunted, misshapen—used all their lives as a beast of burden is used;*
>
> *That the camels were not camels, but farm beasts, such as were kept in the house all winter, their white cow breaths steaming into the cold.*

>And now it was many women, a babble.
>
>One old woman, seamed and bent, began to sing. Swaying, the others joined her, their faces and voices transfiguring as they sang; my mother, through cracked lips, singing too—a lullaby.
>
>For in the shining cloud of their breaths, a baby lay, breathing the universal sounds every human baby makes, sounds out of which are made all the separate languages of the world.
>
>Singing, one by one the women cradled and sheltered the baby.[29]

In our day of woman-created rituals, worn female wisdom figures and a human child are still rare but possible elements; in the days when Olsen's mother and Eva lived, they existed only in dreams.

Olsen brings us back over and over again to the blights that divide individuals and communities from each other. It seems no accident that all her stories are filled with prisons or with places and institutions that function as prisons behind benign facades, trapping violence within their walls and turning friends and trusted companions into traitors. The most striking example of this betrayal is Eva's description of Lisa, her friend and colleague in the Bund, who taught her to read, taught her that "life was holy, knowledge was holy." She was an aristocrat and, says Eva, "noble in herself." The story we piece together from Eva's disjointed memories is that a fellow revolutionary betrays Lisa and many others. In prison, Lisa, "the gentle and tender," kills the informer, "biting at the betrayer's jugular, screaming and screaming." Lisa is pledged to nonviolence, but "because of betrayal, [she] betrayed all she lived and believed" (R 112, 113, 99).

In the racially divided world of "O Yes," Franklin Junior High School is a prison that encourages treachery rather than loyalty, and even the black community into which Parry is initiated is a kind of prison. While this community offers its members the riches of language, ritual, and loving support, racism and economic inequities promise that Parry probably will not finish high school, almost certainly will not go to college. Even as a twelve-year-old she comes home from school to care for younger brothers and sisters and cousins while her mother works the evening shift.

In the meatpacking plant in *Yonnondio*, with its eerie presentiment of Nazi gas ovens, hierarchies exist among the workers: "Girls and women [work] in Casings, where men will not work.

Year-round breathing with open mouth, learning to pant shallow to endure the excrement reek of offal, the smothering stench from the blood house below" (134). Native-born Americans are pitted against "dumb furriners," who are pitted against blacks, who are able to get jobs only if the bosses are sure they will scab in case of a strike (87). Finally, the work itself is an ugly parody of cooperation and solidarity. The workers, like their machines, are "geared, meshed, timed, controlled." As Olsen describes the work in the plant, everyone on the conveyer line depends on everyone else; but the speedup system "choreographed by Beedo" to increase productivity turns this work into a deadly dance.[30]

Yet even these workers, who seem completely at the mercy of the machines and the implacable stopwatches of the bosses, find ways to protect and help each other. Olsen gives us an unforgettable description of a day when it is "104° outside, 112° in casings," at seven in the morning. One might expect each worker to look out for himself or herself in this place. But under the pounding of the machines and the workers' frenzied efforts to keep up, comes the quiet evidence of their attentiveness and their necessarily subversive efforts to spare one another: "By word or gesture or look of the eye, the message goes out in each department: spell Marsalek; spell Lena; spell Laurett; spell Salvatore: however possible, spell, protect those known near their limit of endurance." A man has a heart attack and the silent message passes down the line, "*slow it, we got to slow it.*" A steam pipe bursts, scalding the women working under it; and though the straw boss yells at them to stay at their machines, the workers jump to the women's aid, calming, rescuing, carrying out the pregnant Lena and the women who "fall and writhe in their crinkling skins" (144–46).

In this unlikely place the second element of Olsen's paradigm emerges: across fields blighted by isolation and competition, hands reach out; people feel other's suffering as their own, and the strong find ways to spare the weak. The fruitful yield is this miracle of human community created when people in the most desperate circumstances choose to act in unison against injustice. As Burkom and Williams say, "Suffering creates a coherent human community" in Olsen's writing.[31] These communities in turn yield an expanded selfhood. Olsen shows one character after another freed from the prison of the self by a call to responsible action, issued by and within a community: Eva; Alva Phillips; Carol; the faceless, cogged workers in *Yonnondio* who become Kryckszi, the leader, and Ella, the poet and sustainer.

Setting Olsen's fiction alongside her description of the San Francisco General Strike reveals another yield of communal action—a fierce and lasting joy. Though she faithfully records in "The Strike" the violence of clubs and dogs and guns, and the efforts of police, bosses, and politicians to break the strike, the overwhelming feeling of the piece is one of solidarity and joy. Of her own participation in the strike, she writes, "My heart was ballooning with happiness anyhow, to be back, working in the movement again, but the things happening down at the waterfront, the heroic everydays, stored such richness in me I can never lose it." Later she adds, "These are things one holds like a glow in the breast, like a fire; they make the unseen warmth that keeps one through the cold of defeat, the hunger of despair."

Olsen describes a workers' meeting a few days before the strike, when twenty thousand workers packed into the San Francisco auditorium "to fling a warning to the ship owners." Like the black congregation in "O Yes," these workers give each other momentary safety in a hostile environment, the will to renounce powerlessness, and mutual support within a loving community:

> Spurts of song flaming up from downstairs, answered by us, echoed across the gallery, solidarity weaving us all into one being. 20,000 jammed in and the dim blue ring of cops back in the hall was wavering, was stretching itself thin and unseeable. . . . The thunder of our applause, the mighty roar of it for Bridges, for Caves, for Schumacher. "Thats no lie." "Tell them Harry" "To the Finish" "We're with you" "Attaboy" "We're solid." The speeches, "They can never load their ships with tear gas and guns," "For years we were nothing but nameless beasts of burden to them, but now. . . . " "Even if it means . . . GENERAL STRIKE," the voices rising, lifted on a sea of affection, vibrating in 20,000 hearts.[32]

Joyful as this description is, the blight-fruit-possibility pattern I have been tracing in Olsen's work makes it clear that communities that grow only out of injustice and selves that cannot flower because existing communities force them to renounce some essential part of their history will never satisfy Olsen. At Eva's deathbed, when her son Lennie grieves for "that in her which never lived (for that which in him might never live)" (R 117), readers are invited to share his grief. In Silences Olsen writes, "It has never yet been a world right for love, for those we love, for ourselves, for flowered human life"; and "The changes that will enable us to live together without harm . . . are as yet only in the making" (256). But in Olsen's writing, *yet* is always a hopeful word, and in this case it points toward an imagined world in which every child is a miracle and every life a song. Where many writers see only isolated particles in a hostile landscape, Olsen discerns connecting links reaching in every direction through space and time, across the most seemingly unbridgeable divisions. Although she pictures a splintered world inhabited by fragmented people, Olsen steadfastly brings to light the patterns that connect person to person, individual to community. Or perhaps it is more accurate to say that she creates those patterns by asserting the possibility of identification and responsibility where it does not seem to exist.

The large and small communities Olsen envisions do two seemingly contradictory things: they acknowledge and celebrate differences, yet their members find ways to identify with each other's lives *through* the differences rather than by leaping over them or acting as if they did not exist. As I said earlier, for Olsen community is not a bland collective that erases painful and wonderful differences, and there is nothing generic about her characters. They are strongly marked by appearance and language as members of this family, this nationality or race or class or gender, with a history of work written on their bodies. Olsen makes a special point of the fact that Eva sees her own, David's, and her parents' eyes reflected in the eyes of her grandchildren; and even as Eva is insisting that she is not a member of the Jewish religion and that the only race she belongs to is the human race, Yiddish rhythms and remembered phrases from the Jewish scripture color her speech. Olsen delights in customs and rituals belonging to a culture or a religion (the Mexican funeral rites in "Tell Me a Riddle," for example, and the exuberant black church celebration in "O Yes"). Her careful descriptions preserve them instead of melting them down into an insipid sameness.

Moreover, Olsen insists on the differences among women, showing in such pairs as Carol and Parry, Helen and Alva, Jeannie and Ginger (to cite just those in "O Yes") the importance of race and class in setting horizons and expectations and creating values. Olsen's fiction makes concrete Audre Lorde's powerful statement that "community [among women] must not mean a shedding of our differences, nor the pathetic pretense that these differences do not exist." As Lorde readily admits, when women do acknowledge differences, they often see them "as causes for separation and suspicion rather than as forces for change."[33] Olsen's fiction also acknowledges this danger, not just for women but for all members of society, including children. Yet with all the potentially divisive marks of language, history, culture, gender, class, and race firmly embodied in her characters, Olsen's imagery pushes toward identification rather than isolation.

In every story, Olsen's characters mirror, mime, and shadow each other, as if they are trying to get a kinesthetic sense of what it is like to be a radically different person. It is almost as though bodies reach across the divisions created by ideologies and dogmas. This kinesthetic identification signifies, of course, a deeper emotional and intellectual pantomime—what Carol means in "O Yes" when she says she feels a black classmate's emotions as if they were her own: "She acts so awful outside but I remember how she was in church and whenever I see her now I have to wonder. And hear . . . like I'm her, Mother, like I'm her. . . . Oh why do I have to feel it happens to me too?" (R 70–71). For Emily (in "I Stand Here Ironing") and Stevie (in "Requa"), pantomime is a stealthy way of trying on someone else's face, cough, or way of moving, a way of searching for hidden links between themselves and the people around them. Stevie begins to heal when he moves out of his willed numbness into physical and emotional contact: "Miming Wes's face   Sounding Evans dry ghost cough. . . . Sometimes stopping whatever he is doing, his mouth opening: fixed to the look on [his mother's] dying face" (72). In "Tell Me a Riddle," pantomime is Eva's eager reaching across cultures toward a life more expansive than her own. When Jeannie brings a Samoan friend to visit and perform a native dance, Eva dances too: "Long after they left, a tiny thrumming sound could be heard where, in her bed, she strove to repeat the beckon, flight, surrender of his hands, the fluttering footbeats, and his low plaintive calls" (R 112).

Even "O Yes," that story of the relentless sorting of children by race and class, is filled with the synchronization of bodies. As Carol and Parry sit close together before the church service begins, they are joined by the silent music of an old game that expresses the history of their friendship: "Parry's arm so warm. Not realizing, starting up the old game from grade school, drumming a rhythm on the other's arm to see if the song could be guessed. 'Parry, guess.' . . . As long ago. Parry warm beside her too, as it used to be, there in the classroom at Mann Elementary, and the feel of drenched in sun and dimness and dream. Smell and sound of the chalk wearing itself away to nothing, rustle of books, drumming tattoo of fingers on her arm: *Guess"* (*R* 51, 52). Later in the story, the description of Carol playing with Parry and Parry's little brother combines loose, easy sentence rhythms with a perfect image of unity: "In the old synchronized understanding, Carol and Parry kick, catch, kick, catch. And now Parry jumps on her pogo stick (the last time), Carol shadowing her, and Bubbie, arching his body in a semicircle of joy, bounding after them, high, higher, higher" (65–66). The next moment Carol and Parry have been sorted into the categories labeled white and black, and their friendship dies. Elaine Neil Orr notes that the reader is "not certain whose story this is." The point of view shifts frequently among Carol and Parry, their mothers, and Carol's sister Jeannie. While Orr sees this "lack of a central consciousness" as a flaw in the story,[34] I see it as another of Olsen's important strategies; along with physical images of unity, it suggests that diverse people can form communities even in a deeply racist society.

In Olsen's work this identification-within-difference leads to a careful sifting out of communal guilt and responsibility. Who is innocent? Who is guilty, and of what? Who is responsible for the harm suffered by children, women, the poor, members of despised races and nationalities? Olsen shows many of her characters—men, women, and even children—forced to stand by helplessly and watch loved ones being destroyed by disasters they cannot avert. The phrase *innocent bystander* is an ironically apt description of these characters, for whom the legacy of their witnessing is, instead of innocence, a terrible sense of complicity that erodes self-worth. One of the important tasks she sets for her stories is to lift the burden of guilt from innocent shoulders and at the same time assert community responsibility, which everyone shares by virtue of being human. Some share it doubly, triply, quadruply depending on their life circumstances. For if it is true as I have been saying that her imagery pictures the hidden bonds among people, it must also be true that those bonds implicate everyone to a greater or lesser degree in the making of oppression or justice.

Olsen is especially intent on easing what she calls the "helpless pain" of mothers and children ("Requa" 70). One of her darkest motifs is of children whose childhoods have been stolen by adult cares thrust upon them too soon, forcing them to care for themselves, brothers and sisters, and most sadly, their parents. Stevie, from "Requa," provides the most poignant example. As he tries to fall asleep the first night in his new wilderness home, memories slide through the wall he has built around his feelings. In one of his memories he addresses his dead mother: "You promised   and see I'm someplace else again   dark and things that can get me and I don't know where anything is. Don't expect *me* to be 'sponsible" (57). Those brief sentences sum up the fourteen years of Stevie's life: frequent moves, a working mother having to ask her child to take care of things and hold their lives as well as their possessions together. Though Stevie disclaims responsibility, he feels guilty, not for failing to keep track of their meager belongings, but for failing to prevent his mother's death. Olsen repeats Stevie's plaintive refrain later in the story, clarifying the connection with his mother's death. As he lies in the rain, waiting for his uncle Wes to return from a visit to a prostitute, he remembers another rainy night, and again protests silently, "Don't ask *me* where your umbrella got put, don't expect *me* to be 'sponsible, you in your leaky house." The memories do not respect his protests, and he is forced to remember and mime her dying, her death:

> *Her shiver.* Rain underneath, swelling to a river, floating
> her helpless away   *Her shiver*
>   Twisting from the pain: face contorted, mouth fallen open
> fixed to the look on her dying, dead face. (70)

The opening line of "Requa,"—"It seems he had had to hold up his head forever"—refers on the literal level to Stevie's long jolting trip in his uncle's pickup from San Francisco to Requa. In Stevie's tangled memories, the thought and feeling of having to stay awake, to stay upright and responsible refers to his efforts to care for his mother in the days before she died. He remembers being "afraid to lie down even if she was quiet, 'cause he might fall asleep and not hear her if she needed him" (54). His vigilance cannot prevent her death. But far from concurring in Stevie's guilt, Olsen's story says in his voice, "Don't expect *him* to be responsible," when childhood, poverty, and isolation make responsibility impossible.

In an individualistic vision, where families are isolated, presumably self-sustaining units, one might blame shiftless fathers or immature mothers for laying such burdens on their children. Olsen does not allow so smug an explanation, forcing on us again and again the sight of parents doing the best they can with what they have, and still abandoning their children in one way or another. In "Requa," Olsen shows us the life of Stevie's mother in the few cheap possessions and the memories she has bequeathed to Stevie. He remembers a moment of joy: "Laughing. One of her laughing times. Running fast as her, the bundles bumping his legs. Running up the stairs too. Tickling him, keeping him laughing while she dried his face with the rough towel" (70). But most of his memories are of her "sagged with weariness," her legs swollen and blue-veined. A fragment of remembered conversation tells the story of their helpless love for each other: "(*Are you tired, Ma? Tired to death, love*)" (58). Olsen does not attribute guilt to Stevie's mother any more than she does to him, and in fact, she is especially concerned that mothers be exonerated of accusations of guilt, which she calls "a lie and . . . an oppressive lie. It's a sexist lie. And it's part of that lie to keep us in our place."[35]

Olsen never holds her women characters responsible for all the things women have traditionally been blamed for in life and in literature—for being raped, for having children, for not having children, for failing to protect their children. But having said that, one must quickly add that seen through the filter of her multiple vision, women are responsible, sometimes in the same ways as men, sometimes in ways that are unique to them. In speaking of "I Stand Here Ironing," Olsen recently said that while she did not mean the story to be read in terms of mother's guilt, as some critics have done, the story does place "the responsibilities—sometimes personally, but mostly on that world in which so much shaped and misshaped . . . [Emily's] life."[36] It would be a mistake to slide over that seemingly impersonal *world*. Part of what Olsen says here and shows in her writing is that to varying degrees, women wield power even in patriarchal society and are, therefore, partially responsible for the shaping and misshaping of lives within that society. Depending on their class, nationality, race, and age, her women both "mirror and maim" each other, as Catharine Stimpson says, that combination holding both anguish and the possibility of change. Stimpson finds in *Silences* and in Olsen's biographical essay on Rebecca Harding Davis clear descriptions of "the constraints upon the bourgeois woman that objectify, trivialize, infantalize, and diminish her." In Olsen's work, women of whatever class or race mirror each other since "all . . . share a sense of violation of the potential self, of deprivation."[37] But Olsen's early poetry and her fiction also show women participating, often with genuine or willed ignorance, in the racism and class prejudice that maim girls and women who do not enjoy white middle-class privilege.

From her earliest to her most recent writing, Olsen indicts white women and middle- and upper-class women for failing to identify with their suffering sisters. It is surely significant that her earliest poem, "I Want You Women Up North to Know," is addressed to women rather than to men. While women do not own or run the Texas sweatshops where "maria ambrosa catalina" work, they do clothe their children in delicately embroidered dresses, "dyed in blood" and "stitched in wasting flesh," and sold at "macy's, wanamakers, gimbels, marshall fields."[38] Olsen does not spare the racist woman principal in "O Yes" or the women whose charitable contributions support the convalescent home to which Emily is sent in "I Stand Here Ironing." Emily's mother says that pictures of the children never find their way into the papers, so she does not know whether "the girls still wear those gigantic red bows and the ravaged looks on the every other Sunday when parents can come to visit 'unless otherwise notified'" (R 14). As Catharine Stimpson says, "Helping to underwrite this loveless, demeaning place are charitable balls that 'sleek young women' plan when they are not decorating Easter eggs and filling Christmas stockings for the objects of their sterile philanthropy."[39]

Woven into Olsen's criticism is her denial of women's powerlessness. She shows women as well as men claiming and using power, and then having to face their capacity to destroy. (Lisa, the revolutionary from "Tell Me a Riddle," comes to mind, as well as Eva herself, who asks, even at the end of her life, *"human beings we'll destroy ourselves?"* [R 118]). Peace activist Patricia Mische, in writing of the ambivalence many women feel about power, says, "We women perceived ourselves as being powerless for so long that we came to think of it as one of our *virtues.* 'We women' were not responsible or accountable for the atrocities of history. We, after all, were the anonymous 'innocent women' of history, linked with the 'innocent children.'"[40] Olsen shows that this is a dangerous half-truth: to preserve oneself untouched by disclaiming responsibility means to cut oneself off from the power to bring about change.

Olsen's perception of women's responsibility and her efforts to lift guilt are other elements of her writing that link her to minority women writers. Although more and more writers share these perceptions, not surprisingly I find them expressed most powerfully in the writing of women who are doubly or triply marginal. Many black lesbian feminists, for example, instead of claiming special exemptions for themselves by reason of their triple marginality, not only admit but demand recognition of their responsibility for oppression. Many also offer a sharp critique of any feminist position that denies women's responsibility for class and racial oppression. Of the many voices now expressing this idea, two eloquent ones are Andrea Canaan's and Rosario Morales's, both in essays from the collection *This Bridge Called My Back*. In "Brownness," Andrea Canaan writes that while it is easy and comfortable to label white males or whites in general or men in general as the enemy, that position "negates" her power to bring about change: "When I accept white male power as inevitable and not within my control, I accept my impotence to acquire power and control for myself, through and for my brown community, through and for my world community. To give to brown, white, men, women, etc., the status of all-powerful is to cloak them in mystery and power."[41] In an essay appropriately titled "We're All in the Same Boat," Rosario Morales uses specific language that both acknowledges her own responsibility and insists that her readers face theirs: "I carry within me a vicious anti-semite voice that says jew him down   that says dirty jew   that says things that stop me dead in the street and make the blood leave my face   I have fought that voice for 45 years   all the years that I lived with and among jews who are almost me . . . whose sorrows reach deep inside me."[42]

There are characters in every one of Olsen's stories who "live untouched," refusing to acknowledge entangling destinies and thereby saving themselves from feeling other people's pain or joy as their own. In "O Yes," Carol wonders why she cannot be like her friend Melanie "and not care." In "Tell Me a Riddle," Max and Rosa, immigrants from Russia who have perfectly adapted to the United States of the 1950s, are "smooth and pleasant," talking of their own and their children's cars, houses, and education as if those successes made up the world, and turning hunger, human rights, and betrayal into after-dinner conversation. In *Yonnondio*, the bosses who have moved one step above the workers become their most unsympathetic taskmasters. And in "Requa," the owner of the junkyard where Wes and Stevie work believes that his survival depends on a complete absence of feeling for the homeless migrant families drifting past his door. He says to a man whose car breaks down miles from the salvage yard, "Pay on the line or no tow. . . . I don't care how many kids you got stuck in your jalopy, or how far you had to hitch to get here. Sure we got a used trans-mission. We got a used everything. But for do-re-mi. Don't ask me how you're going to manage without a heap" (67).

Olsen's answer to the question of caring and responsibility comes at the end of "O Yes" as the mother tries to find words to comfort her weeping daughter. She does not say them out loud, but the story says them to its readers: *"Caring asks doing. It is a long baptism into the seas of humankind, my daughter. Better immersion than to live untouched. . . ."* (71) Olsen's verbal and visual echoes pull even those who refuse responsibility into identification, her ironic caricatures revealing by way of opposition the unity that should exist and destroying the complacent notion that one can cut a solitary path through life unmarked by those one has harmed. In *Yonnondio*, the banks "batten on" the farmers "like hogs," says Jim, as they take the profits from the Holbrooks' year of labor and repossess the neighbors' farms; and at Armour's and Cudahy's the poor work to feed "a rare and cherished few." The resulting "fat bellies" of those individuals and institutions mirror hungry, preg-nant mothers and skeleton children, whose stomachs are "pushed out like a ball." In "Requa," Evans's "Don't ask *me* how you're going to manage" echoes Stevie's "Don't expect *me* to be 'spon-sible."

Catharine Stimpson says that Olsen embodies her vision of "generous and egalitarian human relations" in metaphors: "in pictures of small groups that fuse self-expression and group ritual: a family singing; the members of a farm community dancing." Many would agree with Stimpson that Olsen's dreams "seem naive in comparison to a sophisticated ideal of the state" and "idealistic in comparison to the possibility of realizing them."[43] In *Yonnondio*, Olsen seems to undercut her own vision of possibility. The Holbrooks celebrate the Fourth of July with their neighbors. It is a typical American celebration with fireworks, a rare holi-day dinner, fiddle music, and dancing. Mazie thinks, "O it's us again . . . it's us. Then in clenching fear: Now something bad's going to have to happen. Again" (125). I believe Olsen means her readers to share Mazie's perception of the fragility of such mo-ments of community celebration. Joy is too fleeting to trust, and oppression constant and predictable, in part because these small communities are surrounded by people and institutions who re-fuse "immersion in the seas of humankind."

For Olsen that refusal is not inevitable. Her fiction, rather than simply recording isolation and individualism, counters those

forces of "disruption, chaos, and disintegration," as Meridel Le-
Sueur calls them.[44] From the beginning of her writing career,
Olsen has been aware of the danger of turning the sufferings of
her characters into aesthetic objects that allow distance and the
serene resolution of contradictions. In *Yonnondio,* the authorial
voice breaks into the story to address this artistic problem. The
narrator describes women and children waiting after a mine cave-
in to see who will come out alive and who will be buried. Then the
author breaks in:

> And could you not make a cameo of this and pin it onto your
> aesthetic hearts? So sharp it is, so clear, so classic. The shat-
> tered dusk, the mountain of culm, the tipple; clean lines, bare
> beauty—and carved against them, dwarfed by the vastness of
> the night and the towering tipple, these black figures with
> bowed heads, waiting, waiting.
>
> Surely it is classical enough for you—the Greek marble of
> the women, the simple, flowing lines of sorrow, carved so
> rigid and eternal. Surely it is original enough—these gro-
> tesques, this thing with the foot missing, this gargoyle with
> half the face gone and the arm. . . . You will have the cameo?
> Call it Rascoe, Wyoming, any of a thousand mine towns in
> America, the night of a mine blowup. (30–31)

The authorial voice disappears in her later fiction. In its place are
images, rhythms, and spaces that powerfully draw readers into
kinesthetic and emotional identification with "thwarted lives."[45]
Her stories gather around themselves a circle of witnesses, a community whose members are called to acknowledge responsibility,
struggle against futility, and sustain each other in the struggle.

The Power and Peril of Language and Silence

I N EACH OF THE PREVIOUS CHAPTERS, I have discussed the linguistic and literary strategies Olsen uses to bring to light the lives of her characters and the worlds they inhabit. In this chapter, I shall shift the focus from language as Olsen's "incomparable medium," as she often calls it, to language as one of her most important subjects. As I said earlier in this study, I saved the consideration of language as subject until last, because I do not want to relegate the stories Olsen tells or her characters to a faded background. Yet whatever else her writing is about—mothers, families, working people, children, communities—it is also inescapably about the struggle to know and communicate those stories. It is about writers and writing, oral and written language; and because of Olsen's devotion to silenced people, it is also about the desperation and eloquence of silence, gesture, and action.

Olsen's preoccupation with language and silence as subjects is explicit in *Silences* and implicit in the direction her stories take, the characters she creates, even the appearance of her prose. As several critics have pointed out, Olsen's stories can be read analogously as celebrations of writing that comes to fruition and as mourning for writers and their work that do not. Bell Chevigny calls *Yonnondio* "a tribute to the characters hidden in the dusty boxes of other distracted writers."[1] In Deborah Rosenfelt's words, this novel is also an elegy for Olsen's own untold stories, "lost between the midthirties and late fifties," and "for the incompleteness of the novel itself."[2] On a more celebratory note, Blanche Gelfant sees "Requa," published almost ten years after the collection *Tell Me a Riddle,* as a "story of recovery" in which "a child's renewed will to live becomes inseparable from an artist's recovered power to write."[3] Although none of Olsen's characters is a writer or has any hope of becoming one, lovers of words haunt even her earliest fiction; and in every story mute or muted characters struggle to find the confidence to speak, a means of expression, and ardent listeners. One could move from story to story drawing tragic or joyful parallels for the struggling artist in Mazie, in Emily, in Anna, in Wes, in Eva, in Jeannie.

Olsen's language also calls insistent attention to itself by creating "a design upon the page," as Blanche Gelfant says. Gelfant's description of the visual design of "Requa" could apply with few modifications to most of Olsen's other fiction and nonfiction: "Its varied typography creates truncated patterns of print that catch the eye; words placed together as lists or as fragmentary refrains form distinct visual units; blocks of nouns separated from the text produce concrete poems; intervening spaces turn into aesthetic entities."[4]

Olsen's attitude toward language, expressed in both fiction and nonfiction, is similar to her attitude toward the lives and themes the language conveys: for her, language too is a living, many-rooted tree, struggling against blight to bear fruit, yet rich with possibility. She must tell of circumstanced lives in circumstanced language; like those lives, language is marked by its history and shaped by where it has been and the work it has done. Those marks, whether of race, class, or gender, are both its limitation and its glory. Olsen is driven to digging through pawnshops and junkyards to find the precious discarded words, myths, images, rhythms, and metaphors that she must then retool to tell her stories. The language is marred, yet Olsen says about it what she says about the lives she has chosen as her material: the work of salvaging must go on, and that work did and does bear fruit. Looked at from one angle, having to scavenge for language is a pinched and precarious existence; from another, it is the essence of human ingenuity and skill. Olsen looks at this conservative effort from both angles.

In discussing Olsen's work, it is impossible to write about language without also writing about silence; for whether blighted or fruitful, language and silence are inseparable for Olsen. Her life as a writer, the lives of her characters, and the words on the page all hover between speech and silence. As I look at her work I am re-minded of those optical illusions where squinting or tilting the page just right reveals either a vase or two human faces—either the dark or the light spaces. That is what the pages of Olsen's prose are like: squint at them, look at them from a different angle, shift the pages in the light, and it is possible to see either nega-tive or positive space, either black print or the surrounding white-ness, either language or silence. I read this entanglement of word and silence as an ambiguous, triple-layered image—as language shrouded and stifled by silence, as language struggling toward expression, and, tilted in the light, as a promising field of silence from which a future language, now undreamed, might spring.

Finally, any discussion of Olsen's attitude toward language is incomplete without considering also the centrality of nonverbal means of expression and communication in her work and what that centrality might mean. Paradoxically, the same life circum-stances that gave Olsen a deep love of spoken and written lan-guage and an awareness of its power also convinced her of lan-guage's limitations. Her Jewish heritage, the influence of the political Left and the early labor movement, and her life as mother and worker all showed her the importance of "reading" the lan-guage of bodies if she was to understand the stories of illiterate or silenced people. Moreover, Olsen's fiction helps rescue physical means of communication—dance, work, touch, ritual, collective action—from the bias against them in overly rational, word-conscious, middle-class culture.

In the pages that follow, then, I will explore silence, language, and nonverbal communication as subjects of Olsen's fiction and nonfiction. Although I will discuss them separately for clarity's sake, it will be readily apparent that this is a false division; for Olsen uses language to suggest silence and to describe gesture, both of which in turn reveal untold stories and unspoken or un-written words.

I shall begin the discussion of silence as subject in the obvious place, with *Silences*, Olsen's 1978 compilation of two addresses ("Silences in Literature" and "One Out of Twelve: Writers Who Are Women in Our Century"); her biographical interpretation of Rebecca Harding Davis's *Life in the Iron Mills* and an excerpt from that book; and an intriguing after-section called "Acerbs, Asides, Amulets, Exhumations, Sources, Deepenings, Roundings, Expan-sions," in which Olsen liberally documents the ideas presented in the two famous talks that begin the book. Olsen writes that silence should be the natural environment for the word, "that necessary time for renewal, lying fallow, gestation, in the natural cycle of creation" (6). But for most of humanity throughout most of history, silence has not been that fertile environment. "The silences I speak of here are unnatural," Olsen writes, "the unnatural thwarting of what struggles to come into being, but cannot. In the old, the obvious parallels: when the seed strikes stone; the soil will not sustain; the spring is false; the time is drought or blight or infestation; the frost comes premature" (6). In this book, Olsen concentrates most on the societal factors—the silencers—that stifle creativity, and in particular the creation of literature. She says categorically, "Where the gifted among women (*and men*) have remained mute, or have never attained full capacity, it is because of circumstances, inner or outer, which oppose the needs of creation" (17).

The layers of unnatural, blighted silence are heavy in this book, surrounded as it is with the silent voices of those who never wrote and the stories they might have told but did not. These are "the mute inglorious Miltons: those whose waking hours are all struggle for existence; the barely educated; the illiterate; women. Their silence the silence of centuries as to how life was, is, for most of humanity. Traces of their making, of course, in folk song, lullaby, tales, language itself, jokes, maxims, superstitions—but we know nothing of the creators or how it was with them" (10). They are the people who could not think of themselves as writers because they did not belong to the class or race or gender that produces writers.

Silences is also filled with the unwritten work of those who produced only a small part of what they might have, given time, economic and psychological support, the lifting of censorship, and changes in critical attitudes. Olsen describes the "foreground silences" of such writers as Dorothy Richardson, Hortense Calisher, Theodora Kroeber, and herself, who were in their forties or fifties or sixties before they published; the "one-book silences" of writers like Henry Roth, whose only novel is *Call it Sleep,* and Jean Toomer, who published *Cane* and no other novel; and the silences of women like Margaret Walker who spent thirty interrupted years writing *Jubilee.*

Silences also speaks eloquently of those writers, mainly women, whose written works sank rapidly back into oblivion because of the modern publishing climate—"It is always fall in the commercial literary world, and books are its seasonal leaves" (169)—and either negative attention or none at all from critics and academics:

"Eclipsing, devaluation, neglect, are the result of critical judgments, a predominantly male domain. The most damaging, and still prevalent, critical attitude remains 'that women's experience, and literature written by women are, by definition, minor.' Indeed, for a sizable percentage of male writers, critics, academics, writer-women are eliminated from consideration (consciousness) altogether" (40).

Finally, Olsen writes of the gaps—the silences—in literature itself, left by writers who, to meet the demands of critics, censors, readers, and publishers, wrote in the prevailing mode, renouncing large chunks of their experience, including most of what it means to be a woman and/or a worker. She also comments briefly on "our still restrictive, defining sexuality as heterosexual, times," which discourage lesbian women from broaching that "necessary, freeing subject for the woman writer"—"telling the truth about [their] experiences as a body" (254–55). The anger and sense of loss Olsen expresses is equally for silenced writers and for "what has not yet been written into literature" (21).

One early reviewer of *Silences* takes Olsen to task for blaming "everything except that standard ailment known as writer's block, while quoting the lamentations of a number of writers (mostly men) who suffered no other impediment."[5] But *Silences* shows that talk of writing blocks is often a convenient way of turning the difficulties writers face in societies past and present into an individual problem for which no one else need take responsibility. Writers of acknowledged genius reinforce Olsen's claim. She quotes many of them, and that chorus of voices, all of them bearing witness to silence, is one source of the book's power and credibility. One such voice is Katherine Anne Porter's: "I have no patience with this dreadful idea that whatever you have in you has to come out, that you can't suppress true talent. People can be destroyed; they can be bent, distorted and completely crippled" (*S* 166). Other voices are those of Melville, Rilke, Woolf, Kafka, Bogan, Plath—hardly lazy or self-indulgent writers trying to find excuses for their lack of productivity.

In the chapter of *Silences* called "The Literary Situation (1976)," Olsen writes, "What follows is the blues. Writer, don't read it" (169). In a way, all of *Silences* is the blues, in its inexorable piling up of the circumstances that crush literary talent. But far from being one more crushing blow, this book has helped to free beginning writers by naming the societal causes of silence, many of which they instantly recognize. In explaining why she uses this potentially discouraging book as a text in a writing workshop for women, writer and teacher Alix Kates Shulman says that "to remain ignorant of the forces opposing you is to remain forever vulnerable to them."[6] Olsen has remarked that she "didn't say strongly enough [in *Silences*] 'and yet the tree did and does bear fruit.'"[7] Like Shulman, I find the opposite to be true. Even as Olsen expresses anguish over all writers, herself included, who almost did not write at all, or whose work is stunted or scanty, or who spent years writing what should have taken months, she is calling to the attention of her readers the names and works of many little-known writers, setting them side by side with the Jameses and Hawthornes and Conrads. As Shulman says, this juxtaposition helps "demystify creative writing as the exclusive province of the 'great'—those mysteriously talented, biologically privileged, usually white, usually male, successful few."[8] One could easily glean from *Silences* a lengthy reading list composed entirely of women writers, both well known and obscure, all of their work the fruit borne in spite of the blighted silence that surrounded their creative efforts.

If the scope of one's vision is limited to the United States, it is easy to take for granted Olsen's message in *Silences* or to read it as old news. Today, on almost every university campus in the country, teachers and students are questioning the content of the literary canon, standards for judging literature, and the very concept of a canon of privileged works. Books by and about the marginal writers Olsen names in *Silences* now grace publishers' booklists and bookstore shelves. In the last twenty years, women writers have "broken silence" about even formerly unspeakable subjects. But Olsen would be the first to remind us that academic United States is not the world. In *Silences*, her range extends beyond these narrow boundaries to the many places within this country where the full scope for creation does not exist. Under the heading "Restriction: Riveted to the Ground," she quotes Ntozake Shange, contemporary African-American poet and playwright:

> When women finally do begin to try to write . . . we write autobiographically. So autobiographically in fact that it is very hard to find any sense of any other reality. There is no other reality besides my house. There is no other reality outside Chattanooga. St. Louis is the only city that exists. This grammar school where me and my friends went, we chewed bubblegum, and went and got screwed the first time—that's all

that happens. See, the whole thing is that our mobility is limited, our ability to read is limited, our ability to write is limited, our ability—or even the impulse—to dream is limited. (242)

Olsen also reminds us in *Silences* that in many countries literacy belongs only to a few, and that many writers participate in freedom movements "at the price of their writing" and even at the price of their lives. This was true in 1978; it is true today. She includes "Lives of the Poets," a remarkable "found poem." Lillian Robinson, who arranged the poem, found the lines in Margaret Randall's introduction to her translation of Latin American poets who wrote within the last thirty years. The poem names several who were killed for their revolutionary activities: Guatemalan Otto-René Castillo, killed in 1967; Javier Heraud, killed in Bolivia in 1963; and Leonel Rugama, assassinated in Nicaragua in 1970. The last stanza mourns not the death of a poet but the curtailment of his poetry:

> Carlos Maria Gutierrez is
> Uruguayan,
> well known
> as a revolutionary journalist.
> *Diario des Cuatelo*
> came directly out of a
> prison
> experience in 1969
> and is his first
> and only book of poems. His first
> and only book
> of poems. (143–44)

Like all Olsen's writing, *Silences* moves back and forth between blight and fruit. Olsen celebrates the "exhausting (though exhilarating) achievement" of those who "came to writing against complex odds," an achievement that "cannot reconcile for what is lost by unnatural silences" (263, 146, 21). Yet, in one of her epigraphs to this book of "the blues" she quotes André Gide: "I intend to bring you strength, joy, courage, perspicacity, defiance." That is exactly what the book has done and continues to do for countless readers who are also writers. To quote Shulman again, "There is hope in one of the lessons of *Silences:* others have done it, maybe I can too."[9] It is appropriate that *Silences* should end with an excerpt from Davis's *Life in the Iron Mills*, for in writing this book in this way, Olsen is passing on to other writers the gift Davis gave to her.

Silence is also a palpable reality in the lives of Olsen's characters. They are not, any of them, writers; only one (Jeannie in "Tell Me a Riddle") is an artist in the usual sense of the word. Yet most of them suffer under the same contradictions as do Olsen and the writers she describes in *Silences*. As Olsen tells unforgettable stories of forgotten people, she shows them gradually sinking deeper and deeper into silence. In "Tell Me a Riddle," for example, Eva's voice fades from "a girl's voice of eloquence that spoke their holiest dreams," to a "hoarse voice that broke from silence to lash, make incidents, shame [David]," to a "gossamer" voice that sings on her deathbed the melodies her life had silenced (*R* 119). Then there are only the sounds of death.

Most of Olsen's central characters are denied the fruitful silences essential to creative human activity, including the creation of meaning out of the chaotic raw materials of a life. They are stifled by a silence that steals their language, offers them no listeners or none who understand, and denies the validity of their experience. The double cruelty of their lives is that the same circumstances which impose a poisonous silence make a germinating silence unattainable by filling their lives with distraction and noise. The din of the packinghouse in *Yonnondio* is one deafening example of this combination of noise and silencing. The machines rule the place: "Clawing dinning jutting gnashing noises, so overweening that only at scream pitch can the human voice be heard." The only human sounds are the shouts of the straw boss and "a hysterical, helpless laughter" of workers driven beyond endurance. The workers can communicate messages of concern for each other only with a surreptitious "word or gesture or look of the eye" (134, 145, 144). It is, of course, in the best interests of the owners of the plant to prevent the talk that might lead to unified revolt against frightful working conditions. What is more, men and women are robbed of their stories by this kind of labor, arriving home too tired and hopeless for the work of communication, the telling of tales. One night Mazie asks Jim, "Pop, tell Ben and Jimmie when you were little. *But the day at Cudahy's has thieved Pop's text*—his mouth open, he sleeps the sleep of exhaustion" (129).

In Olsen's fiction, women, especially mothers, rarely experience a restful silence. The quiet they might otherwise enjoy is either fraught with danger or heavy with responsibility. The mother in "I Stand Here Ironing" hears the cry of her youngest child and thinks, "That time of motherhood is almost behind me when the ear is not one's own but must always be wracked and listening for the child cry, the child call" (R 17). In *Yonnondio*, besides listening for the cries of children, the miners' wives also listen for the shriek of the whistle announcing a mine explosion: "on the . . . women's faces lived the look of listening" (27). Even at the end of her life, Eva, in "Tell Me a Riddle," still listens for children's voices and the sounds of disaster, and for answers that do not come. In her little room in Los Angeles, Eva listens endlessly to music: "She would lie curled on her side, her knees drawn up, intense in listening (Jeannie sketched her so, coiled, convoluted like an ear), then thresh her hand out and abruptly snap the radio mute—still to lie in her attitude of listening, concealing tears" (R 111).

The story in which the characters' silence is most poignant is "I Stand Here Ironing," for it depicts the gradual silencing of a child, which Olsen describes as the "leeching of belief, of will, the damaging of capacity" that "begin so early" in the lives of most girls (S 127). In this story a schoolteacher or counselor calls or sends a note to the mother-narrator, asking her to come to school to talk about her nineteen-year-old daughter Emily: "I wish you would manage the time to come in and talk with me about your daughter. I'm sure you can help me understand her. She's a youngster who needs help and whom I'm deeply interested in helping" (9). As the mother stands at her ironing board, the teacher's request moving "tormented back and forth with the iron," she tries "to remember, to sift, to weigh, to estimate, to total" the events in Emily's life that have made her a child who rarely smiles, a misfit in school, in many ways a stranger to her mother, shy and silent. The mother thinks back to Emily's babyhood. To her mother, Emily was a miracle, a beautiful baby who "blew shining bubbles of sound," and who "loved motion, loved light, loved color and music and texture" (10). But her father walks out when Emily is less than a year old, in the familiar depression pattern, leaving the nineteen-year-old mother to fend for herself and her child as best she can. Poverty forces the mother to send Emily to relatives or leave her with strangers, "to whom she was no miracle at all" (10).

From the beginning words do not work for Emily. They cannot get her what she wants and needs. When she is a tiny girl, her mother puts her in a nursery that is no more than "a parking place for children," this one run by a cruel teacher. Though Emily does not rebel or cry, every day she thinks up a new reason why they should stay home: "Momma, you look sick, Momma. I feel sick. Momma, the teachers aren't there today, they're sick. Momma, we can't go, there was a fire there last night. Momma, it's a holiday today, no school, they told me" (11–12). But everyday she must go: "It was the only place there was. It was the only way we could be together, the only way I could hold a job" (11). Later, after her mother marries, her parents leave her alone at night, and return one time to find her "rigid awake." Emily says, "I didn't cry. Three times I called you, just three times, and then I ran downstairs to open the door so you could come faster" (13).

When Emily is seven, her mother is persuaded to send her to a convalescent home to recover from measles. As her mother describes it, Emily's eight months there is a time of painful isolation. She is not allowed to have friends. On visiting Sundays "the parents stand below shrieking up to be heard and the children shriek down to be heard, and between them the invisible wall, 'Not To Be Contaminated by Parental Germs or Physical Affection'" (14). Though her parents write every other day, and they and Emily plead with the administrators, Emily is never allowed to hold or keep the letters, and she hears each one read only once.

Later, Emily tells riddles to her sister Susan, and Susan, "quick and articulate and assured," wins applause for them while Emily silently looks on. At school she is always out of place and out of step, "dark and thin and foreign-looking in a world where the prestige went to blondness and curly hair and dimples, . . . slow where glibness was prized" (20). As a teenager, when Emily is happy and feeling communicative, she tells her mother "everything and nothing" (19). Finally, Emily becomes a pantomimist who wins laughter with wonderful but wordless clowning. Even this gift partially turns on her, making her "somebody" but leaving her as "imprisoned in her difference as she had been in anonymity" (10).

Olsen makes Emily's silence seem even more stifling by the words she chooses to describe it. Repetition of the same or related words suggests the pattern of Emily's life. When she is eight months old her mother has to leave her with the woman downstairs. Everyday when the young mother comes home, Emily "would break into a clogged weeping that could not be comforted" (11). Her mother uses the same language to describe Emily's ability to make people laugh: "We have left it all to her, and the gift has as often eddied inside clogged and clotted, as been used and growing" (19). Those words, *clogged* and *clotted*, suggest feelings or imaginative and loving impulses trapped inside, souring and becoming poisonous rather than nourishing for the self and others. They call to mind blocked streams that turn rank; sour and curdled milk; and the trapped, rancid air of tenement hallways. They even suggest what happens when the healthy flow of blood is blocked.

All these connotations combine to say that creative expression and communication are as essential to Emily as food and water, air and her life's blood—and when they are denied, she does not have what she needs to live. "Silence *is* like starvation," says Chicana poet Cherríe Moraga.[10] So too say the images surrounding Emily in this story.

Emily's mother seems as immured in silence as her daughter is. The whole story is cast as a silent dialogue between Emily's mother and her teacher or counselor, the "you" the mother addresses at the beginning and end of the story. The mother tells her own and Emily's story eloquently, shaping conventions and time sequence, inventing images and metaphors. Her story weaves back and forth, in and out, because she has no illusions about being able to sum up a human life with linear neatness. She is anything but inarticulate, but we soon discover that this effort to put her own and her daughter's lives into words will go nowhere, at least within the story. She will not go to talk with Emily's teacher, perhaps because she cannot imagine anyone listening with understanding to the complex mesh of circumstances that made Emily "a youngster who needs help." In each of Olsen's stories, people who find sensitive listeners also find a language. But the listeners are few, or they arrive too late, or are removed by death or the rootlessness that often accompanies poverty. There is no hint that the mother in this story will turn her experiences into writing. As a mother/worker, she is always busy, always distracted, never has time to ponder, to gather, to sift. Her daughter asks her, "Aren't you ever going to finish the ironing, Mother? Whistler painted his mother in a rocker. I'd have to paint mine standing over an ironing board" (19). Even if she could find the time, the mother, like the "mute inglorious Miltons" that Olsen describes in *Silences,* does not belong to the gender and class whose members can easily imagine themselves as writers. Even the mother's powerful last words, "Only help her to know—help make it so there is cause for her to know—that she is more than this dress on the ironing board, helpless before the iron," is a plea that resounds only within the mother's mind and heart.

Like most of Olsen's muted characters, Emily and her mother

emerge from silence only through Olsen's unforgettable prose. In the world of "I Stand Here Ironing," words are dammed up and serve neither Emily nor her mother. But the mother's final statement breaks out of the plot, becoming the author's plea to her story and the story's plea to the readers. It is as if Olsen were saying to the words on the page, "Be powerful enough to ease the press of circumstance that crushes or limits the burgeoning creativity of children like Emily."

In addition to being an important subject, silence is also a crucial element of Olsen's style. Through fragmented lines, the use of italics and parentheses, and the arrangement of words on the page, Olsen lets us see and feel silence, expressing irrevocable loss yet filled with unexpressed meanings and unexplored lives.

Words on Olsen's pages are often adrift in white space. They are fragments of thought and feeling broken by ellipsis marks or blanks, rarely achieving coherence or bridging the full distance between the characters. In her dissertation, "Recent Voices in American Feminist Literature," Kathleen Halischak says that Olsen's fiction conveys the discontinuity that characterizes the lives of most women, especially mothers. "There is," she says, "little fluidity, but many questions, repetitions, listings, and refrains."[11] These listings have a spareness about them, like shopping lists or the hurried jotting of ideas made while a mother stands in line at a checkout counter or rides a bus. One example from "Tell Me a Riddle" is Eva's description of the life of her friend, Mrs. Mays, and the other old people who live in California beach settlements:

> Once you went for coffee   I walked   I saw   A Balzac   a Chekhov to write it   Rummage Alone On Scraps. . . .
> Singing.   Unused   the life in them.   She   in this poor room   with her   pictures   Max   You   The children Everywhere   unused   the life   And who has meaning? Century after century   still all in us   not   to grow? (R 108)

Eva's speech is broken because she is gasping for air. But the brokenness also suggests lifetimes lived without what Melville calls "the calm, the coolness, the silent grass-growing mood" that allows ideas to germinate and grow (S 7).

"For all victims," writes Catharine Stimpson, "there may be periods between silence, or its equivalents, and the full articulation of their dreams—periods of stammering, of fragmented speech."[12] Like many of Olsen's characters, Eva lives in just such a painful though hopeful moment, with the very incompleteness of her utterances suggesting how rich her inner life is and how important her past experiences. Mary DeShazer describes Eva's attempt to explain why she cannot hold her new grandson as "pregnant with incomprehensible emotional turmoil." Eva only says, "I cannot, cannot. . . ." Even her thoughts are broken: "Not that way. Not there, not now could she, not yet . . ." (92–93). As DeShazer suggests, at the end of a life like Eva's no words are eloquent enough to say what has gone unsaid during forty-seven years of marriage and motherhood.[13]

Often the very appearance of the words on the page makes visible the urgency of unspoken thoughts and feelings and makes the silences between her characters weightier. They have so much to say, so much to say to one another. What is between them is silence, but the silence is as loud as a cry or a shout. For example, Olsen's liberal use of italics reveals the long years of silence between Eva and her children, and especially Clara, her oldest daughter. We overhear Clara's thoughts:

> *Pay me back, Mother, pay me back for all you took from me.*
> *Those others you crowded into your heart. The hands I needed to be*
> *for you, the heaviness, the responsibility. . . .*
>
> *She hears that music, that singing from childhood; forgotten*
> *sound—not heard since, since . . . And the hardness breaks like a*
> *cry; Where did we lose each other, first mother singing mother?*
>
> *Annulled: the quarrels, the gibing, the harshness between; the fall*
> *into silence and the withdrawal.*
>
> *I do not know you, Mother. Mother, I never knew you.* (116)

How many muffled years of silence between mother and daughter are in those words, and how much sorrow in the realization that nothing can break that silence now. Those few words—"*the quarrels, the gibing, the harshness between; the fall into silence and the withdrawal*"—tell the life story of Clara and Eva and at the same time suggest with painful accuracy the life stories of countless mothers and daughters in our society whose lives are wrenched apart by the interlocking circumstances accompanying poverty, migration, and patriarchal family life.

I am even more intrigued by Olsen's use of italics and parentheses together. This combination suggests that important ideas and feelings are simultaneously emerging from silence and being pulled back into it. DeShazer points out that in "Tell Me a Riddle,"

Olsen uses this odd combination to "paradoxically understate yet reinforce key motifs and themes."[14] Here are a few of those emphatic asides, all of them from Eva's thoughts: It is, she thinks, "(*A long travel from, to, what the feel of a baby evokes*)" (91). When her grandson climbs a tree, "hanging exultant, free, with one hand at the top," while his sister hunches over "in pretend-cooking," Eva silently urges her granddaughter, "(*Climb too, Dody, climb and look*)" (95). Whether she is holding one sleeping child or listening to another ask her parents which disaster plan to check in case of atomic attack, Eva's mental comment is "(*Children trust*)" (96). The italics assert the importance of what has traditionally been considered parenthetical—mere cultural discards. The parentheses say the opposite: while the words contained between them are crucial to the life of the character whose thoughts they express and, in Olsen's view, crucial to human life, they are irrelevant asides in the dominant thought of the surrounding society and in most of Western literature.

In depicting the rich lives of her characters, Olsen suggests centuries of untold stories. The white spaces in and around her stories reverberate with the lives of millions of Evas and Davids, Jims and Annas, Mazies and Emilys and Stevies: revolutionaries, women who stood next to their husbands during strikes, working men and women, aging immigrants living in smelly rooms, mothers, silent children. Most of these life stories will never be told. Olsen begins and ends *Yonnondio* with Whitman's line, "unlimn'd they disappear." Even as her skillful words are telling one story, the white spaces between the words are filled with other stories sinking into silence, "blank and gone and still, and utterly lost."

But in spite of societal attitudes and ideologies that turn whole groups of people into parenthetical comments, at most, in the history and literature of our culture, the white spaces/silences in Olsen's writing vibrate with possibility. I would apply to all Olsen's fiction and nonfiction Elizabeth A. Meese's description of *Silences:* "The pages' blank spaces, open invitations to the reader to participate in the text's creation, to break the silences by inscribing themselves, further reinforce Olsen's remarkable accomplishments."[15] "Requa," for example, ends with open parentheses and no final period. Stevie has just spent Memorial Day visiting cemeteries with Mrs. Edler, the owner of the boardinghouse where he and Wes live. When they come home, Wes asks Mrs. Edler what she did to make Stevie so playful and attentive, so unlike his withdrawn self:

When I heard where you went, I expected sure he'd come
back near dead, bad as in the beginning. But he's been frisky
as a puppy all day. Chased me around the junk heaps.
Rassled   went down to the river on his own   throwed skim-
mers   sharped a saw perfect   Paid attention. Curled up and
fell asleep on the way home.
   That's where he is—still sleeping. Lay down second we
got home and I can't get him up. Blowing the biggest bubble
of snot you ever saw. Just try and figger that loony kid.
                              (stealthily   secretly reclaiming
                                                    (74)

That open ending invites Olsen herself to complete this story and
her readers stealthily to reclaim the lives and parts of lives that are
parenthetical in our culture. This story, primarily about a man and
a boy, further suggests that the lives of certain men or parts of the
lives of all men are among those valuable discards.

   Even Olsen's *Mother to Daughter, Daughter to Mother* offers similar encouragement. Described as a daybook and reader, it is set up
as many calendars are, with text on one page and a week's calendar on the facing page. Of course, one is free to fill those ruled
spaces with doctors' appointments and grocery lists. But because
the calendar spaces are not dated, because the writing by and
about mothers and daughters is so provocative, and because Olsen introduces the book with her regret that mothers still have not
told their stories in their own words, the book seems to ask insistently, "And you, what is your story? What are the stories of your
mother, your daughter?" I see the book with its small spaces as
Olsen's particularly gracious invitation to mother/writers during
"non-writing times," as she calls the periods when women are
simply too busy and distracted for sustained writing. As Olsen
does in talks and interviews, the book seems to urge mothers to
"keep faith with their writing selves" by jotting notes that capture
fleeting impressions. "Something happens in that process," Olsen
says. "A deposit of that is going to remain with you."[16]

   As I have said, Olsen loves language, yet she faces in *Silences*
and in her fiction the question feminist writers and critics must
face: Is it enough for women to break their silence, to "come to
writing" or speech, or is language itself the most insidious silencer
of women? In interviews and lectures, Olsen defends the language
of the Western world against the accusation that it has been poi-
soned by male domination.[17] But her fiction convinces me that this

question began to trouble her back in the 1930s when she first drafted *Yonnondio*, and that it has been broadened by her multiple vision to include all marginal people. Rephrased, Olsen's question about language as silencer might ask whether our language and literature are blighted not only for women but also for working people and for racial, cultural, and sexual minorities. As we might expect, Olsen's answer is both yes and no, as she finds even in language's blighted condition an impetus to creativity.

Silences contains inexorable catalogues of the silencers within the language that define whole groups of people and their experiences out of existence. *Silences* also describes the limiting and destructive myths that tell marginal people who they are with such authority that the people accept the myths as reality and disown themselves. In her fiction, Olsen shows these destructive linguistic forces at work eroding the confidence of her characters and limiting their horizons.

In *Yonnondio*, for example, racist, sexist, elitist language reaches into her characters' lives, denying them access to the power of self-naming. The Holbrook children soon discover that they cannot find a trace of themselves in books. One day Anna Holbrook takes her children to the library, a marvel to a woman who has never learned to read. But Mazie and Will do not share her wonder; like other packingtown kids, they turn from the books "in outraged self-respect, for is it not through books, the printed word, or so it seemed, that they had been judged poor learners, dumb, dumb, dumb? Told: what is in us has nothing to do with you" (125–26). Mazie and Will reject the books the librarian selects for them— "onceuponatime and theylivedhappyeverafter fairy tales" for Mazie and "adventure and magic books" for Will. They turn instead to the magical worlds of the movies and the city dump where "children—already stratified as dummies in school, condemned as unfit for the worlds of learning, art, imagination, invention— plan, measure, figure, design, invent, construct, costume themselves, stage dramas; endlessly . . . live in passionate absorbed activity, in rapt make-believe" (121). But this world of make-believe and its language, patterned as they are on movies and movie magazines, betray the children, providing them with no more validation for their lives than do the silly library books.

A bit of human wreckage from this world is Gertrude Skolnick, in real life a Polish girl with broken nails who washes dishes in her aunt's diner and must listen to her mother yell at her in a guttural, foreign-sounding tongue. But in the imaginary world she creates in her tent on the dump, she is Jinella, a glamorous composite of all the movie queens she has ever seen. The tent becomes "Jinella's mansion, Jinella's pagan island, Jinella's palace, whatever Jinella wills it to be that day," until her mother's voice calls her back to her sordid life.

From one point of view one must marvel at the power of Jinella's imagination, which creates with a few discarded trinkets and some borrowed dialogue the worlds of *The Sheik of Araby, Slave of Love,* and *The Fast Life,* and which turns a dump in a stinking town into a fragrant pleasure palace: "Luxuriously on her rug, pretend silk slinking and slithering on her body, turbanned, puffing her long pretend cigarette: Say vamp me, vamp me. I'm Nazimova. Take me to the roadhouse, I want to make whoopee. Hotcha. Never never never. O my gigolo, my gigolo. A moment of ecstasy, a lifetime of regret." She creates illusions not only for herself but also for Mazie and the other little girls who fight for the privilege of being admitted into Jinella's world, where for a moment they too are transformed: "And once alone, smelling sweet of Blue Waltz and moist flesh, her arms tight around Mazie, passionately: whisper to me: Jeannine my queen of lilac time. Jeannine I dream of lilac time. Whisper it. Kiss me. Forever never to part, my pagan love" (128).

But from another point of view Gertrude/Jinella's life is pathetic. She yearns for what she will never have; in her imagination, "slender white fingers with talon fingernails float unattainable in the dust mote air." She wants to be "classy," not a drudge, not "Human Wreckage" (148). An added irony is that the only classiness she has ever seen is Hollywood glitter. Jinella is caught in her dream world, and, by contrast, the real world of Gertrude Skolnick seems unbearably sordid. She calls her home, her mother's Polish accent, Mazie, a crippled girl, and herself "ugly" and "fishface." Mazie passes Jinella's cruel names on to her little brother Ben: " 'Fishface,' she heard herself saying in Jinella's inflection, 'why don't you close your mouth, fishface?' " (141). Jinella's world and the language that creates it are by turns funny, cruel, and impoverished, for they teach her to devalue herself and her hardworking people; but they are also Gertrude Skolnick's rebellion against the real ugliness of a narrow, corrosive, evil-smelling world.

With only a small shift of viewpoint, Olsen becomes one of the figures who haunt her stories: the "peerers, combers and escavators" hunting for treasure in rummage sales, ragbags, and salvage yards. And Jinella, that young thwarted artist, becomes a warning to the writer herself not to settle for shoddy myths and images of love and beauty. Ironically, not all the cheap glitter Olsen must reject comes from *Silver Screen* magazines and Valentino movies. As she makes clear in *Silences,* much of the shoddiness is enshrined in the canonical literature of the Western world, whose stereotypes about love women writers must resist. Her list includes: " 'Love is a woman's whole existence.' Centrality of the male. Centrality of sexuality. Confinement to biological (sex-partner) woman. The trap of biological analogy: glorifying womb, female form imagery; or softness, the inner. Earth mother, serving vessel, sex goddess, irresistible romantic heroine; victim; 'do with me as you will' stereotype" (252–53). Despite these inbred dangers, Olsen's love of language and her respect for its power are so deep she cannot simply leave it on the patriarchal junkheap.

This love comes to Olsen as a triple heritage. It comes from her Jewish ancestors, for whom the written word was so sacred that they did not use newspapers to wrap herring. In *Number Our Days,* Myerhoff quotes an old man from the Aliyah retirement center: "For us all books are religious. Study is religious. Each page and each letter on the page has its own special character, even the white spaces between the letters are holy. . . . When a book is left open, we put a cover over it, for respect. When it is worn out we give it a burial. It's like a living thing. All writing has something of holiness."[18] I do not intend to pull Olsen into a religious tradition to which she has never belonged. But the love of the written word rooted in Jewish religious tradition was an enduring value for socialist Jews both in Eastern Europe and in the United States. In fact, it was education—the influence of the written word—that helped bring about the rise of the workers' movement in Russia. According to Baum, Hyman, and Michel, the earliest leaders of the movement were not workers at all but "the children of middle-class families who had been influenced by the *Haskalah* [the nineteenth-century Jewish Enlightenment] and who were financially able to provide their children with the secular education that often led to revolutionary activism."[19]

For Jews, not just religious words but hexes, charms, curses "change things around." As another Jewish man tells Myerhoff, "When you have the right word, you have power over something." If this was true of Hebrew, the language of religion and law, it was even more true of Yiddish, the *mama-loshen,* or *mother's tongue*, the language of everyday life in Eastern European *shtetls*. Myerhoff adds that Jews have always "treasured the spoken word" and that stories "are a renewal of the word, made alive by being spoken, passed from one to another, released from considerations of correctness and Law."[20] Olsen does not know Yiddish (most American Jews did not teach it to their children), but she shares this belief in the power of words and in the spoken and written *mother tongue* as the rightful possession of the groups of people she is most interested in. She uses in her fiction what she calls "the language of our first years," and "of the deepest, purest emotion, language that does not come primarily out of books, but the language of first thought, emotion."[21]

Olsen's love of language also comes to her from her socialist parents and their colleagues, for whom words were actions and calls to action. From her earliest years, Olsen listened to the voices around her, even considering it part of her good luck that she stuttered when she was young, because that made her listen to "what she still considers an intoxicating richness of speech. 'Just the music, the varieties, the ways of speaking. . . . it all had a magical tone.' "[22] As Erika Duncan says, Olsen listened to the "speech of the powerful socialist orators who had such a profound influence on her own use of language, revealing to her early how language was able to affect and move people." She especially admired immigrants, "who did not yet know all the words they needed in order to express themselves, who had to somehow make do with the words they did know, stretching them," and working people, many of them also recent immigrants and most of them without formal education.[23] Olsen says of them, "The people of the packing-house strike were not masters of language . . . but when they would get up to speak, they would speak with such beauty . . . the sodders, the sod farmers used the language of the prairie when it was all grass and no trees, wind." Olsen also listened to her black neighbors, whose linguistic rhythms she "could not fully enter, yet longed for."[24]

The third part of Olsen's legacy comes from a lifetime of reading and absorbing the rhythms of what she calls "the whole range" of the written word. Only one generation and one migration removed from illiteracy, her devotion to books is that of someone who almost did not have access to them.[25] For Russian Jewish women of her mother's generation and class, learning to read could be a punishable act; like Eva, they would have had to find a willing teacher and often brave a father's wrath.[26] Reading and writing look different from this perspective.

But the contradictions embodied in every one of the literary and oral traditions out of which she writes are not lost on Olsen. She writes those contradictions into her fiction. As Eva tells David, the Hebrew holy language was denied to women and often used to denigrate them. While the language of socialist orators espoused the "holiest dreams" of women and men workers, it was also marked by sexism and championed an equality that seldom reached beyond the walls of the labor hall. The "common language" of sodders and miners also passsed on entrenched lessons about men and women, blacks and whites. Olsen fills Jim Holbrook's talk with terrible phrases: "Keep your damn brats from under my feet"; "furrin scum and niggers"; "Can't screw my own wife." Even the "mother tongue" that speaks the language of "first emotion" is blighted, transmitting from mother to daughters and sons our culture's controlling myths. When Mazie protests, "Why is it always me that has to help? How come Will gets to play?" her mother answers with finality, "Willies a boy" (Y 142).

Western literature presents Olsen with an even more difficult contradiction. Even as she was eagerly reading her way through the Omaha library, she soon discovered that "not only the speech but so much else of the lives of human beings around me was not in literature."[27] Olsen shows Eva struggling with this same conflict. For Eva, as for her Jewish ancestors, the word is sacred. The lesson she learns from her friend Lisa, who taught her to read, has the force of an equation: "life was holy, knowledge was holy" (112). What is more, Eva's spirit is kept alive in part by her memorized authors—Hugo, Chekhov, Balzac, Dostoyevsky—all of them writing firmly within patriarchal traditions. She struggles to free herself from the sexist attitudes reinforced by this literary tradition, but for one who narrowly missed being illiterate, giving them up would be an unthinkable poverty.

Olsen chooses to salvage all these languages, blighted though they are, as a way of countering the idea that educated white men, who have "only a thimbleful of experience," own a monopoly on language and literature.[28] Olsen borrows that phrase, as well as Silences' last, hopeful words, from Woolf: "Literature is no one's private ground; literature is common ground. Let us trespass freely and fearlessly and find our own way for ourselves. It is thus that English literature will survive if commoners and outsiders like

ourselves make that country our own country, if we teach ourselves how to read and how to write, how to preserve, and how to
create" (264). For Olsen, literature is common ground, not in the
sense that it expresses common meanings but in the sense that
anyone can go there and plant her or his feet. In *Silences*, Olsen quotes Elaine Showalter's assessment of the damage done to
women by the literature usually taught in colleges: "Women [stu-
dents] are estranged from their own experience and unable to
perceive its shape and authenticity, in part because they do not see
it mirrored and given resonance in literature." This is, Olsen adds,
a harm "difficult to work through." But then she gives an accurate
description of herself as a writer: "Nevertheless, some young
women (others are already lost) maintain their ardent intention to
write—fed indeed by the very glories of some of the literature that
puts them down" (29). Though she was not college-educated,
Olsen was "incited to literature" by both the glories and the gaps
she found in her reading. As she puts it, "The factor that gave me
the confidence was that *I* had something to contribute, *I* had
something which wasn't in there yet."[29]

"Requa" provides good examples of the fruitful results of Olsen's salvaging of language. Gelfant says that in Olsen's prose
"everything can be recycled, and anything broken and discarded
put to new use. Nothing is beyond the human imagination that
can create even out of waste, the 'found' objects in a junkyard, a
poetic text."[30] The junk Gelfant refers to is the waste products of
technology that overflow the salvage yard where Wes and Stevie
work, which Olsen's work of reclamation turns into concrete poetry. I find even more exciting Olsen's skillful interweaving of the
tools and tasks of Wes's work with Shakespearean rhythms:[31]

> Hasps   switches   screws   plugs   faucets   drills
> Valves   pistons   shears   planes   punches   sheaves
> Clamps   sprockets   coils   bits   braces   dies
>
> How many shapes and sizes; how various, how cunning in
> application. Human mastery, human skill. Hard, defined, en-
> during . . . they pass through his hands. (65)

Behind these lines lie Hamlet's: "What a piece of work is a man!
How noble in reason! How infinite in faculties! In form and moving, how express and admirable!" (II.ii.315–17).[32] In this brilliant

recombination, the making of poetry and everyday, skilled labor are bound together as manifestations of human intelligence. Both Shakespeare and technological waste become pieces of junk that need to be and can be reclaimed and retooled by "human mastery, human skill." Later in the story Olsen picks up the Shakespearean echoes again, suggesting a rough correspondence between the crafting and recrafting of tools and the crafting and recrafting of language and literary strategies:

> accurately threaded, reamed and chamfered Shim Imperial flared
>   cutters benders grinders beaders
>   shapers notchers splicers reamers
>
> > > how many shapes and sizes
> > > how various, how cunning in
> > > application
> > > (71)

At a 1986 talk at the University of Minnesota, Olsen said that women's ingenuity has created a hundred forms of pasta when practicality and nutrition demanded only one. Where others see only pasta, Olsen sees a manifestation of the human "artistic capacity that will create art forms out of domestic materials and other necessities of life."[33] Where others see discarded tools and junked cars, Olsen sees technological mastery and concrete poetry and hears Shakespearean echoes. And where others see a language hopelessly colonized by the patriarchy, Olsen sees both language and literature as "various and supple enough" to express an infinite range of human experience.[34]

The subtext of Olsen's writing, then, is not the denial of language's ability to communicate the lives and reality of people outside the mainstream; it is rather the possibility of such communication. Along with such earlier writers as Virginia Woolf and Rebecca Harding Davis, this attitude toward language closely aligns Olsen with those contemporary women poets Alicia Ostriker calls "the thieves of language," who see language "as plurally generated and diffuse at any given time and subject to change at all times" rather than as the creation and exclusive possession of the patriarchy.[35] Like them Olsen is engaged in an exhilarating wrestling match with all the resources of language to make it express her whole reality. In addition, Olsen's multiple vision leads her to reclaim and retool linguistic and literary strategies rather than to create an exclusive women's language, which would inevitably raise new barriers between working women and men, black women and men, and women of different classes and cultures. The concept of a women's language, whether playfully or seriously proposed, denies, or at least ignores, the other determining circumstances that preoccupy Olsen. While one important part of her life's work has been putting women's inner and outer lives into words, an equally important part has been forging linguistic bonds between people of different genders, races, and classes, and acknowledging those that already exist.

Olsen shares with women of color in particular a grasp of the dangers inherent for them in language, as well as a determination to face the dangers and to "trespass freely and fearlessly" on the common ground of literature (S 264). An example from the collection *This Bridge Called My Back* traces one woman's struggle to become a writer, the betrayal she then discovers in language, and finally her decision to claim language, the enemy, as her own. In the angry essay titled "Speaking in Tongues: A Letter to 3rd World Woman Writers," Gloria Anzaldúa describes the barriers to writing that Olsen made familiar in *Silences:*

> How dare I even consider becoming a writer as I stooped over
> the tomato fields, bending, bending under the hot sun, hands
> broadened and calloused, not fit to hold the quill, numbed
> into an animal stupor by the heat.
>   How hard it is for us to *think* we can choose to become
> writers, much less *feel* and *believe* that we can.

This self-described "little chiquanita from the sticks" does become literate and does begin to think of herself as a writer; but then she must face the power that language has to distort her perceptions of herself, her family, and her people. She quotes Cherríe Moraga's poem "It's the Poverty" as an accurate description of her own ambivalent feelings toward language:

> *I lack imagination* you say,
> No. I lack language
> The language to clarify
> my resistance to the literate.
> Words are a war to me.
> They threaten my family.
>
> To gain the word
> to describe the loss

I risk losing everything.
I may create a monster
the word's length and body

Swelling up colorful and thrilling
looming over my *mother*, characterized.
Her voice in the distance
unintelligible illiterate.

These are the monster's words.

Yet later in the same essay, right in the teeth of that "monster," Anzaldúa says, "The writing is a tool . . . [that] shields us, gives a margin of distance, helps us survive." In words reminiscent of Olsen's, she exhorts her radical sisters of color to "forget the room of one's own—write in the kitchen, lock yourself in the bathroom. Write on the bus or the welfare line, on the job or during meals, between waking and sleeping. . . . No long stretches at the type-writer unless you're wealthy or have a patron—you may not even own a typewriter. While you wash the floor or clothes listen to the words chanting in your body."[36]

A logical corollary of Olsen's belief in the elasticity of language might be that for her the possibilities within language and litera-ture are infinite. In one sense that is true, for she models and encourages the expansion of literary boundaries to admit new stories and forms. In another sense her knowledge and love of words have also taught her their limits, and the most fertile pos-sibility she suggests is a rhythm in which language neither re-places nor overwhelms silence and non-verbal means of expres-sion and communication.

As I said earlier, I suspect that Olsen's sense of the crucial interplay between language, silence, and action came from her life as mother and worker. I believe this perception is also another part of Olsen's rich inheritance from the literary and political Left. In the socialist tradition, words call to action and celebrate it, but they do not replace "the muscular event," as LeSueur calls actual par-ticipation in a strike. Simply stated, essays and speeches about unjust labor practices must be accompanied by bodies on the picket line. A paragraph from LeSueur's description of the 1934 Minneapolis Truckers' Strike sheds light indirectly on Olsen's par-ticular blend of word and action. LeSueur had intended to cover the strike as a journalist detached from the fray, but in spite of her fears she ended up participating in a collective action for the first time in her life:

> I have never been in a strike before. It is like looking at something that is happening for the first time and there are no thoughts and no words yet accrued to it. If you come from the middle class, words are likely to mean more than an event. You are likely to think about a thing, and the happening will be the size of a pin point and the words around the happening very large, distorting it queerly. . . . When you are in the event, you are likely to have a distinctly individualistic attitude, to be only partly there, and to care more for the happening afterwards than when it is happening.[37]

Olsen describes an opposite tension in "The Strike." No detached reporter, she is pulled away from the action on the waterfront, "the battlefield," as she calls it, to write an account of the events leading up to the 1934 San Francisco General Strike. She sits at her typewriter, "making a metallic little pattern of sound in the air, because that is all I can do, because that is what I am supposed to do." Olsen obviously knows that it is important for a worker who is also a skilled writer to record these events, "so that the beauty and heroism, the terror and significance of those days, would enter your heart and sear it forever with the vision." But her written words are no substitute for action; they are rather part of a rhythm in which word and action inspire each other. A week earlier Olsen had been present at a mass meeting of workers where "solidarity" wove them all "into one being" and had gone down to the waterfront where she could stand, "watching, silent, trying to read the lessons the moving bodies . . . were writing." "The Strike" ends with these hurried words: "The rest, the General Strike, the terror, the arrests and jail, the songs in the night, must be written some other time, must be written later. . . . But there is so much happening now. . . ."[38] As if inspired by her own words, Olsen left her typewriter to join the picket line and was arrested with three hundred other strikers.[39]

Besides political action, Olsen presents in her fiction myriad other nonverbal means of expression and communication. Her works are filled with images of sight, touch, and taste. One might read the physicality of Olsen's writing as despair over language's ability to represent the lives of women and other marginal people, but I find that interpretation too somber to do justice to Olsen's belief in the flexibility of language and the eloquence of nonverbal expression.

The physicality of Olsen's writing responds to the necessity of learning to read silent forms of communication if one wants to know the history of silenced people. For those who have never had access to pen and paper, much less to the printing press, and for people like Jim Holbrook, whose spoken text has been stolen by exhausting work, one must read the stories of lives transcribed on bodies or miss them altogether. Elaine Neil Orr says that in Olsen's fiction "bodies are texts that tell of terror," and hands speak when voices cannot.[40] Varicose veins and aching feet, arthritic, swollen hands twitching in sleep—those are the texts that tell life stories. Moreover, Olsen's faith in human capacity and adaptability leads her to assert that people will create, and if one medium is denied them, they will find another. Denied language, Emily becomes a mime. Denied the resources of education, the young "FrankLloydWrights of the proletariat" construct fantastic shapes on the dump (*Y* 61). But Olsen also affirms the wisdom and grace of physical means of expression and communication, not just as poor substitutes for language but as ways of knowing and creating. And the loss of those means is as tragic for her characters as the loss of language. In "Tell Me a Riddle," for example, David's and Eva's bodies know something about the bonds between them that their words contradict. Despite their words to each other— David's sarcasm and Eva's bitter curses—their bodies speak an unbreakable oneness. When in her anger Eva leaves their bed to sleep on a cot, David cannot sleep: "After all the years, old harmonies and dependencies deep in their bodies; she curled to him, or he coiled to her, each warmed, warming, turning as the other turned, the nights a long embrace" (83–84).

Similarly, in "Requa" Stevie has been so traumatized by the loss of his mother that he cannot be healed by words. He is "reclaimed," in the language of the story, by his uncle's rough touch, a Memorial Day ritual, and the steady rhythms of work in the salvage yard:

> *The dead things, pulling him into attention, consciousness.*
> *The tasks: coaxing him with trustworthiness, pliancy, doing as he*
>   *bids*
>
>   having to hold up
>   (65)

Though this story recreates the world of the Great Depression in which poverty has made all the characters desperate for any work at all, this is not the blind, driven toil of *Yonnondio*. On the contrary, the tasks Wes teaches Stevie are varied and useful, requiring skill and attentiveness:

> sharpening   hauling   sorting   splicing
> burring   chipping   grinding·   cutting
> grooving   drilling   caulking   sawing
> *the tasks, coaxing*
> rust gardens   (72)

To reveal their potency to her readers, Olsen transforms the names of tools and manual skills into a chant or healing charm. Within the story, however, it is not words but the sturdy heft of the tool in the hand and the trustworthy rhythms of work that ground Stevie's life. Or, to shift to Olsen's witty metaphor, tools and tasks are "rust gardens" that promise to bloom.

The perception that words are not enough to express a life runs through the works of many other writers but is almost a constant in the works of black women writers. I think, for example, of Toni Morrison's *Bluest Eye*, in which a mother's love smells to her daughter like wintergreen cough syrup and feels like rough hands readjusting a quilt and resting for a moment on the forehead of a sick child. Zora Neale Hurston's *Their Eyes Were Watching God* fairly bursts with wordless joy, and in Paule Marshall's *Praisesong for the Widow*, the main character sheds her middle-class pretensions and is reconnected with her black heritage by a dance and the "laying on of hands."[41]

Like these novels by black women, Olsen's fiction asserts that words have their limits because of the physicality of the human person, which cries out for bodily expression. Nor is that expression a frill. For Olsen it is essential in creating and sustaining the lives of individuals and communities. Without words and the right to say them, mothering, work, most human activity are bondage.[42] But words without free bodily expression are their own kind of bondage. This is especially true for women, who for centuries were denied the right to tell the truth about the body, as Olsen says in *Silences*. But in addition to that, they often also have been denied the body's free use. One of Olsen's parenthetical comments in *Silences* notes this seldom mentioned but crucial distinction between men and women: "Knowledge of one's body that comes

only through free use of it, . . . denied. (Thoreau's birthday wish
for himself one year: 'to inhabit his body with inexpressible satisfaction.' Never possible for his sister Sophia. He could swim—and
naked, walk to exhaustion, 'dithyrambic leap' about; all physical
activity was open to him. Never for Sophia—or any woman—that
inexpressible satisfaction)" (254).

With her usual unsentimental clarity, Olsen shows the ways in
which circumstances blight bodily expression, spoiling the sense
of joy and power and unity it could provide. In "I Stand Here
Ironing," for example, one of the first things the mother remembers is that the simple, loving act of nursing her child was dictated
by some nameless experts, and instead of creating a bond between
her and Emily, it was a source of pain and frustration for both of
them: "With all the fierce rigidity of first motherhood, I did like the
books then said. Though her cries battered me to trembling and
my breasts ached with swollenness, I waited till the clock decreed"
(*R* 10). In *Yonnondio,* lovemaking becomes rape or at best the only
thing women are good for; and in "Tell Me a Riddle," David comes
home from his meetings to find Eva nursing one baby, holding
another, and trying to read in the only scrap of time she has. "She
would feel again the weather of the outside on his cheek when . . .
he would find her so, and stimulated and ardent, sniffing her skin,
coax: 'I'll put the baby to bed, and you—put the book away, don't
read, don't read' " (76). A beguiling lure, but a lure nevertheless,
away from language and into the only role her husband and her
society can imagine for her. Also in *Yonnondio,* Mazie learns not to
trust her body's daring grace in jumping onto ice trucks. The old
taunt, "Girl go to London, go to France / Everybody sees your
pants," makes her self-conscious. "Twice she misses, almost goes
under the wheels. No more for her that lithe joy, that sense of
power" (127).

Yet the language Olsen uses to describe all kinds of nonverbal
expression presents a different view. Under the blight, Olsen offers the language of possibility. Free movement gives Mazie "lithe
joy, that sense of power"; and one of the most exuberant scenes in
Yonnondio pictures Baby Bess banging a fruit-jar lid on the table, "in triumphant, astounded joy" at noise and movement and
power: "Release, grab, slam, bang, bang. Centuries of human
drive work in her; human ecstasy of achievement; satisfaction
deep and fundamental as sex: *I can do, I use my powers; I! I!*
Wilder, madder, happier the bangs. The fetid fevered air rings
with Anna's, Mazie's, Ben's laughter; Bess's toothless, triumphant

crow. Heat misery, rash misery transcended" (153). Olsen's language says that bodily expression is as important as breathing and thought and the words used to describe it. It is "lightning in her brain" (Y 153).

This interplay in Olsen's work of written and spoken language, silence, and nonverbal communication lays certain dangers in the path of a woman writer. In her essay "Women and Fiction," Lynn Sukenink argues that when woman associates herself with feeling, intuition, and empathy—the allegedly irrational and inexpressible human powers—she comes to be seen as "all body, undivided by the particulars of language. She may express a wisdom through her body, but she is not, since she is non-reflective . . . capable of perceiving that wisdom. Because she is not a composite being, any imaginative rearrangement of self, i.e., composition—has to be accomplished from outside." This age-old perception creates a dilemma for women writers, says Sukenink, some of whom "make a special plea for [their] rationality and ability to speak," while others choose "to turn toward emotion as a rule of response, and to stress the difficulties of utterance, the higher bliss of speechlessness."[43]

Olsen obviously refuses both of these narrow channels. On the one hand, her writing is anything but a romantic flight into wordlessness, and her struggle to give silenced people a spoken and written voice continues against such old and new obstacles as functional illiteracy and the critical opinion that women's story has now been told and there is no need for more books on the subject.[44] On the other hand, while Olsen claims for herself and other marginal people language's full resources, she is too much aware of mystery and the rhythms of creation to abandon silence or nonverbal communication.

Like many of the writers Olsen quotes in *Silences*, she knows that one of the circumstances creation "demands for full functioning" is protected, uninterrupted, quiet time (S 11). What is perhaps more important for writers is an inner receptiveness, with the buzz of cliché and stereotype at least momentarily stilled, so that individuals, communities, and events can reveal themselves. Olsen finds strong, intelligent words to describe the mysteries of death, love, friendship, pain; but those words grow out of and lead back into a listening silence. Moreover, Olsen's love of language and sure reliance on its possibilities have taught her its limits. For Olsen, language must neither replace nor overwhelm physical means of communication; words alone cannot bridge the distance between people or bind them together, nor can they fully express or define an embodied life rooted in history and grounded in community.

In her essay "Resisting Amnesia: History and Personal Life," Adrienne Rich writes:

> Our theory, scholarship, and teaching must continue to refer back to the flesh, blood, violence, sexuality, anger, the bread put on the table by the single mother and how it gets there, the body of the woman aging, the pregnant body, the body running, the body limping, the hands of the lesbian touching another lesbian's face, the hands of the typist, of the midwife, of the sewing machine operator, the eyes of the woman astronomer, of the woman going blind on the transistor as-sembly line, of the mother catching the briefest expression on the child's face: the particularity and commonality of this vast turbulence of female becoming, which is continually being erased or generalized.[45]

In her resistance to amnesia and her commitment to the future, Olsen shows clearly that the greatest peril for women, as for any group of marginal people, does not lie in silence or in language, though they hold peril enough. It lies rather in splitting mind from body, reason from emotion, and language from silence, touch, and action. Power comes from authoritatively claiming the right to all sources of knowledge and all forms of expression.

But that ringing affirmation raises an immediate and troubling question: Why has Olsen apparently not claimed the power of written language these past fifteen years? While she is a powerful speaker, reader, and teacher, and while she still generously en-courages other writers, she herself has not written any substantial fiction or nonfiction since *Silences* in 1978. These years raise new questions about the circumstances necessary for the full exercise of creativity and for the authoritative claiming of language. To an outside observer, Olsen has had during these years the conditions for harvesting that she describes in *Silences*: protected, uninter-rupted time; freedom from the fragmentation that marked her life as a writer-worker-mother; an audience that is at least partially sympathetic and receptive; and the impetus to write new stories or continue old ones. The stories Olsen knows and wants to tell—about mothers and mothering, about working people, the young, the old—still make up only a small proportion of literature. Olsen has not lost her sense of community or her belief that suffering anywhere is everyone's—and especially the writer's—responsibility. Nor has she lost her belief in the power of language. In 1984 at the University of Northern Iowa in Cedar Falls, Olsen addressed a group of high school and college students who had written prize-winning critical essays. Her talk, entitled "The Word Made Flesh," begins with this affirmation: "It is I who am honored, to be here with you, young co-workers in the medium I love: the medium of language, of thought, of the recording of human experience which encompasses all on earth, and the infinite."[46]

As I said at the beginning of this study, some people might surmise that it is the very easing of silencing circumstances, the healing of blights, that has taken away Olsen's subject and perhaps even her reason to write. I think that is unlikely. When I look at the past fifteen years of Olsen's life, as when I look at her writing, I still see positive and negative space, language and silence, luck, enabling circumstances, and irreparable damage. I still see blight, fruit, and possibility.

First, the positive space, the language. While they still face plenty of obstacles, many of the people who were in the margins when Olsen wrote *Silences* are now putting their own stories down on paper, finding publishers, winning interested readers. As Olsen says of these writers, "We have a possibility for literature in our country as we've never had before. In the '30s, writer after established writer was going out and discovering America. . . . It's different now, because we have the writers who've lived that life, who know that life, whose people's life it is. It's so important for us because this literature has never been established for us in our own voices, our own tongue, with our own comprehensions."[47] If one thinks of writing as a collaborative rather than an individual or competitive activity, as both Olsen and I do, then it is not fanciful to say that Olsen's body of work includes all those books written by women and men who were inspired and heartened by her, just as Rebecca Harding Davis's body of work includes *Yonnondio*, *Tell Me a Riddle*, and *Silences*. And, with lovely reciprocity, Davis's *Life in the Iron Mills*, which Olsen brought to the attention of the Feminist Press, belongs in some way to Olsen, too.

But there is also the negative space, which this communal body of work cannot fill. As I said earlier, Olsen sees herself as a writer who has been irreparably harmed by the circumstances of her life. And though most of those harmful circumstances were in the past rather than the present, it seems to me that they offer oblique explanations for this latest silence. She writes that "we are not only beings seeking to change; changing; we are also that which our past has made us" (S 258). She is writing here about women and men struggling to reshape gender and family relationships and to balance the claims of love and work. But this statement also applies forcefully to writers and, I think, to Olsen herself, who has carried the silencing of the past into her present. Some well-known lines from *Silences* describe this entanglement: "The habits of a lifetime when everything else had to come before writing are not easily broken, even when circumstances now often make it possible for writing to be first; habits of years—response to others, distractibility, responsibility for daily matters—stay with you, make you, become you. The cost of 'discontinuity' . . . is such a weight of things unsaid, an accumulation of material so great, that everything starts up something else in me; what should take weeks, takes me sometimes months to write; what should take months, takes years." Olsen is speaking of herself as well as the many "one-book" authors she names in *Silences* when she says sadly, "Time granted does not necessarily coincide with time that can be most fully used, as the congested time of fullness would have been" (S 21).

Another entanglement of past and present has to do with censorship. While I marvel at the four great stories Olsen wrote during the fifties, I cannot help but wonder about the stories she did not dare tell either then or since. She recently described 1955–56, the year of her Stegner fellowship at Stanford and one of her most fruitful as a writer, as "a presage year for our country." It was the year "of Rosa Parks, Birmingham, Little Rock. Year of the first happenings of freedom movements, movements against wrong, which were to convulse and mark our nation and involve numberless individual lives." But it was also, she writes, "year that began still in the McCarthyite shadow of fear; of pervasive cynical belief that actions with others against wrong were personally suspect, would only end in more grievous wrong; year of proclamation that the young were a 'silent generation,' future 'organization men.' "[48] Olsen certainly is not the only person harrassed by McCarthy and the House Un-American Activities Committee in the fifties to live in fear of reprisals to herself and her family. Charlotte Nekola and Paula Rabinowitz report that even as recently as 1987 a few women were reluctant to have their or their relatives' work included in *Writing Red*, an anthology of radical writing by American women in the thirties. Some of these women "had suffered, or had seen their friends suffer, the outrages of the McCarthy era. For them, this persecution remained a bitter memory." While the selections in the anthology diverge in every direction from the Communist party line, the very title frightened these women.[49] Several of Olsen's early pieces appear in this anthology; moreover, the stories contained in *Tell Me a Riddle* hint at all the ways in which voices of protest were silenced in the United States. But nowhere, not even in *Silences*, does Olsen name directly the governmental censorship of artists and radical thinkers during the fifties. She only says obliquely that while political censorship sometimes "spur[s] inventiveness," it is "most often (read Dostoyevsky's letters) a wearing attrition" (*S* 9).

The brutal silencing of dissent in the Soviet Union, beginning in the 1930s with Stalin, might have been another "wearing attrition" on Olsen's work. As I have said, Olsen departed in many important ways from the literary and political dictates of the American Communist party, and she stopped being a member by the end of the thirties.[50] But while Olsen's anguish over the Holocaust and the bombing of Hiroshima are important elements in "Tell Me a Riddle," and the racial divisions in the United States before the civil rights movement form the background for "O Yes," nowhere in Olsen's fiction, nonfiction, talks, or interviews do I find her expressing a similar anguish over the events that took place in the Soviet Union during Stalin's regime and after: the curtailment of personal freedom, the repression of intellectual and artistic dissent, the exile, imprisonment, or murder of millions of people, and the seizing of the countries of Eastern Europe. I can well understand that Olsen would be reluctant to fuel anti-Communist feeling among her readers or listeners. Yet for a person of her great integrity, her apparent silence in the face of these atrocities is hard to understand. One of the most powerful statements in *Silences* is Rilke's: "It is the great quantity of what is not done that lies with all its weight on what wants to come out of the soil" (152). I do not mean to dictate Olsen's politics or the content of her stories; yet it is possible that the stories she has not told, the things she has not said, are almost a physical weight crushing the stories she might have written in her later life.

But I do not want this speculation on Olsen's nonwriting times to overshadow the great value of what she has written and what she still might write. As I have been saying throughout this study, I find Olsen's work painful but insistently, courageously hopeful. Like Catharine Stimpson, I think that Olsen "is doing more than

measuring wrongs. She also desires a future world—new, recreated, right." Her works are therefore texts in the schoolroom
sense, because she sets for them the "profoundly educational
function" of bringing that world about.[51] I will turn in my conclusion to the question of whether her writing performs that great
task.

The Politics of Change

T HE FINAL, INEVITABLE QUESTION raised by Olsen's pattern of blight, fruit, and possibility is whether her fiction and nonfiction suggest ways to make the possible real, the "not yet" the here and now.[1] Does she tell us in one way or another how mothering can spread a feast for both mothers and children; how the gnarled and twisted relationships within families can become a sheltering embrace; how ghettos can become communities, and communities sources of strength and justice where difference is celebrated rather than hated and feared; how language of all kinds can be a means of liberation rather than confinement? Those are certainly fair questions to ask of a writer like Olsen, for whom literature is neither propaganda nor detached aestheticism but rather useful beauty that lays bare the intolerable contradictions of modern life in order to heal them.

The most obvious answer to the question is no, if we are looking for success stories or blueprints for change. Within the boundaries of Olsen's stories, the characters and, even more important, the communities to which they belong rarely get to enjoy the recreated worlds Olsen envisions. Some readers stop with the pain, finding it almost too unrelenting to bear. Others, while asserting that Olsen's work holds more than pain, claim that the most radical hope she offers is a humanistic vision. Some critics do so to save Olsen from what they perceive as the narrowness of feminism or Marxism. Burkom and Williams, for example, believe that "Olsen is importantly connected with both women's and proletariat literature; to read her entire canon is to recognize that she is neither sexist nor leftist but a passionately committed humanist."[2] For Ellen Cronan Rose, Olsen's fiction, and "Tell Me a Riddle" in particular, "is far more than a feminist document." It escapes, she says, "the Procrustean feminist aesthetic Olsen propounds in 'One Out of Twelve,'" by describing not merely "'common female realities'" but also "'common *human* realities.'"[3]

Critics who are sympathetic to Olsen's feminist and socialist views, among them Rosenfelt and Stimpson, argue that Olsen cannot, or at least does not, imagine a political or economic solution to the catalog of injustices she documents. Stimpson says that Olsen must therefore settle for "an aroused humanism" that stresses "the conscience, the sensibility, the worth, and the capabilities of the marginal and the dispossessed."[4] Rosenfelt says of *Yonnondio* that the novel's most persuasive hope "is less a vision of political and economic revolution than an assertion that the drive to love and achieve and create will survive somehow in spite of the social forces arraigned against it, because each human being is born with it afresh." Rosenfelt adds that "it is with this 'humanistic' rather than 'Marxist' optimism that the novel now ends."[5]

The words *humanism* and *humanistic* are usually meant as high praise, and there is no denying the admiration in the critical voices I have just quoted. Yet I think that proposing faith in the enduring human spirit as Olsen's most hopeful idea short-circuits the radical energy of her thought and takes us only halfway to the vision of possibility her writing insists on.

It is true that Olsen's characters show great ingenuity in adapting their tools to the tasks at hand and themselves to their surroundings; as Rosenfelt points out, this is especially true of her young characters. In *Yonnondio*, for example, the Holbrook children, fresh from the prairie where they had been like bread browning in an oven, find the packinghouse city alien until its "mammoth stone beauty has carved itself into their blood" (61). In "Requa" Olsen reverses the pattern. Stevie, the San Francisco boy who had "rocked his nights high on a tree of noise, his traffic city," "whose sleep came gentled in streetlamp glow," and whose plaything had been a lamppost "he could hug and swing himself round and round," at first finds in nature only terrifying reminders of his mother's death: "The trees *were* red, like blood that oozed out of old meat and nobody washed the plate," and they "tower and lean as if they might fall on him" (54, 65). Eventually Stevie comes to love the sound of rain on earth—"this soft murmurous receiving"—and the sharp fragrance of wet pine needles and wild lilac. Olsen's characters also show great courage and will, as children and adults alike set out doggedly, hunger and stagnation at their backs, their faces turned toward some fragile promise of a better life.

But for Olsen there is as much sorrow and rage as there is hope in the spectacle of human resilience, adaptability, and creativity being continually reborn into a society that does not yet "afford them scope" (S 261). That she shows creativity and the assertion of power more often in children than in adults attests to her belief that these qualities are often "[ground] down to an exhausted dust," as Annie Gottlieb says, before people reach maturity.[6] The talk on which the essay "Silences" is based was originally entitled "The Death of the Creative Process," and it included these paragraphs:

> Not many would accede to creativity as an enormous and *universal* human capacity (let alone recognize its extinction as the question of the age). I am one of those who, in almost unbearable, based conviction, believe that it is so.
>
> To establish its truth incontrovertibly would require an ending to the age-old denial of enabling circumstances— because of one's class, color, sex—which has stunted (not extinguished) most of humanity's creativity. Few of us have been permitted "the exercise of vital powers along lines of excellence." (S 261)

To say that this stunted condition offers a humanistic hope leaves the "age-old denial of enabling circumstances" intact. I have an uneasy sense that critics who propose humanism as an alternative to the limitations of feminism or Marxism want to leap over the economic and political realities of people's lives and sidestep the differences these realities create. But Olsen's multiple vision keeps those differences firmly before us as she undertakes the difficult but essential task of pushing out narrow boundaries and working toward a synthesis of feminism and other forms of radical analysis. Or, to return to the image with which I began, Olsen sets differences on top of each other like richly colored transparencies through which the light can shine.

The synthesis Olsen desires makes many routes from prose to possibility untenable for her. She does not, for example, envision for women an existence separate from men or one that adopts stereotypically male patterns of " 'sexual liberation' (genitally de-fined)" and detachment from the everyday needs of family and community—in short, freedom from the work of the "essential angel" (S 254–55). She cannot accept the common solution of carving out a safe niche for oneself and one's family and friends and leaving the rest of the world to fend for itself. Nor does she offer as a solution for struggling artists isolation from the clamor-ings of everyday life or the exaltation of uniqueness with its ac-companying denial of relationships and history. Olsen takes ref-uge neither in a heavenly paradise nor in an earthly one. Of the former she says, "We don't know about the next life. We do know about this one—and we want to make it as long, as beautiful as possible."[7] And only in her earliest poems did the young Tillie Lerner write of Russia's "heaven . . . brought to earth in 1917."[8] In spite of her many acknowledged debts to early socialist thought, she refuses to praise the achievement of economic equality for working men if that equality leaves women isolated in their homes, subservient to their husbands and far from the sources of power. Olsen shows clearly that each of these solutions would heal one wound only to open others near the scar.

If each of those solutions is incomplete or individualistic, what does Olsen suggest to change the crippling circumstances of gen-der, race, class, nationality, age? I see two answers, both of them based on Olsen's strong sense of community and her view of history. The first is the simple but fundamental idea that change is possible if people gather together, with all their differences intact, to create it. Olsen is true to what she calls "the lessons [of] the 'thirties"—"that so-called ordinary people can in their own time make changes with their pool of strength, that people resist, that they make as much of life as they can."[9] The second answer Olsen offers is the experience of joy as a source of community and power. These two beliefs, while they do not provide a blueprint for the "revolutionary, subversive movement in our time" that Olsen calls for, do provide an impetus toward it.[10]

While Olsen rejects a cyclical interpretation of history and the sense of isolation and impotence it breeds, the alternative she offers is by no means a simplistic faith in human progress. Olsen was not deluded by the material prosperity of the fifties and six-ties, for example, into thinking that the Great Depression was over. It is significant that "Requa," completed in 1970, is set during the depression, allowing Olsen to reveal to the current generation of readers the endurance of the people of the thirties. But more important, situating the story in the depression expresses Olsen's view that the poverty and terror of that time continue into the present for many people in the United States, whose lives are still invisible and who are unemployed or working at jobs that do not pay them a living wage, much less the honor she accords them, their work, and their tools. The depression setting also reveals Olsen's understanding of the extent to which women's position in the United States, as elsewhere, is determined by economic fluctuations and inequities. The gains won for some women by the most recent feminist movement did not even touch the lives of many others. What single mother in 1970, working, living in poverty, raising her children, could not say in the voice of Stevie's mother, *"I'm tired to death, love"* (58)?

In addition, while Olsen often praises "the people of that generation" for their sense of kinship and their responsibility for each other, she is obviously aware that not everyone learned the same lessons from the thirties that she and her parents did. Many Americans carried away from the Great Depression "a legacy of fear, but also a desire for acquisition," according to historian Susan Ware; "the great majority reacted by thinking money is the most important thing in the world. Get yours. And get it for your children. Nothing else matters. Not having that stark terror come at you again." Because many blamed themselves for their financial failures, they did not push for societal changes, and they certainly did not offer a radical challenge to capitalism.[11] Olsen hints at these other "lessons of the thirties" in "Hey Sailor, What Ship?" when Whitey mourns the deterioration of the labor movement and in "Tell Me a Riddle" when David reflects on the difference between his and his son's values. David thinks to himself, *"I had wanted to leave you each a few dollars to make life easier, as other fathers do."* Then he imagines his son's thoughts: *"(Failure! you and your 'business is exploitation.' Why didn't you make it when it could be made? Is that what you're thinking, Sammy?)"* (R 87).

Given the persistence of misery and the resistance to radical, communal solutions, some might say that the promise of societal change is a cruel illusion to dangle before oppressed people or before the oppressed and despairing parts of each of us. Olsen convinces me of the opposite viewpoint: that the cruelest illusion, the one most protective of the status quo, is that humans are locked into unchangeable cycles of poverty and pain. In "The Word Made Flesh," Olsen counters the image of the future that ends George Orwell's *1984*—"a boot stamping on a man's face forever"—which she says is for some also the image of the past. She sets against that deadly image what she calls "our bedrock of reality." This bedrock is ordinary people's resistance to oppression that she sees all through history: the "will, courage, capacity to change what degrades, harms, limits."[12]

When Olsen speaks in a linear, logical way about her hope for the future, as she does in this talk, she often describes a general kind of endurance that sounds like nothing other than or more than humanism. But fiction allows her to present a more radical, metaphorical, and historically specific picture. Olsen embodies her rejection of absurdity and a cyclical theory of history in the figure of Sisyphus, who appears and reappears under various guises in her stories. In "Tell Me a Riddle," Eva ponders the "ancient man who fought to heights a great rock that crashed back down eternally—eternal labor, freedom, labor" (R 99). In Olsen's hands, amazing things happen to this ancient man and his rock, as she draws him into human history. In "Hey Sailor, What Ship?" Sisyphus becomes a procession of men carrying children. As Whitey watches Len carry Allie upstairs, "the fire leaps up, kindles Len's shadow so that it seems a dozen men cradle a child up endless stairs" (R 32). Then, in "O Yes" Sisyphus becomes a black woman, Alva, to whom Jesus says in a vision, *Mama Mama you must help carry the world.* Although Alva is fifteen at the time, "sin-sick," poor, pregnant, and alone, she responds, *Free, free, I am so glad* (R 61). Finally, in the section of "Dream Vision" I quoted in Chapter 4, the Sisyphus figure appears as many worn, bent women who have carried burdens all their lives. Now they sing a lullaby and their burden is a child: "Singing, one by one the women cradled and sheltered the baby."

As I have said, Olsen never borrows Christian or classical myths without revising their meaning in startling ways. Her Sisyphus is not the Greek trickster-king eternally punished for trying to cheat death; nor is he Camus's existential hero, engaged, as Erika Duncan puts it, in a "fiery and futile rebellion against . . . an unalterably anguished human condition."[13] As with all of her revised myths, Olsen has folded many meanings into this one. Some of those meanings *are* dark and futile. In Whitey's sad vision, the stairs lead nowhere and "the rain traces the windows, beseechingly, ceaselessly, like seeking fingers of the blind" (R 32). But any futility in Olsen's writing is not rooted in her despair over "the human condition," in which we are all "bound slaves . . . immured in immanence," as Ellen Cronan Rose says.[14] I agree rather with Duncan that Olsen is railing not against mortality or immanence in her adaptation of the Sisyphus myth, but against the circumstances that deform the time between birth and death. There is a world of difference between Olsen's final dedication to "Tell Me a Riddle"—

> *For two of that generation*
> *Seevya and Genya*
> *Infinite, dauntless, incorruptible*
> *Death deepens the wonder*

—and nineteen-year-old Emily's words in "I Stand Here Ironing," when, half flippantly, half cynically she says she is not worried about midterm tests because "in a couple of years . . . we'll all be atom-dead" (*R* 20).

The stone Sisyphus pushes up the hill in Eva's imagination is also the stone that holds the fossilized remains of previous generations. But amnesia cuts each generation off from crucial stories of the past, and the deliberate silencing of writers who might tell those stories lets the stone fall back again. Even in the 1990s, young people are often cut off from their ancestors by an education that ignores the history of socialism, labor, and feminism in this country. Without knowing that history, we are doomed to believe that our efforts for justice are always isolated trudges up that hill. Worse yet, this wiping clean of memory guarantees that cycles of poverty and violence will continue, and that the patterns locking whole groups of people out of creativity and power will appear natural or, at best, unchangeable. In "Tell Me a Riddle," for example, a great source of despair in Eva's life is the fact that her daughters and even her granddaughters repeat the surface patterns of her life in America but know little of its depths, because she has not had the time or the words to teach them.

But Olsen's writing says that history need not be this dreary treadmill. She transforms Sisyphus into a woman, a "babble of women," a man, a procession of men, and changes her/his/their stony burden into human stories retold or told for the first time, a child, and the world. This startling transformation challenges an absurdist view of history and also suggests ways to break out of cycles.

I have been saying throughout this study that Olsen both practices and teaches the importance of bringing to light individual and communal lives. But as Elaine Neil Orr says, Olsen's preoccupation with history does not come out of a "romantic infatuation with the struggles of earlier times."[15] It is on the contrary a way of linking the present struggles with those of the past so that the connections become a source of courage and solidarity. In her introduction to *Seven Women: Portraits from the American Radical Tradition*, Judith Nies writes: "In many ways it is awareness of tradition that allows people to overcome personal despair. Without a sense of tradition people act without consciousness or form. Tradition provides connections, and connections give courage. Courage was one trait these women had in common." The seven radical women whose stories Nies tells are Sarah Moore Grimke, Harriet Tubman, Elizabeth Cady Stanton, Mother Jones, Charlotte Perkins Gilman, Anna Louise Strong, and Dorothy Day. What she discovered through her research contradicts the traditional portrayal of these women as "lone strugglers, isolated voices speaking to an empty audience." She found instead that they and many others like them were at least "aware of one another, asked similar questions about American society, and built on what others had done before them." Most important, Nies says, "they were sustained by knowing that there were a few others like them—somewhere." These women activists knew the power of history not only to bolster their own courage but also to support and animate whatever radical cause they were espousing. According to Nies, every speech Mother Jones gave was a "history lesson in the labor struggle."[16]

It goes without saying that if history lessons are important for workers, they are crucial for women in any field, whose words and works have been for so many centuries "muted voices on the patriarchal wind," to borrow Annis Pratt's excellent phrase.[17] Olsen therefore urges women in particular but also the members of any oppressed minority group not to throw away as if they were worthless the lives and the hard, creative work of their mothers and fathers. In fact, her confidence that people can make "changes on what [is] wrong about the hard times" comes in part from her honest yet loving historical look at her working-class, immigrant ancestors.[18]

"The difference between radicals and other people," writes Nies, "is that radicals *see* differently, and . . . cannot rest until they act."[19] Olsen's permutations on Sisyphus imply several essential shifts of vision. The first concerns women's lives. In Olsen's writing, women cradle and sing to a child in the traditional way, but they also carry the world as artists and activists. Annie Gottlieb describes this shift of vision best when she says that Olsen, among others, "has given us another gift: the shift of viewpoint that transforms the stark contradictions of our lives into fruitful, if painful, tensions—sources of art, solace and understanding."[20] Gottlieb is talking about the apparent contradiction between mothering and writing, but Olsen also transforms the supposed contradiction between the private life of bearing and rearing one's own children and the public life of creating a world fit for all children, all life.

I want to say emphatically that this shift in viewpoint is not a treacherous call to adapt oneself to humanly intolerable circumstances while allowing the circumstances to reign. Rather, the shift presented by Olsen demands the end of such adaptation and refutes the belief that mothering, other creative work, and work for social change are mutually exclusive activities. Olsen never suggests that women must bear children in order to be "fulfilled," and she resists in *Silences* the "societal coercion" that would make family life "the only suitable way of life for a female" (202); still, she asks for free choice rather than the opposite coercion: "Them lady poets must not marry, pal," as John Berryman elegantly puts it (*S* 31n). In *Silences* she gives evidence of the real changes that follow such a change in viewpoint, listing first "that long roll of childless woman writers" from the twentieth century as well as from earlier centuries, and then an even longer list of writers, mainly from the 1960s and 1970s, who "are assuming as their right fullness of work and family life" (200, 31–32).

But Olsen goes a step further in analyzing the relationship between the various kinds of women's work. Rosenfelt writes: "In according . . . creative capacity especially to women and children, as in detailing the impact of social circumstance on the dailiness of family life, Olsen adds a significant dimension to the largely masculine-public world of the proletarian novel. Women's work in preserving and nurturing that creative capacity in the young is shown . . . to be an essential precondition to social change." In other words, Olsen believes that because women who care for children see most clearly their creative energy, they also see most clearly the ways in which poverty, sexism, and racism dry up that creativity or contain it in safe and stagnant pools. Rosenfelt says that for Olsen "the loss of creative capacity is not, as Wordsworth would have it, the inevitable price of growing up, but rather the price of growing up in a society *like this one*."[21] In her fiction, Olsen challenges what Chevigny calls "the paradox confronting women: that children, who most identify and confirm the values women want to bring to the transformation of the world, most surely bind them away from such action."[22] For Olsen, this is not a paradox—an apparent contradiction. It is a real contradiction, and she challenges it by calling for another shift of vision, this time turning women's work into men's work too or, more accurately, into everyone's work—the work of the community.

No longer a lonely mother or an isolated and impotent family, her Sisyphus becomes a procession of men and a singing cluster of women. In "O Yes," Alva gladly accepts the burden of the world. As that story makes clear, however, the support of the black religious community is so strong that Alva accepts the burden not only by and for herself, but also in the name of the community, knowing that "gloved and loving hands" will help her carry it. In this story, Olsen also creates breaches in the ghetto walls which surround the black community and make it both isolated and vulnerable. She does this by showing black and white people, old and young, men and women being baptized into the seas of humankind, into caring and doing. The "eternal labor, freedom, labor" of the classical Sisyphus then becomes the community's labor of bringing the world's children to the fullest possible life and the community's freedom to choose and choose again life over death. Eva's desperate question in "Tell Me a Riddle"—"*78,000 in one minute* (whisper of a scream) *78,000 human beings   we'll destroy ourselves?*"—necessarily goes unanswered. It *is* a question, nevertheless, and not a statement. Through it Olsen implies her belief that we humans are free to choose the destruction or the survival of the race.

I said earlier that Olsen wants to write in such a way that her readers will fill with their own lives the blank spaces in her prose. She wants to trigger her readers' memories and pull potential writers from silence to speech. I think she also wants her stories to collect around themselves communities of intent listeners, mimes of the suffering and joy she depicts. Within her stories most of her characters appear trapped in cycles of poverty and oppression, but Olsen pushes her readers to become radicals like Nies's seven women, who "*see* differently" and who "cannot rest until they act." The writer/artist then becomes the bridge between what is and what might be, between prose and possibility. For of course Sisyphus is also the artist and his burden the word. Eva's seemingly disjointed ponderings on this mythical man contain her parenthetical thought, "(stone will perish, but the word remain)"

(99). That burdensome word, heavy with futility and power and constantly in need of recreation, demands of writers the utmost freedom and effort; through it they must reveal the "fossil memory" of human history and at the same time imagine and inspire change.

I think Olsen would agree with Denise Levertov, a poet with whom she has much in common, that the language of change and change itself create each other. In "Making Peace," a recent poem of Levertov's, "A voice from the dark" asks poets to "give us / imagination of peace, to oust the intense, familiar / imagination of disaster." But the poem's speaker answers that

> peace, like a poem,
> is not there ahead of itself,
> can't be imagined before it is made,
> can't be known except
> in the words of its making,
> grammar of justice,
> syntax of mutual aid.
> A feeling towards it,
> dimly sensing a rhythm, is all we have
> until we begin to utter its metaphors,
> learning them as we speak.

For Olsen and Levertov, the things they desire most—peace within and between countries, healing between women and men and children, just economic and political structures—are not out there waiting, like new continents, to be discovered; rather, they must be imagined and lived by people whose vision ranges far beyond what now exists. Levertov's speaker continues, "A line of peace might appear / if we restructured the sentence our lives are making."[23] Olsen writes in the same vein in *Silences*, "The changes that will enable us to live together without harm . . . are as yet only in the making" (258). Creating these changes is, she says, an essential writer's task as well as an essential human task (258).

Like Levertov, Olsen resists the seductiveness of despair, that most individualistic of emotions. By creating simultaneously in her life and in her writing a "believable language of affirmation," she gives fleeting glimpses of the world she desires.[24] Olsen does this by setting down scenes of joy even in the bleakest landscapes of her fiction, not as a cruel hoax, an otherworldly dream, or a golden ring to be snatched by a few fortunate *only's* (S 39n), but as a powerful impetus to action by the community gathered around her stories.

The joy Olsen recounts from her own life and creates in the lives of her fictional characters often comes out of suffering or, more accurately, out of people banding together to oppose it. "The Strike" and David and Eva's memories of revolution in Russia are good examples. But Olsen resists a second common temptation, one that leads us to believe that only suffering can bind people together, and that joy from any source other than the struggle against oppression will rupture community bonds. In 1930, Meridel LeSueur wrote in her journal, "Whittle oneself down on the edge of suffering. We do not know ourselves except when we suffer. . . . In joy I know only myself, in sorrow I know others. . . . In happiness we are seperete [*sic*]. . . . In suffering we are fused."[25] To be fair to LeSueur, she was reacting against the urgings of leftist critics that she stress opportunities for women rather than their sufferings. Moreover, her writing does not hew to her own line. I quote her because she is expressing a view that is both common and understandable, given our narrow and individualistic conceptions of the sources and consequences of happiness.

But Olsen banishes quietly, with a line or two, all those old, illusory, competitive sources of happiness: alcohol, casual visits to prostitutes, Jinella's movie magazine dreams in *Yonnondio*, Max and Rosa's all-American dream of prosperity and success in "Tell Me a Riddle." Without resorting to cynicism, she also drains away the power of romantic love, that great domesticator of women in Western life and literature. In "Tell Me a Riddle," we see Jeannie transformed with happiness in caring for her grandmother. David assumes she is in love, just as he assumes she must be getting married when she tells him she plans to quit her job as a public health nurse. In an almost offhand upsetting of expectations, Olsen presents not romance or sex or marriage as the source of Jeannie's happiness but rather her devotion to the Mexican-American people she works with and her love for her dying grandmother. For Jeannie, Eva is "my darling escape . . . my darling Granny" (116).

In contrast to the shallowness and predictability that often characterize literary depictions of happiness, Olsen's fiction provides glimpses of an intense and liberating joy. It comes from an almost infinite array of experiences—friendship, teaching and learning, play and celebration, sexual love, work with the hands and the mind, family life of every shape and kind, the care of children, no matter who tenders it. It is true, as Stimpson says, that Olsen often shows women bound in "a community of sorrow."[26] On the other hand, the friendship between Jeannie and Eva is one of several examples in which Olsen depicts women joined in a wide variety of joyful experiences that bridge distances and differences of all kinds—race, religion, class, age, education. In fact, in *Yonnondio* she shows not suffering but joy bringing Mazie and Anna together for an unforgettable moment that heals at least momentarily the pain between mother and daughter.

Anna takes her children on a long walk to collect dandelion greens. Having seen a nutrition wheel at a clinic which commands the impossible—*One Serving: Green Leafy Vegetable Daily*—she sets out on the excursion for a purely motherly and utilitarian reason. But before long the beautiful day and the unaccustomed pleasure of walking free Anna from her role. "A remote, shining look was on her face, as if she had forgotten . . . [her children], as if she had become someone else, was not their mother any more." At first Mazie is frightened by her mother's remoteness. Then Anna puts her arms around Mazie, strokes her hair, and sings to her. She is so radiant and so loving that Mazie is drawn into her transformed and transforming world. Olsen's description of this moment—of Anna and Mazie moving in perfect harmony, mother and daughter but also two separate and momentarily whole selves—is so skillfully written no summary can do it justice:

> A fragile old remembered comfort streamed from the stroking fingers into Mazie, gathered to some shy bliss that shone despairingly over suppurating hurt and want and fear and shamings—the harm of years. River wind shimmered and burnished the bright grasses, her mother's hand stroked, stroked. Young catalpa leaves overhead quivered and glistened, bright reflected light flowed over, 'lumined their faces. A bee rested on Mazie's leg; magic!—flew away; and a butterfly wavered near, settled, folded its wings, flew again.
>   I saw a ship a sailing
> her mother sang.
>   A sailing on the sea
>   Mazie felt the strange happiness in her mother's body, happiness that had nought to do with them, with her, happiness and farness and selfness.

> I saw a ship a sailing
> And on that ship was me.
> The fingers stroked, spun a web, cocooned Mazie into hap-
> piness and intactness and selfness. Soft wove the bliss round
> hurt and fear and want and shame—the old worn fragile bliss,
> a new frail selfness bliss, healing, transforming. Up from the
> grasses, from the earth, from the broad tree trunk at their
> back, latent life streamed and seeded. The air and self shone
> boundless. Absently, her mother stroked; stroked unfolding,
> wingedness, boundlessness. (119)

The closeness between Mazie and Anna does not last. They
return to the constricting roles decreed for mothers and daughters,
and there is no indication within the story that the memory of
having been whole and united with another loved person will lead
Anna or Mazie to work for social change. Yet, for me, this scene is
the glowing center of *Yonnondio;* its power reaches backward and
forward through the gritty darkness of the story, making poverty
and fragmentation seem even more intolerable, simply because
we have caught a glimpse of this rich unity. In the depression
economy that prevails in Olsen's writing, not only material goods
but also love, recognition, daily care, time, and the chance to learn
and grow are scarce commodities; and one person's or one group's
happiness, freedom, and power are almost inevitably achieved at
the price of someone else's misery. In such an economy, moments
of intense shared happiness are doubly valuable because they are
rare and fleeting. But besides preserving the moment, it is pre-
cisely this economy of scarcity—an economy as prevalent now as
it was when she wrote these stories—that Olsen wants to change.

Levertov ends "Making Peace" with the hope that

> peace, a presence,
> an energy field more intense than war,
> might pulse then,
> stanza by stanza into the world.[27]

That is Olsen's hope too. The harsh beauty of her prose asks her
readers to come together in resisting every kind of oppression.
Even more radically, her life and her writing challenge us to give
up the sorry comfort of resignation, powerlessness, and despair
and to join her in imagining and living a happiness so deep that it
becomes indispensable to life.

Notes

INTRODUCTION

1. Alice Walker, "Saving the Life That Is Your Own: The Importance of Models in the Artist's Life," in her *In Search of Our Mothers' Gardens: Womanist Prose,* p. 14.
2. Citations of Olsen's major works appear in the text. I have used the following editions and abbreviations: *Mother to Daughter, Daughter to Mother* (Old Westbury, N.Y.: Feminist Press, 1984); *Silences* (New York: Dell, 1980), designated as *S; Tell Me a Riddle* (New York: Laurel-Dell, 1981), designated as *R; Yonnondio: From the Thirties* (New York: Laurel-Dell, 1981), designated as *Y;* and "Requa," *Iowa Review* 1 (Summer 1970): 54–74. "Requa" is sometimes referred to as "Requa-I," indicating that Olsen considers it the first part of an unfinished novella that she is still working on. Throughout this study I refer to the story as "Requa," since I discuss it as a self-contained work.
3. Olsen, quoted in Marilyn Yalom, "Tillie Olsen," in *Women Writers of the West Coast,* ed. Marilyn Yalom, p. 64.
4. *Women's Studies Newsletter* (Old Westbury, N.Y.: Feminist Press) 2 (Winter 1972); 3 (Spring 1973); 4 (Summer 1973). Reprinted in Gail Baker, "Excavations: Tillie Olsen's Reading List: A List out of Which to Read, Extend Range, Comprehension," pp. 76–79.
5. Alice Walker, "Zora Neale Hurston: A Cautionary Tale and Partisan View," in her *In Search of Our Mothers' Gardens,* p. 92.
6. Annie Gottlieb, "A Writer's Sounds and Silences," p. 5.
7. Tillie Olsen, lecture/reading, Univ. of Minnesota, Minneapolis, 5 June 1986.
8. Olsen, quoted in Margaret Miles, "Talking with Tillie Olsen," p. 10.
9. For lists of the fellowships, honors, degrees, and appointments Olsen has received, see Mickey Pearlman and Abby H. P. Werlock, *Tillie Olsen,* pp. xv–xviii.
10. Olsen, quoted in Christina Van Horn, "Writer Tillie Olsen: Upbeat on Women's Future."

11. Joan Kelly, "The Doubled Vision of Feminist Theory," pp. 263–65.

12. Olsen, quoted in Pearlman and Werlock, *Tillie Olsen*, p. 2.

13. Olsen, quoted in Yalom, "Tillie Olsen," p. 64.

14. Audre Lorde, "The Master's Tools Will Never Dismantle the Master's House," in *This Bridge Called My Back: Writings by Radical Women of Color*, ed. Cherríe Moraga and Gloria Anzaldúa, pp. 98–99.

15. "Robin Morgan, Interviewed by Helen Cooper," in *Women Writers Talking*, ed. Janet Todd, pp. 108–10.

16. Elaine Neil Orr, *Tillie Olsen and a Feminist Spiritual Vision*, pp. 119–37, 85–92; Pearlman and Werlock, *Tillie Olsen*, pp. 63–76.

17. For a good overview and critique of theorists who, to varying degrees, ignore the author and her or his life, see Cheryl Walker, "Feminist Literary Criticism and the Author," pp. 551–71. Fortunately for Olsen, most of her critics bring to her work a keen interest both in her life and in the mutual influences of literature and social, economic, and political history. The work of such critics as Deborah Rosenfelt, Erika Duncan, Blanche Gelfant, Elaine Neil Orr, Catharine Stimpson, and Marilyn Yalom has been invaluable to me in this regard.

18. Marilyn Farwell, "Adrienne Rich and an Organic Feminist Criticism," p. 193.

19. Olsen, quoted in Van Horn, "Writer Tillie Olsen."

20. "Tillie Olsen: A Profile," interview by Susan Stamberg for "All Things Considered," National Public Radio, 1980.

21. Catharine R. Stimpson, "Tillie Olsen: Witness as Servant," p. 6.

22. Farwell, "Adrienne Rich," p. 199.

23. "Germaine Greer, Interviewed by Joseph Kastner," in *Women Writers Talking*, ed. Janet Todd, p. 144.

24. Orr, *Tillie Olsen*, p. 135.

25. Olsen, quoted in Yalom, "Tillie Olsen," p. 64.

26. Erika Duncan, "Tillie Olsen," in *Unless Soul Clap Its Hands: Portraits and Passages*, p. 41.

27. Bell Hale Chevigny, review of *Yonnondio: From the Thirties*, pp. 38, 39; Deborah Rosenfelt, "From the Thirties: Tillie Olsen and the Radical Tradition," pp. 390–94.

28. Tillie Olsen, telephone interview with the author, 3 April 1985.

29. Rich, quoted in Farwell, "Adrienne Rich," p. 198.

30. John Leonard, quoted in "Tillie Olsen: A Profile," interview by Susan Stamberg.

31. This important distinction is Adrienne Rich's. She wrote in 1984 that "one task for the nineteen- or twenty-year-old who wrote the earliest poems . . . [in the volume she was working on] was to learn that she was neither unique nor universal, but a person in history, a woman and not a man, a white and also Jewish inheritor of a particular Western consciousness, from the making of which most women have been excluded." Quoted in Sandra M. Gilbert and Susan Gubar, eds., *The Norton Anthology of Literature by Women*, p. 2025.

32. John Clayton, "Grace Paley and Tillie Olsen: Radical Jewish Humanists," p. 45.

33. The works I found most valuable were those examining the overlap of two or more of the life circumstances that preoccupy Olsen. I am especially indebted to Charlotte Baum, Paula Hyman, and Sonya Michel; Barbara Myerhoff; Joan

Kelly; Alice Kessler-Harris and Paul Lauter; Deborah Rosenfelt; and Susan Ware.

34. Stimpson, "Tillie Olsen," p. 10.

35. Alicia Ostriker, "The Thieves of Language: Women Poets and Revisionist Mythmaking," pp. 330–31.

36. Olsen, quoted in Rosenfelt, "From the Thirties," p. 383.

CHAPTER 1

1. Olsen, quoted in Rosenfelt, "From the Thirties," pp. 379, 405 n. 8. According to Rosenfelt, this quotation is from a cover letter for several of Olsen's early poems, written when she was in her late teens or early twenties. Rosenfelt reports that the letter was addressed to Harriet Monroe, editor of *Poetry: A Magazine of Verse*. In correspondence with me (8 March 1992), however, Olsen writes that the excerpt is from a 1931 diary entry.

2. Rosenfelt, "From the Thirties," p. 378.

3. Olsen, quoted ibid., p. 400. Rosenfelt writes that this quotation is from a 1938 journal entry. In correspondence with me (8 March 1992), Olsen indicates that it comes from a diary entry that she cannot date accurately.

4. Chevigny, review of *Yonnondio*, p. 38.

5. Margaret Atwood, "Obstacle Course," review of *Silences*, p. 27.

6. Yalom, "Tillie Olsen," p. 59.

7. Olsen, quoted in Sally Cunneen, "Tillie Olsen: Storyteller of Working America," p. 573.

8. Orr, *Tillie Olsen*, pp. 23–25. For the influence of Olsen's Jewish background on her writing, see also Naomi Rubin, "A Riddle of History for the Future," pp. 1, 4, 18; and Clayton, "Grace Paley and Tillie Olsen," pp. 37–52.

9. Charlotte Baum, Paula Hyman, and Sonya Michel, *The Jewish Woman in America*, pp. 77–78.

10. Duncan, "Tillie Olsen," p. 36.

11. Olsen, quoted in Rosenfelt, "From the Thirties," p. 376.

12. Duncan, "Tillie Olsen," p. 38.

13. Olsen, quoted in Yalom, "Tillie Olsen," p. 57.

14. Rosenfelt, "From the Thirties," p. 376.

15. Elaine Hedges, introduction to *Ripening: Selected Work, 1927–1980*, by Meridel LeSueur, p. 8.

16. Rosenfelt, "From the Thirties," pp. 386, 383.

17. Meridel LeSueur, quoted in Alice Kessler-Harris and Paul Lauter, introduction to *The Unpossessed*, by Tess Slesinger, p. x.

18. Duncan, "Tillie Olsen," p. 35.

19. Rosenfelt, "From the Thirties," pp. 376, 382, 385; Yalom, *Women Writers*, p. 578.

20. Olsen, quoted in Yalom, "Tillie Olsen," p. 58.

21. Duncan, "Tillie Olsen," pp. 40–41.

22. Olsen, quoted ibid., p. 39.

23. Rosenfelt, "From the Thirties," p. 374.

24. Orr, *Tillie Olsen*, pp. 31, 38.

25. Cunneen, "Tillie Olsen: Storyteller," p. 573.

26. Olsen, quoted in Kay Mills, " 'Surviving Is Not Enough': A Conversation with Tillie Olsen," p. 3.

27. Stimpson, "Tillie Olsen," p. 10.
28. Blanche Gelfant, "After Long Silence: Tillie Olsen's 'Requa,'" p. 69 n. 8.
29. Olsen, quoted in Rosenfelt, "From the Thirties," p. 404.
30. Carolyn Heilbrun, *Reinventing Womanhood*, p. 210.
31. Ibid., pp. 53, 21, 31–32.
32. Marion Glastonbury, "The Best Kept Secret—How Working Class Women Live and What They Know," p. 173.
33. Kessler-Harris and Lauter, introduction to *The Unpossessed*, p. xi.
34. Rosenfelt, "From the Thirties," pp. 394, 391.
35. Kessler-Harris and Lauter, introduction to *The Unpossessed*, p. xi.
36. Tess Slesinger, *The Unpossessed*, p. 349.
37. Tillie Lerner, "The Iron Throat," p. 2.
38. Pearlman and Werlock, *Tillie Olsen*, pp. 25–27.
39. Elaine Tyler May, *Homeward Bound: American Families in the Cold War Era*, pp. 3–15.
40. Kessler-Harris and Lauter, introduction to *The Unpossessed*, p. xiii.
41. Catharine Stimpson, "Three Women Work It Out," p. 565.
42. Olsen, quoted in Rosenfelt, "From the Thirties," p. 404.
43. Audre Lorde, *Uses of the Erotic: The Erotic as Power*, unpaginated pamphlet [p. 5].
44. See, for example, Nina Auerbach, "Women on Women's Destiny: Maturity as Penance," pp. 328–29.
45. Gelfant, "After Long Silence," p. 64.
46. The Blake quotation is from a letter to William Henley dated 7 October 1803: "Please to pay my best thanks to Miss Poole: tell her I wish her a continued excess of Happiness—some say that Happiness is not good for Mortals, and they ought to be answer'd that sorrow is not fit for Immortals and is utterly useless to any one; a blight never does good to a tree, and if a blight kill not a tree but it still bear fruit, let none say that the fruit was in consequence of the blight." Earlier in the letter, Blake talks about his need for employment and wonders why, with his hard work and intelligence, he does not do as well as others seem to with little or no work. *Complete Writings with Variant Readings*, ed. Geoffrey Keynes, p. 830.

    The Emily Dickinson line begins poem 657 in *The Complete Poems of Emily Dickinson*, ed. Thomas H. Johnson, p. 327:

> I dwell in Possibility—
> A fairer House than Prose—
> More numerous of Windows—
> Superior—for Doors—
>
> Of Chambers as the Cedars—
> Impregnable of Eye—
> And for an Everlasting Roof—
> The Gambrels of the Sky—
>
> Of Visitors—the fairest—
> For Occupation—This—
> The spreading of my narrow Hands
> To gather Paradise—

47. Olsen, quoted in Miles, "Talking," p. 10.
48. Gelfant, "After Long Silence," p. 64.
49. Maya Angelou, lecture/reading, Westminster Town Hall Forum, Westminster Presbyterian Church, Minneapolis, October 1984.
50. Olsen, quoted in Linda Park-Fuller, "An Interview with Tillie Olsen," p. 76.
51. Olsen, telephone interview with the author, 3 April 1985.
52. Adrienne Rich, "Resisting Amnesia: History and Personal Life," p. 67.
53. See Gerda Lerner's definition of patriarchy in her *Creation of Patriarchy*, pp. 239–42.
54. Heilbrun, *Reinventing Womanhood*, p. 139.
55. Rich, "Resisting Amnesia," p. 66.
56. Kessler-Harris and Lauter, introduction to *The Unpossessed*, p. xv.
57. Rosenfelt, "From the Thirties," pp. 390–91.
58. Tillie Lerner, "I Want You Women Up North to Know," reprinted in Selma Burkom and Margaret Williams, "De-Riddling Tillie Olsen's Writings," pp. 67–69.
59. Stimpson, "Tillie Olsen," p. 1.
60. Kessler-Harris and Lauter, introduction to *The Unpossessed*, p. xv.
61. Chevigny, review of *Yonnondio*, p. 38.
62. Cunneen, "Tillie Olsen: Storyteller," p. 571.

CHAPTER 2

1. Adrienne Rich, *Of Woman Born: Motherhood as Experience and Institution*, p. 237.
2. For example, Edith Sumner Kelly's *Weeds* was published in 1923 and was not reprinted until 1972, in the appropriately named Lost American Fiction series of the Southern Illinois University Press. Agnes Smedley's *Daughter of Earth*, published in 1929 and reprinted in a shortened version in 1935, did not reappear until 1973 when the Feminist Press reprinted it.
3. Valerie Miner, "The Light of the Muse," p. 7.
4. Sue Standing, "Cellar Door," quoted in Olsen, *Mother to Daughter, Daughter to Mother*, p. 33.
5. Olsen, quoted in Lisa See, "PW Interviews: Tillie Olsen," p. 79.
6. Charlotte Nekola and Paula Rabinowitz, eds., *Writing Red: An Anthology of American Women Writers, 1930–1940*, pp. 11–12.
7. John L'Heureux, preface to *First Drafts, Last Drafts: Forty Years of the Creative Writing Program at Stanford University*, p. 63.
8. Tillie Lerner, "I Want You Women Up North to Know," reprinted in Burkom and Williams, "De-Riddling," pp. 67–69.
9. Linda Kathryn Yoder, "Memory as Art: The Life Review in Contemporary American Fiction," pp. 97–98.
10. Erika Duncan, "The Hungry Jewish Mother," p. 232.
11. Olsen, lecture/reading and correspondence, 8 March 1992.
12. Olsen, quoted in See, "PW Interviews," p. 79.
13. The Jerusalem Bible, 1966.
14. Stimpson, "Tillie Olsen," p. 5.
15. Mary K. DeShazer, " 'In the Wind of the Singing': The Language of Tillie Olsen's 'Tell Me a Riddle,' " pp. 21–22.
16. Rebecca Harding Davis, *Life in the Iron Mills; or The Korl Woman*, pp. 31–33, 64.

17. Olsen, quoted in Linda Matchan, "The Staggering Burden of Motherhood," p. 98.
18. Meridel LeSueur, "Annunciation," in *Ripening: Selected Work, 1927–1980*, ed. Elaine Hedges, p. 128.
19. See Yoder, "Memory as Art," p. 100; and Judith Arcana, *Our Mothers' Daughters*, p. 188.
20. Tillie Lerner, "The Strike," reprinted in *Years of Protest: A Collection of American Writings of the 1930s*, ed. Jack Salzman, p. 139.
21. Annie Gottlieb, "Feminists Look at Motherhood," p. 51.
22. Ibid., pp. 51, 52.
23. Ibid., p. 53.
24. Ibid., p. 52.
25. Duncan, "The Hungry Jewish Mother," p. 232.

CHAPTER 3

1. Stimpson, "Tillie Olsen," pp. 2–3.
2. Andrea Canaan, "Brownness," in *This Bridge Called My Back*, ed. Moraga and Anzaldúa, p. 235.
3. Rosenfelt, "From the Thirties," p. 403.
4. LeSueur, "Women Know a Lot of Things," in *Ripening*, p. 172.
5. Judith Kegan Gardiner, "A Wake for Mother: The Maternal Deathbed in Women's Fiction," p. 162.
6. Phoebe-Lou Adams, "PLA," p. 96.
7. Joan Wood Samuelson, "Patterns of Survival: Four American Women Writers and the Proletarian Novel," p. 153.
8. Stimpson, "Tillie Olsen," p. 2.
9. Ibid., pp. 6–7.
10. Ibid., p. 4.
11. Gelfant, "After Long Silence," p. 64.

CHAPTER 4

1. Olsen, quoted in Rosenfelt, "From the Thirties," p. 404.
2. Tillie Olsen, "Dream Vision," in *Mother to Daughter, Daughter to Mother*, pp. 263–64.
3. Dexter Fisher, ed., *The Third Woman: Minority Women Writers of the United States*, pp. 140–44.
4. Lorde, "The Master's Tools," in *This Bridge Called My Back*, ed. Moraga and Anzaldúa, p. 99.
5. Burkom and Williams, "De-Riddling," p. 76.
6. Susan Cory Everson, "Bodyself: Women's Bodily Experience in Recent Feminist Theology and Women's Literature," p. 175.
7. Gardiner, "A Wake for Mother," p. 176; see also Orr, *Tillie Olsen*, p. 103, and DeShazer, "'In the Wind of the Singing,'" p. 22.
8. Jacqueline Mintz, "The Myth of the Jewish Mother in Three Jewish, American, Female Writers," p. 348.
9. DeShazer, "'In the Wind of the Singing,'" p. 24.
10. Ibid., pp. 26–27.
11. Emily Dickinson, "There is a solitude of space," in *The Complete Poems of Emily Dickinson*, p. 691, no. 1695.

12. H. D., "The Walls Do Not Fall," in *Trilogy*, p. 9.

13. Heilbrun, *Reinventing Womanhood*, p. 181.

14. Annette Bennington McElhiney, "Alternative Responses to Life in Tillie Olsen's Work," p. 83.

15. Henry J. Tobias, *The Jewish Bund in Russia: From Its Origins to 1905*; Baum, Hyman, and Michel, *The Jewish Woman*, pp. 74–89.

16. Tobias, *The Jewish Bund*, p. 44.

17. Baum, Hyman, and Michel, *The Jewish Woman*, p. 87.

18. Ibid., pp. 78–83.

19. Judith Nies, *Seven Women: Portraits from the American Radical Tradition*, p. 110.

20. Susan Ware, *Holding Their Own: American Women in the 1930s*, pp. 46–47; LeSueur, "I Was Marching," in *Ripening*, pp. 158–170; and Tillie Lerner, "The Strike," reprinted in *Years of Protest*, ed. Salzman, pp. 138–44.

21. Ware, *Holding Their Own*, p. 47.

22. Barbara Myerhoff, *Number Our Days*, pp. 75–89.

23. Ibid., pp. 255–56.

24. Ibid., p. 86.

25. Ibid., pp. 258–59.

26. Ibid., pp. 259–61.

27. Telephone interview with the author, 3 April 1985; see also Orr, *Tillie Olsen*, for a thorough discussion of Olsen's religious sense. Pages 23–27 and 139–83 are especially helpful.

28. Telephone interview with the author, 3 April 1985, and written correspondence, 8 March 1992.

29. Olsen, "Dream Vision," in *Mother to Daughter, Daughter to Mother*, pp. 262–63.

30. Olsen's Beedo system is a fictionalized version of a method for greater efficiency and speed devised by a Frenchman named Charles E. Bedaux. Factory workers who produced more than a set number of units per hour received a bonus for themselves and for overseers and higher officials. Carolyn Rhodes writes that "Bedaux's method of payment had the obvious advantage of making his system very attractive to management, including the lowest level of bosses. And it had a corresponding and equally obvious disadvantage for workers: it meant that the bosses at every level, even those who directly supervised the workers, had a vested interest in speeding up production" ("'Beedo' in Olsen's *Yonnondio*: Charles E. Bedaux," pp. 23–25).

31. Burkom and Williams, "De-Riddling," p. 73.

32. Tillie Lerner, "The Strike," reprinted in *Years of Protest*, ed. Salzman, pp. 138, 139–40.

33. Lorde, "The Master's Tools," in *This Bridge Called My Back*, ed. Moraga and Anzaldúa, p. 99.

34. Orr, *Tillie Olsen*, p. 94.

35. Olsen, quoted in Mills, "'Surviving Is Not Enough,'" p. 3.

36. Olsen, quoted in Miles, "Talking with Tillie Olsen," p. 10.

37. Stimpson, "Tillie Olsen," p. 8.

38. Olsen, "I Want You Women Up North to Know," reprinted in Burkom and Williams, "De-Riddling," pp. 67–68.

39. Stimpson, "Tillie Olsen," p. 8.

40. Patricia Mische, "Women and Power," pp. 41–42.

41. Canaan, "Brownness," in *This Bridge Called My Back,* ed. Moraga and An-zaldúa, pp. 235–36.

42. Rosario Morales, "We're All in the Same Boat," in *This Bridge Called My Back,* ed. Moraga and Anzaldúa, pp. 92–93.

43. Stimpson, "Tillie Olsen," p. 5.

44. LeSueur, "I Was Marching," in *Ripening,* p. 159.

45. Davis, *Life in the Iron Mills,* p. 69.

CHAPTER 5

1. Chevigny, review of *Yonnondio,* p. 38.

2. Rosenfelt, "From the Thirties," p. 390.

3. Gelfant, "After Long Silence," p. 69.

4. Ibid., p. 68.

5. Adams, "PLA," p. 96.

6. Alix Kates Shulman, "Overcoming Silences: Teaching Writing for Women," p. 530.

7. Olsen, quoted in Mills, " 'Surviving Is Not Enough,' " p. 3.

8. Shulman, "Overcoming Silences," p. 532.

9. Ibid., p. 532.

10. Cherríe Moraga, "La Güera," in *This Bridge Called My Back,* ed. Moraga and Anzaldúa, p. 29.

11. Kathleen Halischak, "Recent Voices in American Feminist Literature," p. 12.

12. Stimpson, "Tillie Olsen," p. 6.

13. DeShazer, " 'In the Wind of the Singing,' " p. 24.

14. Ibid., p. 22.

15. Elizabeth A. Meese, *Crossing the Double Cross: The Practice of Feminist Criticism,* p. 112.

16. Olsen, quoted in Mills, " 'Surviving Is Not Enough,' " p. 3.

17. Telephone interview with the author, 3 April 1985; lecture/reading; Yalom, "Tillie Olsen," p. 63.

18. Myerhoff, *Number Our Days,* pp. 91–92.

19. Baum, Hyman, and Michel, *The Jewish Woman,* p. 75.

20. Myerhoff, *Number Our Days,* p. 271.

21. Olsen, quoted in Yalom, "Tillie Olsen," p. 63.

22. Kenneth Turan, "Breaking Silence," p. 56.

23. Duncan, "Tillie Olsen," p. 37.

24. Olsen, quoted ibid., pp. 37–38.

25. Telephone interview with the author, 3 April 1985.

26. Baum, Hyman, and Michel, *The Jewish Woman,* pp. 59–62, 78–79.

27. Turan, "Breaking Silence," p. 56.

28. Olsen, lecture/reading.

29. Olsen, quoted in Turan, "Breaking Silence," p. 56.

30. Gelfant, "After Long Silence," pp. 62–63.

31. Burkom and Williams, "De-Riddling," p. 81.

32. William Shakespeare, *Twenty-three Plays and the Sonnets,* ed. Thomas Marc Parrott, p. 692.

33. Olsen, lecture/reading, and written correspondence, 8 March 1988.

34. Telephone interview with the author, 3 April 1985.

35. Alicia Ostriker, "Comment on Homans's ' "Her Very Own Howl": The Ambiguities of Representation in Recent Women's Fiction,' " p. 600.

36. Gloria Anzaldúa, "Speaking in Tongues: A Letter to Third World Women Writers," in *This Bridge Called My Back*, ed. Moraga and Anzaldúa, pp. 166, 170.

37. LeSueur, "I Was Marching," in *Ripening*, p. 158.

38. Tillie Lerner, "The Strike," in *Years of Protest*, ed. Salzman, pp. 142, 138, 140, 144.

39. Orr, *Tillie Olsen*, p. 48.

40. Ibid., pp. 47, 63.

41. Toni Morrison, *The Bluest Eye*, p. 7; Zora Neale Hurston, *Their Eyes Were Watching God*, p. 250; Paule Marshall, *Praisesong for the Widow*, p. 249.

42. Gottlieb, "Feminists Look at Motherhood," p. 53.

43. Lynn Sukenink, "Women and Fiction," pp. 37–38, 44.

44. Shulman, "Overcoming Silences," pp. 532–33.

45. Rich, "Resisting Amnesia," p. 67.

46. Olsen, "The Word Made Flesh," prefatory essay to *Critical Thinking / Critical Writing: Prizewinning High School and College Essays*, p. 1. This essay is the written version of the Twelfth Annual H. W. Reninger Lecture, compiled from Olsen's lecture notes, the transcribed text, and later additions and corrections by Olsen.

47. Olsen, quoted in Mills, " 'Surviving Is Not Enough,' " p. 3.

48. Olsen, quoted in L'Heureux, preface to *First Drafts, Last Drafts*, p. 64.

49. Nekola and Rabinowitz, preface to *Writing Red*, p. xii.

50. Duncan, "Tillie Olsen," p. 34.

51. Stimpson, "Tillie Olsen," pp. 1, 10.

CONCLUSION

1. Monza Naff, my colleague at the College of St. Benedict, posed this question.

2. Burkom and Williams, "De-Riddling," p. 66.

3. Ellen Cronan Rose, "Limning: or Why Tillie Writes," pp. 8, 9.

4. Stimpson, "Tillie Olsen," p. 2.

5. Rosenfelt, "From the Thirties," p. 398.

6. Gottlieb, "A Writer's Sounds and Silences."

7. Olsen, lecture/reading.

8. Olsen, quoted in Burkom and Williams, "De-Riddling," p. 69.

9. Olsen, quoted in Park-Fuller, "Interview with Tillie Olsen," p. 76.

10. Olsen, lecture/reading.

11. Ware, *Holding Their Own*, pp. xx, xiii.

12. Olsen, "The Word Made Flesh," p. 6.

13. Duncan, "Tillie Olsen," p. 34.

14. Rose, "Limning," p. 9.

15. Orr, *Tillie Olsen*, p. 107.

16. Nies, *Seven Women*, p. xv.

17. Annis Pratt, "Review: Blackbirds in a Pie: Feminist Scholarship and Women's Experience," p. 462.

18. Olsen, quoted in Park-Fuller, "Interview with Tillie Olsen," p. 76.

19. Nies, *Seven Women*, p. xvi.

20. Gottlieb, "Feminists Look at Motherhood," p. 53.

21. Rosenfelt, "From the Thirties," p. 399.
22. Chevigny, review of *Yonnondio*, p. 39.
23. Denise Levertov, "Making Peace," quoted in Michael True, "The Indispensable Arts: The Persistent Humanity of Denise Levertov," p. 38.
24. True, "Indispensable Arts," p. 39.
25. LeSueur, quoted in Elaine Hedges, introduction to LeSueur's *Ripening*, p. 11.
26. Stimpson, "Tillie Olsen," p. 8.
27. Levertov, "Making Peace," quoted in True, "Indispensable Arts," p. 38.

Works Cited

TILLIE OLSEN SOURCES

"The Iron Throat" (Tillie Lerner). *Partisan Review* 1 (April–May 1934): 3–9.

"I Want You Women Up North to Know" (Tillie Lerner). *Partisan* 1 (March 1934): 4. Reprinted in Burkom and Williams, "De-Riddling Tillie Olsen's Writings," pp. 67–69.

Lecture/reading. University of Minnesota, Minneapolis. 5 June 1986.

Mother to Daughter, Daughter to Mother: A Feminist Press Daybook and Reader. Edited by Tillie Olsen. Old Westbury, N.Y.: Feminist Press, 1984.

Mothers and Daughters: That Special Quality, an Exploration in Photography. Edited by Tillie Olsen with Julie Olsen Edwards and Estelle Jussim. New York: Aperture Foundation, 1987.

"Requa." *Iowa Review* 1, no. 3 (Summer 1970): 54–74. Reprinted as "Requa-I" in *Best American Short Stories,* edited by Martha Foley and David Burnett, pp. 237–65. Boston: Houghton Mifflin, 1971.

Silences. New York: Delacorte Press/Seymour Lawrence, 1978. Reprint New York: Dell, 1980.

"The Strike" (Tillie Lerner). *Partisan Review* 1 (September–October 1934): 3–9. Reprinted in *Years of Protest: A Collection of American Writings of the 1930s,* edited by Jack Salzman, pp. 138–44. New York: Pegasus, 1967.

Telephone interviews with the author, 3 April 1985, 15 February 1992.

Tell Me a Riddle. Philadelphia: Lippincott, 1962. Reprint New York: Laurel-Dell, 1981.

"The Word Made Flesh." Prefatory essay to *Critical Thinking/Critical Writing: Prize-winning High School and College Essays,* pp. 1–8. Cedar Falls, Iowa: University of Northern Iowa, 1984.

Yonnondio: From the Thirties. New York: Delacorte Press/Seymour Lawrence, 1974. Reprint New York: Laurel-Dell, 1981.

OTHER SOURCES

Adams, Phoebe-Lou. "PLA." Review of *Silences*. *Atlantic Monthly*, September 1978, p. 96.

Angelou, Maya. Lecture/reading. Westminster Town Hall Forum, Westminster Presbyterian Church, Minneapolis. October 1984.

Arcana, Judith. *Our Mothers' Daughters*. Berkeley: Shameless Hussy Press, 1979.

Atwood, Margaret. "Obstacle Course." Review of *Silences*. *New York Times Book Review*, 30 July 1978, pp. 1, 27.

Auerbach, Nina. "Women on Women's Destiny: Maturity as Penance." *Massachusetts Review* 20 (Summer 1979): 326–34.

Baker, Gail. "Excavations: Tillie Olsen's Reading List: A List out of Which to Read, Extend Range, Comprehension." *New America* 2, nos. 1–2 (1976): 76–79.

Baum, Charlotte, Paula Hyman, and Sonya Michel. *The Jewish Woman in America*. New York: New American Library, 1975.

Blake, William. *Complete Writings with Variant Readings*. Edited by Geoffrey Keynes. London: Oxford Univ. Press, 1972.

Burkom, Selma, and Margaret Williams. "De-Riddling Tillie Olsen's Writings." *San Jose Studies* 2, no. 1 (February 1976): 65–83.

Chevigny, Bell Gale. Review of *Yonnondio: From the Thirties*. *Village Voice*, 23 May 1974, pp. 38–39.

Clayton, John. "Grace Paley and Tillie Olsen: Radical Jewish Humanists." *Response: A Contemporary Jewish Review* 46 (1984): 37–52.

Cunneen, Sally. "Tillie Olsen: Storyteller of Working America." *Christian Century* 97 (21 May 1980): 570–74.

Davis, Rebecca Harding. *Life in the Iron Mills; or The Korl Woman*. Old Westbury, N.Y.: Feminist Press, 1972.

DeShazer, Mary K. " 'In the Wind of the Singing': The Language of Tillie Olsen's 'Tell Me a Riddle.' " Paper presented at the symposium "Tillie Olsen Week, The Writer and Society," 21–26 March 1983. Sponsored by St. Ambrose College, Davenport, Iowa; Augustana College, Rock Island, Illinois; Marycrest College, Davenport, Iowa; Scott Community College, Bettendorf, Iowa; Black Hawk College, Moline, Illinois.

Dickinson, Emily. *The Complete Poems of Emily Dickinson*. Edited by Thomas H. Johnson. Boston: Little, Brown, 1960.

Duncan, Erika. "The Hungry Jewish Mother." In *The Lost Tradition: Mothers and Daughters in Literature*, edited by Cathy Davidson and E. M. Broner, pp. 231–41. New York: Frederick Unger, 1980.

———. "Tillie Olsen." In *Unless Soul Clap Its Hands: Portraits and Passages*, pp. 31–57. New York: Schocken Books, 1984.

Everson, Susan Corey. "Bodyself: Women's Bodily Experience in Recent Feminist Theology and Women's Literature." Ph.D. diss., Univ. of Minnesota, 1984.

Farwell, Marilyn R. "Adrienne Rich and an Organic Feminist Criticism." *College English* 39, no. 2 (October 1977): 191–203.

Fisher, Dexter, ed. *The Third Woman: Minority Women Writers of the United States.* Boston: Houghton Mifflin, 1980.

Gardiner, Judith Kegan. "A Wake for Mother: The Maternal Deathbed in Women's Fiction." *Feminist Studies* 4, no. 2 (June 1978): 146–65.

Gelfant, Blanche H. "After Long Silence: Tillie Olsen's 'Requa.'" *Studies in American Fiction* 12, no. 1 (Spring 1984): 61–69.

Gilbert, Sandra M., and Susan Gubar, eds. *The Norton Anthology of Literature by Women.* New York: Norton, 1985.

Glastonbury, Marion. "The Best Kept Secret—How Working Class Women Live and What They Know." *Women's Studies International Quarterly Forum* 2, no. 2 (1979): 171–81.

Gottlieb, Annie. "Feminists Look at Motherhood." *Mother Jones,* November 1976, pp. 51–53.

———. "A Writer's Sounds and Silences." Review of *Yonnondio: From the Thirties. New York Times Book Review,* 31 March 1974, p. 5.

Halischak, Kathleen. "Recent Voices in American Feminist Literature." Ph.D. diss., Univ. of Notre Dame, 1982.

H. D. *Trilogy.* New York: New Directions, 1973.

Heilbrun, Carolyn G. *Reinventing Womanhood.* New York: Norton, 1979.

Hurston, Zora Neale. *Their Eyes Were Watching God.* Philadelphia: Lippincott, 1937. Reprint Urbana: Univ. of Illinois Press, 1978.

Kelly, Joan. "The Doubled Vision of Feminist Theory." In *Sex and Class in Women's History,* edited by Judith L. Newton, Mary P. Ryan, and Judith R. Walkowitz, pp. 259–70. Boston: Routledge and Kegan Paul, 1983.

Kessler-Harris, Alice, and Paul Lauter. Introduction to *The Unpossessed,* by Tess Slesinger, pp. vii–xvi. Old Westbury, N.Y.: Feminist Press, 1984.

Lerner, Gerda. *The Creation of Patriarchy.* New York: Oxford Univ. Press, 1986.

LeSueur, Meridel. *Ripening: Selected Work, 1927–1980.* Edited and with an introduction by Elaine Hedges. Old Westbury, N.Y.: Feminist Press, 1982.

L'Heureux, John. Preface to *First Drafts, Last Drafts: Forty Years of the Creative Writing Program at Stanford University,* prepared by William McPheron with the assistance of Amor Towles. Stanford: Stanford University Libraries, 1989.

Lorde, Audre. *Uses of the Erotic: The Erotic as Power.* Trumansburg, N.Y.: Out and Out Books, 1978.

McElhiney, Annette Bennington. "Alternative Responses to Life in Tillie Olsen's Work." *Frontiers* 2 (Spring 1977): 76–91.

Marshall, Paule. *Praisesong for the Widow.* New York: Putnam, 1983.

Martin, Abigail. *Tillie Olsen.* Boise, Idaho: Boise State Univ. Press, 1984.

Matchan, Linda. "The Staggering Burden of Motherhood." *Boston Sunday Globe,* 11 May 1986, pp. 95, 98.

May, Elaine Tyler. *Homeward Bound: American Families in the Cold War Era.* New York: Basic Books, 1988.

Meese, Elizabeth A. *Crossing the Double Cross: The Practice of Feminist Criticism.* Chapel Hill: Univ. of North Carolina Press, 1986.

Miles, Margaret. "Talking with Tillie Olsen." *Minnesota Daily,* 2 June 1986, p. 10.

Mills, Kay. " 'Surviving Is Not Enough': A Conversation with Tillie Olsen." *Los Angeles Times,* 26 April 1981, pt. 4, p. 3.

Miner, Valerie. "The Light of the Muse." Review of *The Magnificent Spinster,* by May Sarton. *Women's Review of Books* 3, no. 3 (December 1985): 7–8.

Mintz, Jacqueline A. "The Myth of the Jewish Mother in Three Jewish, American, Female Writers." *Centennial Review* 22 (1978): 346–55.

Mische, Patricia. "Women and Power." *Benedictines* 37, no. 1 (Spring/Summer 1982): 38–48.

Moraga, Cherríe, and Gloria Anzaldúa, eds. *This Bridge Called My Back: Writings by Radical Women of Color.* Watertown, Mass.: Persephone, 1981.

Morrison, Toni. *The Bluest Eye.* New York: Holt, 1970.

Myerhoff, Barbara. *Number Our Days.* New York: Dutton, 1978.

Nekola, Charlotte, and Paula Rabinowitz, eds. *Writing Red: An Anthology of American Women Writers, 1930–1940.* New York: Feminist Press, 1987.

Nies, Judith. *Seven Women: Portraits from the American Radical Tradition.* New York: Viking, 1977.

Orr, Elaine Neil. *Tillie Olsen and a Feminist Spiritual Vision.* Jackson: Univ. Press of Mississippi, 1987.

Ostriker, Alicia. "Comment on Homans's ' "Her Very Own Howl": The Ambiguities of Representation in Recent Women's Fiction.' " *Signs* 10, no. 3 (Spring 1985): 597–600.

———. "The Thieves of Language: Women Poets and Revisionist Mythmaking." In *The New Feminist Criticism,* edited by Elaine Showalter, pp. 314–38. New York: Pantheon, 1985.

Park-Fuller, Linda. "An Interview with Tillie Olsen." *Literature in Performance* 4, no. 1 (November, 1983): 75–77.

Pearlman, Mickey, and Abby H. P. Werlock. *Tillie Olsen.* Boston: Twayne Publishers, 1991.

Pratt, Annis. "Review: Blackbirds in a Pie: Feminist Scholarship and Women's Experience." *College English* 49, no. 4 (April 1987): 459–64.

Rhodes, Carolyn. " 'Beedo' in Olsen's *Yonnondio:* Charles E. Bedaux." *American Notes and Queries* 14 (October 1976): 23–25.

Rich, Adrienne. *Of Woman Born: Motherhood as Experience and Institution.* New York: Bantam, 1976.

———. "Resisting Amnesia: History and Personal Life." *Ms.,* March 1987, pp. 66–67.

Rose, Ellen Cronan. "Limning: or Why Tillie Writes." *Hollins Critic* 13, no. 2 (April 1976): 1–13.

Rosenfelt, Deborah. "From the Thirties: Tillie Olsen and the Radical Tradition." *Feminist Studies* 7, no. 3 (Fall 1981): 371–406.

Rubin, Naomi. "A Riddle of History for the Future." *Sojourner,* July 1983, pp. 1–18.

Samuelson, Joan Wood. "Patterns of Survival: Four American Women Writers and the Proletarian Novel." Ph.D. diss., Ohio State Univ., 1982.

See, Lisa. "PW Interviews: Tillie Olsen." *Publishers Weekly,* 23 November 1984, pp. 78–79.

Shakespeare, William. *Twenty-three Plays and the Sonnets.* Edited by Thomas Marc Parrott. Rev. ed. New York: Charles Scribner's Sons, 1953.

Shulman, Alix Kates. "Overcoming Silences: Teaching Writing for Women." *Harvard Educational Review* 49, no. 4 (November 1979): 527–33.

Slesinger, Tess. *The Unpossessed.* Old Westbury, N.Y.: Feminist Press, 1984.

Standing, Sue. "Cellar Door." In her *Amphibious Weather.* Somerville, Mass.: Zephyr, 1981. Quoted in Olsen, *Mother to Daughter, Daughter to Mother,* p. 33.

Stimpson, Catharine R. "Three Women Work It Out." *Nation* 219 (30 November 1974): 565–68.

———. "Tillie Olsen: Witness as Servant." *Polit: A Journal for Literature and Politics* 1 (Fall 1977): 1–12.

Sukenink, Lynn. "Women and Fiction." In *The Authority of Experience: Essays in Feminist Criticism,* edited by Arlyn Diamond and Lee R. Edwards, pp. 34–44. Amherst: Univ. of Massachusetts Press, 1977.

"Tillie Olsen: A Profile." Interview by Susan Stamberg for "All Things Considered" series. National Public Radio, 1980.

Tobias, Henry J. *The Jewish Bund in Russia: From Its Origins to 1905.* Stanford, Calif.: Stanford Univ. Press, 1972.

Todd, Janet, ed. *Women Writers Talking.* New York: Holmes and Meier, 1983.

True, Michael. "The Indispensable Arts: The Persistent Humanity of Denise Levertov." *Milkweed Chronicle* 7, no. 2 (Spring/Summer 1986): 38–40.

Turan, Kenneth. "Breaking Silence." *New West,* 28 August 1978, pp. 55–59.

Van Horn, Christina. "Writer Tillie Olsen: Upbeat on Women's Future." *Boston Globe,* 31 May 1981, p. 6A.

Walker, Alice. *In Search of Our Mother's Gardens: Womanist Prose.* San Diego: Harcourt, 1983.

Walker, Cheryl. "Feminist Literary Criticism and the Author." *Critical Inquiry* 16 (Spring 1990): 551–71.

Ware, Susan. *Holding Their Own: American Women in the 1930s.* Boston: Twayne, 1982.

Yalom, Marilyn. "Tillie Olsen." In *Women Writers of the West Coast: Speaking of Their Lives and Careers,* edited by Marilyn Yalom, pp. 57–66. Santa Barbara, Calif.: Capra, 1983.

Yoder, Linda Kathryn. "Memory as Art: The Life Review in Contemporary American Fiction." Ph.D. diss., West Virginia Univ., 1983.

Index